# Crashing

## I love You. Forgive Me.

Mark L. O'Brien

LiveLife**Happy**
Publishing

# LiveLife**Happy** Publishing

Library of Congress Cataloging-in-Publication Data

O'Brien, Mark L.

Crashing: I Love You. Forgive Me.

\ Mark L. O'Brien

Nonfiction > Family & Relationships > Death, Grief, Bereavement

Nonfiction > Psychology > Grief & Loss

E-Book 978-1-990461-42-2

Paperback 978-1-990461-41-5

Live Life Happy Publishing

Printing: April 2023. Printed in The USA

Cover Art Credit: The cover artwork for Crashing: I Love You. Forgive Me. was produced by Peter Bruun as part of his 2019 project "Beyond Beautiful: 1000 Love Letters." Learn more about Peter, his life, and work by visiting his website at www.bruunstudios.com.

Publisher's Note & Author DISCLAIMER

This publication is designed to provide accurate and authoritative information concerning the subject matter covered. It is sold with the understanding that the publisher and author are not engaging in or rendering any psychological, medical or other professional services. The contents of this book are the opinions and perspectives of the author alone and not necessarily those of the publishing house. If expert assistance, support or counselling is needed, seek the services of a competent professional or medical professional. For immediate help, call your local crisis line.

*Mark L. O'Brien's powerful memoir, Crashing, takes readers on a heartbreaking journey through his pain and anguish as he comes to terms with his role in his girlfriend's death. It's a powerful reminder of the human spirit's capacity to choose redemption, and also an excellent primer on how substance use and addiction needs to be treated--with scientific evidence and compassion.*

— Leana Wen, M.D., CNN Medical Analyst and author, Lifelines.

*When [Mark] first shared his story with me, I was aghast. I was obviously shocked by the details of the moment that changed Mark's life forever, but I was equally shocked by Mark's transparency and authenticity, which is on full display in this book. Crashing is not only a book about tragedy and heartbreak, but it's also about love, forgiveness, and hope. Mark's courageous memoir is a true illustration of growth after trauma.*

— Devon Still, former NFL player, founder of the Still Strong Foundation, and author, Still in the Game: Finding the Faith to Tackle Life's Biggest Challenges.

*Mark L. O'Brien's courageous memoir, Crashing, is a poignant narrative of choosing growth in the face of devastating tragedy, loss, and uncertainty. O'Brien sheds light on what it is to live through our deepest nightmares and go on, healing through the power of relationships, forgiveness, and a unifying orientation toward bettering the world.*

— Jordyn Feingold, M.D., Wellbeing Expert and co-author, Choose Growth.

This book describes my present recollection of painful and poignant events from the past, including a graphic description of a fatal car collision and scenes related to grief, trauma, suicide, and incarceration that may be troubling for some readers. To the best of my ability, I have recreated events and chronologies as they occurred. In writing this story, I reviewed public records and consulted with many of the individuals involved, some of whom offered contradictory accounts. Trauma affects memory, and that is a part of this story too, so where multiple accounts differed, I've let my memory of events stand. Some names and characteristics of individuals have been changed to protect their privacy.

*To Finnegan, Charlie, and Penny*

*Never forget that in the soil of despair*
*may grow the seeds of meaning.*

# CHAPTER 1

It's so cramped in the car, all crushed around me, and the seat belt is digging into my shoulder. But my first thought isn't to wonder why I'm hanging upside down, why there's blood all over the dashboard, or even why there's a paramedic shining a flashlight in my face. It's that I really, really need to pee.

"Where were you headed?" the paramedic asks me.

"I was going home from work." Right? At least I think I was.

*What happened after work?* I don't even remember leaving.

There's an opening where the windshield used to be. The metal is bent and jagged, but it looks like I could squeeze through if I released the seatbelt.

"Just hang tight. We'll get you out of there."

"I really have to pee." I'm not sure why the peeing matters so much to me.

The paramedic reaches in and tries to free me, but he can't. He walks away, and I hear him talking to another first responder on the scene.

"He's gone," he says.

When I hear it, I figure I must already be a lost cause, dying but not quite dead, hanging upside down in my car with the certainty that it will soon be over. I don't feel like I'm dying, or what I'd expect dying to feel like. But I suppose he has no reason to lie, and he's the pro, right?

Everything I've ever done, everything I'm in the middle

of doing, and everything I plan to do in the future plays like a high-speed movie reel, the scenes flying by and overlapping before my mind's eye. I think about Laura and the pain she'll go through when she learns of my death. I'm supposed to graduate from law school in a few months and ask her to marry me so we can  start our life together. She'll never get to see me win a case, I'll never get to watch her walk down  the aisle to me, and we'll never have the three children we both want. I've wasted all this time preparing for our life together, and now it's over. I'd do anything for just one more day with her. Even one more minute.

❖

I wake up in the hospital, groggy and disoriented. I'm sore and nauseated, and I have a horrible headache. My left ear is burning, and when I reach up to touch it, it's swollen and tender. I feel gashes on the side of my head.

*I didn't die.* I was in an accident. It must have been bad. How did it happen? Am I going to be okay?

I ask a nurse, but she doesn't tell me anything useful. "This is the University of Maryland Shock Trauma Center."

"Was anyone else hurt in the crash?" She doesn't reply.

A while later, a hospital chaplain approaches my bed and introduces herself.

"The nurses told me you've been asking about what happened last night, about whether there were other injuries. Mark, there was a passenger in the car with you."

*Who would be in the car with me after work?*

The truth circles my consciousness like a lion stalking its prey, ready to leap unseen from the grass. I sense the danger, the hairs standing up on my arms, and search uneasily for some clue in my fragmentary recollection of the day before.

It started like any other Friday. I woke up and got out of bed, careful not to disturb Laura in her sleep. She gets grumpy in the morning if she's awakened suddenly. She's taught me to wake her gently, like her parents did when she was growing up, by brushing her hair with my fingers and softly rubbing her back, letting her rise slowly to consciousness.

She always sleeps with her hand curled up on her chin, her long brown hair cascading over the pillow. I stared at her for a moment. It's been three years since we started dating, but I still can't believe she's mine. I wanted to wake her up, to be in her arms before starting my day, but I knew I'd be late for work if I did.

Sighing, I walked out of our room, and on my way to the bathroom noticed that the smell of the carrot cake she made for my birthday still lingered in the air. I don't have classes on Friday, so I went straight to the tax court where I work as a law clerk editing court opinions before their publication. I grabbed lunch at Starbucks up the street from the court, ran into one of my classmates, and had a short chat. On the way back to the court, I gave half of my sandwich to one of the men outside the shelter on E Street. I got off at four o'clock and walked the mile back across town to the free parking on D Street near the Capitol.

*That's odd.* I can't remember driving home. Most days, Laura would have been waiting for me, smoking a cigarette on the low stone wall that surrounded our front porch. I don't remember her greeting me after work though.

And then, all at once, the lion pounces. The night before comes flooding back. The birthday party Laura had for me. Celebrating with friends until the bar closed. Leaving Chris's so she could drive us home. She must have been next to me in the driver's seat.

"Where's Laura?" I panic. "Where is she? Is she okay?"

A wave of nausea floods over my entire body as the realization dawns.

*They wouldn't be acting like this if she were okay.*

"She didn't make it, Mark. I'm so sorry."

The chaplain leaves, and I don't know if it's from the IV drugs I'm getting, the head injury I must have suffered, or the shock of finding out Laura is dead, but I drift into a dream-like state. I'm not really asleep, but I'm also not aware of what's happening around me.

❖

*It's my sophomore year of college, and I'm meeting Laura for the first time. She's just moved into an apartment with her best friend, Theresa, who is in the group of friends I met in the dorms last year.*

*Laura and I quickly bond and become the closest of friends. We sit on the couch in her apartment playing SSX Tricky on the PlayStation. She always gets the high score. Then we're at the house she rented with Theresa the next year, dodging cicadas in the summer when the seventeen-year brood and the thirteen-year brood emerged at the same time. There are thousands of them in the yard, and I'm untangling one that's caught in her hair. Now we're at Fridays, hanging out with her work crew from the Rainforest Cafe where she waits tables. She's wearing her rainforest safari guide uniform, which isn't very flattering, but I admire the curve of her hips anyway, stare across the bar and unconsciously smile when she laughs, her eyes squinting with mirth.*

*Now it's Valentine's Day of my senior year. For three years of our friendship, I've had a crush, but I haven't had it in me to let her know. She's had a few boyfriends along the way, and I've been jealous. I haven't had any girlfriends, just a few random college hookups.*

*Laura tells me she's upset she didn't receive Valentine's flowers from anyone. I go home and order some for her, but I don't have the courage to have the florist put my name on the card, as if not signing them leaves me a little wiggle room to call the whole thing off if she isn't interested.*

*"Do you think he sent them?" she asks me after she receives the delivery. She means the boy at work who kind of creeps her out.*

*"It was me," I say. "I didn't mean to freak you out—"*

*"Aww, Mark. That was so sweet. You didn't need to do that, but I'm glad it was you, not him. Why didn't you sign them, you weirdo?"*

*I thought the flowers would make my feelings clear, but I was wrong. A week later, I ask if I can stop by after work to talk to her. She says yes. "But why do you think you need permission to come over?" I usually just stop by unannounced.*

*I walk down the stairs to the basement and find her sitting on the sofa watching a show. I don't look to see what's on. I'm too focused on what I came to do. She's sitting cross legged with her elbow on her leg and her hand on her chin, wearing her at-home uniform— an oversized hoodie and baggy sweatpants. The smell of cocoa butter and cigarette smoke surround her.*

*"I need to tell you something," I feel so awkward, like I'm reliving middle school, asking my first girl to hold hands at the skating rink. "I didn't send you those flowers because I felt bad that you didn't get any. I sent them because I like you, like, I like you, like you."*

*"How is this not completely obvious to you?" I wonder to myself.*

*I spend the next three hours convincing her that we should start dating, that it won't destroy our friendship, and that I'm serious enough about it that it's worth a shot.*

*"I'm sorry. I've just never even thought about you like that, Mark." She doesn't say it to be cruel, but it stings anyway. "I've never thought about it, so I don't see how it would work."*

*"Then you should just follow my lead, because I've thought about it a lot." I always fall back on humor when I'm uncomfortable.*

*"But you're Mark. You're, like, my best friend."*

*"I still will be. There'd just be more. And I'd get to kiss you," I smile and blush.*

*It doesn't work. By two in the morning, I'm out of good arguments and about to fall asleep.*

*"Well, I'm gonna go home," I say, feeling more than a little embarrassed, distraught, and defeated.*

*"And you're going to come back tomorrow night so we can finish this conversation." I'm still in the game!*

*I return the next night for another marathon conversation, but this time I'm more confident. She must be open to the idea of being together. Why else tell me to come back? Now it's just a matter of negotiating the terms and not talking so much that I screw it up. Exhausted from several more hours of discussion, we stop talking and sit there quietly. I start to doze on the couch in her living room with my head in her lap.*

*"Okay," she finally says. I sit up straight, heart racing.*

*"Okay what?"*

*"Let's give this a try. How do we start?"*

*My heart leaps. I put my hand in her hair and kiss her softly.*

*"Like this."*

*February 15th, the day I sent the flowers, becomes our Valentine's Day.*

❖

I distinctly remember the paramedic saying "he's gone" when I'd heard him at the crash scene. But now I think I must have misheard him. He must have said "she's gone," and *she* was Laura, the center of my universe, the girl I loved and planned to spend the rest of my life with.

*She's gone.*

I sit in total despair, staring into the curtain that surrounds the hospital bed but seeing only Laura's face. The brutal truth repeats in my head. *She's gone. She's gone. She's gone.* How can she be gone? The divide between "she is here" and "she is gone" is infinite, yet it's only the difference of a few hours. Now she is here. Now she is gone.

I think I'm going to be sick, and not from the heavy drinking at my birthday party last night. I'm coming unhinged, and the adrenaline pumping through my veins is making my skin tingle and crawl. I don't know whether to weep, scream, or laugh hysterically at the madness consuming me.

*This can't be real. It must be a demented joke of some kind.*

I reach for my phone to call Laura, and in the moment I realize I don't have my phone and can't call her anyways, a nurse pulls back the curtain around my bed. She's accompanied by two state troopers, and the more senior of the two informs me that I'm required to provide a blood sample.

"It's required by state law as part of our investigation of the crash."

The younger one starts to ask about the night before. She's a petite mid-twenties brunette, and she looks so much like Laura that I can't even talk. All I can say is "you look just like her."

She quickly switches places with her partner, who brusquely informs me she needs to take my statement.

"Were you drinking?"

"Yes."

"How much?"

"I don't know. A lot. It was my birthday party."

I watch as my blood begins to flow through the syringe in my arm. I've never been squeamish, but the sight of it churns my stomach. Without any memory of her from the wrecked car, the image of Laura conjured in my mind is gruesome and bloody.

The trooper continues with her questioning. I probably should have known sooner, but it hasn't occurred to me until now because I know Laura was driving: *They think I did this.*

I've driven drunk before. And like a lot of people who've

driven drunk before, I knew it wasn't smart but occasionally did it anyway. But it wasn't supposed to happen last night. Laura and I are growing up and being more responsible. We don't do that anymore. I'm in my last semester of law school, and I'm so busy that I don't go out very much. Last night was a special night. We had a plan. Laura was our designated driver.

*I couldn't have been driving. I wasn't driving.*

The troopers leave, and my bed is moved to another part of the hospital for a test or for doctors to examine me or maybe for a CT scan. At some point, I stop being a part of it. I separate from the situation, like I'm floating near the ceiling, looking down on myself and the doctors examining me. I don't feel sad or scared. I don't feel anything except a little bit of curiosity and pity for the man I am watching, me. It's interesting and intriguing, like a movie or a story. But it isn't *my story*.

When I come back to my body again, they tell me I have a concussion and ask me to try standing and walking. I don't know why they're so concerned about my concussion and wish they'd focus on the more pressing matter: a terrible mistake has been made. Laura can't be dead.

The next couple of hours are like that. Sometimes I'm experiencing being in my body in the hospital, panicking and desperate for someone to understand that this is all a big mistake. Other times I'm just distantly observing my body and the doctors and the nurses. I don't understand why it's happening, but at the moment, the periodic detachment from the enormity of the situation is saving me from losing my mind.

*I couldn't have been driving. Could I?*

❖

My concussion is minor, and I leave the hospital on the same morning as the crash. On the way out, I realize I'm leaving through the same door where I used to pick Laura up when she'd been an assistant in the hospital and explored her career interest in psychology and health. It's a place I would have passed before without thinking of its role in our life together, but now it sends a jab of sharp pain from my stomach and up through my chest.

Laura's been gone for eight hours. I've known for four. But none of it seems real. She was here, right here in my arms, just last night. I have no idea how I'm supposed to be in a world without Laura. Am I supposed to act differently now? What should I be feeling? My emotions are all over the place, and I can barely identify what's happening in me from one moment to the next. It's complete emotional chaos, like when you spin around so fast you can't see anything clearly, the world whirling by in streaks of color.

My dad says he'll take me to his house. In the car, I vomit all over myself. I don't even try to control it. I don't care about anything.

*What's there to care about now?*

After we stop at Target for cleaning supplies and do our best to get the puke off me and the upholstery of the car, I'm completely exhausted from the late night, the long morning in the hospital, and the crushing weight of loss that has descended on me. I close my eyes as we pull back onto the highway.

# CHAPTER 2

*"This can't be real. It has to be a dream," I say to her.*

*"I'm not sure, babe. Those cops seemed pretty real to me," she replies.*

*"I don't want to be in the world without you."*

*"Do you remember our first summer together?" she asks.*

*"How could I ever forget?"*

*We basked in the time together, knowing we would be apart when I left for law school in the fall. We'd promised each other that night on her couch when I first kissed her that we would give the relationship a try, but we wouldn't let it ruin our friendship, we wouldn't let it get too serious too fast. But how could it not? We'd already been best friends; the emotional stakes were high from the start. Neither one of us wanted to be the one to admit that it had become serious. I didn't want to scare her away, but I knew I was falling in love even before we started dating. She didn't want to acknowledge that it was serious enough that she could get hurt again. Her last breakup had been painful. We didn't talk about what we would do when I left for law school, whether we'd stay together or break it off am-icably. When we did discuss it, we both agreed long distance relationships never worked, but maybe we could be the exception. By July, I couldn't take it anymore, and I told her I would visit as often as I had to if it kept us together.*

*"There was no way I could imagine living without you even then," I tell her now in my dream.*

*With a month to go before I'd leave for law school, we spent a week at the beach in North Carolina. The Outer Banks in August were packed with vacationers. Laura and I were young and still living with roommates, and it felt luxurious to have our own space even though the hotel we stayed at was nothing fancy. Our room was on the first floor, and we could walk out of the sliding glass door right onto the beach. The cheery yellow of the shower curtain and wallpaper matched our lighthearted happiness.*

*The sun was high, and the sand was hot on our feet when we walked out the sliding glass door for the first time. We were falling in love, carefree and in the moment. Laying there on the beach, listening to the sound of the waves crashing, we soaked ourselves in the glow of being together.*

*We laid on the beach the whole first day we were there. At one point, Laura rolled onto her side and looked at me, her long brown hair falling over her shoulder and onto the top of her green and white paisley bikini. She was so cute, a real girl next door type, petite but spunky. The ocean seemed to bring out the green in her eyes. The strap on her top shifted a little, revealing the white tan lines on her bronzed skin. Staring at her, I could hardly breathe.*

*"Hey, mister. What are you thinking about?" she asked playfully, flirting with her smile and her eyes. She had a way of being so sweetly innocent and so mischievous at the same time. I couldn't resist it.*

*"Nothing. I just love it here," I said. There was no obligation to keep, no deadline to meet, no plans, no future or past, nobody and nowhere else. There was only her. And it was perfect. I reached my arm around her waist and pulled her toward me. "I could stay here forever."*

*"Or go back to the hotel room," I'd thought lustily.*

*"I knew I loved you then," I say.*

*"I knew it too. I wondered when you would say it." She has that playful look in her eye again now.*

*"It wasn't too long after."*

*A month passed from that perfect day on the beach, and there was only a day until I left for law school in Virginia. I would be three hours away from Laura, and I planned to drive home to Maryland every weekend to see her. I would be away for only a few days at a time, but it felt like it would be forever.*

*The night before I left for, we laid together in her bed, my head resting in her lap, talking about how hard the distance would be.*

*"I love you," I told her for the first time. I'd never said that to a girl before and known what it meant. I had a girlfriend in high school, and we said we loved each other, but it was nothing like this. I didn't need to eat or sleep or anything as long as I was with Laura. When she looked at me, I felt like I was taller, stronger, and about to melt into a puddle all at the same time.*

*"I was nervous you might not say it back," I tell her. She was more experienced in love, and I worried saying it would push her away and that we weren't that serious to her.*

*"You're a silly, foolish man. With two sisters, I would have thought you could read a girl better than that," she says.*

*She had said it back—"I love you too"—then leaned down and kissed me, and the anxiety and excitement of the moment turned to pure and complete contentment.*

*"I wished I could just linger in that moment and never leave, never spend a second away from you and the softness of your eyes looking down at me," I tell her.*

*The next morning, we held each other by the front door of Laura's house, wanting to make the goodbye last a little longer and the time apart a little shorter. I was the first to start crying. "You can't cry," she whispered. "You'll make me cry." But she already was.*

*"I honestly don't think I can live without you, Laura. Being away*

*from you for a week at a time was agonizing."*

"*I'll never leave you,*" *she promises me.*

❖

The car stopping in the driveway wakes me, and I drag myself into the house.

"Maybe you should take a shower," my dad suggests. "I'll grab you some clothes."

I turn the water as hot as I can stand it. Glass and blood fall from my scalp as I desperately scrub, trying to wash away the horror. I put my head against the wall and cry, the tears mixing with the near-scalding water, blood, and glass running down my face.

The lion having sprung on me in the hospital and subdued its prey, it toys with me now. I alternate between hysterical grief and calm reflection. I spiral downward in hopelessness and anguish, and at the moment that I'm on the verge of collapse, the lion lets me go so I can catch my breath and enjoy the fleeting sensation of escape. I know I should be losing it. I remember that just a minute ago *I was losing it.* And yet, for just that moment, I am removed from the pain. I know what has happened, and I consider it with academic detachment. *Laura is dead. The police think I killed her. It's not an ideal situation.*

I step out of the shower as the hot water runs out. They cut my clothes off in the hospital, so I left in a hospital gown. Now I put on one of my dad's shirts and a pair of his pants. I take as long as I can to dress and brush my teeth, removing

CRASHING I LOVE YOU. FORGIVE ME.

the residual chunks of vomit from the car ride home. I have to call Laura's parents, and I'm putting it off as long as I can. I wish I could just never speak to them again, pretend they never existed, but I know that isn't an option. I've been part of their family for three years. David, Laura's dad, knows I've been planning to ask his permission to propose.

They are my family, but according to the police, I've just destroyed their family. I can't imagine that I'd been driving, but it seems unlikely the police would be confused about that. It seems like an important detail for them to get right. On the other hand, I know from my criminal law classes that mistakes happen.

I pick up the phone, unsure of whether Laura's parents know what has happened and terrified they already hate me, that they'll forbid me from attending her funeral, and that they wish I was dead too. If I were them, I'd hate me just for living, whether or not I was driving.

*Are you supposed to make small talk at the beginning of a "sorry your daughter is dead because of me" call?*

David answers on the first ring.

"David, I'm so sorry. I don't know what to say. I don't know how this happened. I am so sorry."

I ask if I can come to Laura's funeral but say I understand if they don't want me there. I don't expect any compassion. I don't expect anything but anger.

David interrupts me. "Mark, we were so worried we lost you too. Thank God you're alright."

The state troopers had come to his house in Florida to

notify him of Laura's death, but they wouldn't tell him what happened to me.

"We know how happy you made Laura, how much the two of you loved each other," David says. "Laura wouldn't want us to be angry at each other, Mark. We're going to need each other."

I don't know what to say. I don't deserve to be treated like this. I deserve to be dead. Their little girl is dead, and it was my job to keep her safe. The police say she's dead because of me. And her family is *worried about me*. I'm so grateful and astonished. And I also want to scream: "HATE ME! Please, hate me!"

*I hate me.*

❖

The first thing I notice is that our house feels like a different place than before: eerie, quiet, sacred. The happiness and comfort of it are gone. As I walk through the front door and into the living room, I'm tiptoeing in a graveyard and whispering to Laura's parents who just arrived from Florida. We're here to go through Laura's belongings and divide them among us.

After a year of law school in Virginia, I transferred to Georgetown to be closer to Laura. We rented this small house together in Magothy Manor outside Annapolis. Manor makes it sound fancier than it actually is, but it's a nice little neighborhood. Our house has four small square rooms, all about 15 feet by 15 feet, a small bathroom, and a small kitchen. The landlord said we could paint as long as we used light colors. We made a blue room, a yellow room, a pink room, and a green room. In the backyard, there's a little patio, and last summer we planted giant sunflowers that grew seven feet tall with flowers that were a foot across. Now their stalks hang limply toward the ground, the weight of their dead blooms too much to bear.

The second thing I notice is that the house smells like her, like us, in a way I'd never noticed before. Our pillows smell like her. The couch. The air. Smell is so strongly tied to our memories. It's like inhaling every moment we ever shared. I can hear her voice and see her face more clearly here.

Every year for my birthday, Laura made me a carrot cake with her family recipe that used jarred baby food and homemade cream cheese frosting. It's my favorite dessert, and there it is, sitting on the kitchen counter where we left it, the two pieces we'd eaten the only parts missing. *Everything* is just as we left it: Nintendo remotes on the couch from the last time we played our favorite snowboarding videogame, outfits Laura tried on for my birthday party and tossed on the floor, dinner plates in the sink with the hardened sauce from her homemade manicotti stuck to them.

"Anything that you want to keep is yours," David says solemnly, putting an arm around my shoulder. "She'd want you to have some things to remember her."

"Thanks," I mutter. "I appreciate that." They know I don't remember driving the car the night of the crash, and they know Laura was supposed to be our designated driver, but I still don't understand how they can be so kind.

I pick out some souvenirs from places Laura and I went together—tickets to Georgetown basketball games, matches from the bar we went to in Las Vegas, cards we'd sent each other when we were apart, a shamrock headband one of the bars had given out on St. Patty's Day two years back. I'd hidden eighty love notes around our house when we moved in so she would find them randomly. I keep the ones she found and collect the ones she never saw. I find a sheet of Limericks I'd written for her, some sweet and some smutty. I'll put it all in the scrapbook she started but never finished for us.

I want to protect Laura's honor and virtue even in death. And I want to protect her parents' memory of her innocence. I hope they won't notice the half-smoked joints buried in the planter by our bed—they do—or the *Cosmo Magazine* version of the *Kama Sutra* on our bookshelf—they don't.

"I'm going to go outside for a minute," I tell them, stepping toward the front door. I need a minute alone and some fresh air.

I walk to the end of our street, to our neighborhood's little beach on the Magothy River. We spent so many sunny afternoons and warm evenings here with our dog, Rocko. The Magothy is a slow-moving river and deepens gradually from the banks. Rocko can walk out far into the river without the water going over his shoulders. He doesn't like to swim, but as long as he can walk, he's happy to be in the water. He especially loves chasing the ducks, even though the ducks never pay him much attention.

I got Rocko before Laura and I started dating. Her house

was broken into, and while she was on vacation, I decided to get her a dog to keep her safe. He was still a puppy and already over 70 pounds. He was sweet, but he looked tough and would scare off anyone who might hurt her. But then I realized on the way home from the shelter that I probably shouldn't have gotten her a dog without asking her if she wanted one. I decided I would keep him but offer to let her borrow him whenever she wanted. I was at her house most of the time anyways. So Rocko went from being her dog to being my dog in a matter of minutes, and then became our dog about eight months later when we started dating. We rounded out our little family when we adopted Boots, a black kitten with white paws who loved to snuggle up with Rocko in his bed.

Staring at the river and knowing we'll never sit there together again, watching the waves lap gently against the shore, I realize I can't live in the house without her. I'll see her in every corner, and I can't be alone with the memories. As a practical matter, I totaled my car in the accident, and the house is far from my school and my job. I can't afford the place without Laura's income either. *So that settles it.* Rocko, Boots, and I will have to move out. I call the landlord and tell him I'm planning to break the lease. He already knows about the crash.

"I'll keep paying the rent while you find a new tenant." It's the least of my problems, but I hope it won't take long because I don't have the savings to pay the full rent by myself for more than a month or two.

"Thanks for letting me know, Mark," he replies kindly. "Hang in there."

I walk back inside to finish the macabre work of dividing Laura's possessions. The experience is surreal, like a dream. It still doesn't feel real that she's gone. I keep expecting her to walk out of our bedroom or call to me from the front of the house. She should be helping pack up our things. We always split the housework 50-50. Then it hits me again. We're doing this because she's gone. She isn't coming back. There's no more Laura, and there's no more Laura and Mark.

# CHAPTER 3

It's February 14th, Valentine's Day, and Laura's funeral is later this afternoon. I'm sure people think it's odd to have her funeral on Valentine's Day, especially when they've heard it's her boyfriend's fault she's dead. Maybe they think it's her family's way of rubbing salt in my wound, retaliation for what I've done. But David knows our Valentine's Day is tomorrow, February 15, and he planned it so it wouldn't be on *our* special day.

When David arrived from Florida, he'd asked me if Laura and I ever talked about her funeral wishes. He assumed we hadn't, but I told him we'd discussed it many times, including the night before she died. Ironically,—or coincidentally; I've never understood the difference—one of our friends had been injured in a drunk driving crash two days before Laura died, and we talked about how lucky she was to be alive. Our friend's accident motivated our firm decision that Laura would be our designated driver the night of my birthday party. It also started a conversation about what each of us would want to happen if we died. Laura wanted to be cremated, and she was adamant that she didn't want a viewing. She didn't want people to see her if she was dead. She thought it would be creepy to have people seeing her like that.

"The viewing isn't for you. It's for the people you leave behind." I'd told her. "It's how people begin healing when they lose someone." The conversation seemed academic when it happened. We didn't expect *this* to be the immediate future. *Or did she somehow know?* But in this alternate reality where she was dead, the one where we were now living, Laura's family and I wanted deeply to see her one final time.

The funeral director told us that instead of a viewing, we could have something called an identification.

"Basically, five or six of you can come into the viewing room and see her. It's not a full viewing. There are no visitors. It's not public," he explained.

I knew Laura didn't want to be seen, but I also knew it wasn't my decision. When her parents decided to do the identification, I was relieved that I'd get to touch and see her. I was also relieved that I wasn't the one to make the choice to ignore her wishes.

Two days later, we walked into the room where Laura's body was lying in a casket with a blanket pulled up to her collar bone. There was a place to kneel in front of her and two benches a few yards away. I first sat in the front row of the benches, too overwhelmed to approach her.

"How can this be the last time I see her?" I thought. We were supposed to have decades, two best friends in love and growing old together.

After several minutes, I stood up and walked to her casket. I knew she died from a head injury, and I was surprised to see that she still looked like herself. You could barely tell she'd been hurt, let alone killed. She was still so beautiful. I put my head on her chest and began to weep.

"I love you, Laura. I'm so sorry. I'm so sorry. I'm so sorry. I will never not love you."

"Did I do this to you?" I asked her quietly. "I wish I was with you. I wish I was dead instead of you. This is because of me, isn't it? This is all because of me."

I kissed her on her nose three times like I'd always done. It was one of our rituals. Her nose was chilly, the warmth of her life absent, and it surprised me how cold she was. It was irrational, but I worried she was too cold, that she might be uncomfortable. I tried to shake it off and remind myself that her body wasn't her anymore. The body didn't care if it was cold. I stayed there kneeling for a few more minutes.

"Can you move her arm so her hand is resting on her cheek before the cremation?" I asked the funeral director. "That's how she likes to sleep."

He said that he would, but I imagined he thought I was ridiculous and wouldn't actually do it.

At the bar on the night of the crash, Laura and I shared a pepperoni pizza. I haven't eaten anything in the five days since. I'm pretty sure I'm not trying to starve myself to death; it's just comforting to know my last meal was one I shared with her, like as long as I don't eat anything else, we just had dinner together. Most of the time, I haven't been hungry anyway. But now I'm starving, and I'm afraid if I don't eat, I'll collapse on the altar during her funeral while giving her eulogy. I finally give in and eat an apple. It's delicious after so long without food. But I'm mad at myself for liking it.

*I shouldn't enjoy anything ever again, not without her.*

I need to get dressed before we drive to the church. I've been wearing Laura's sweatshirt since the day after the crash.

She was ten inches shorter and seventy pounds lighter than me, so it doesn't zip, and it only reaches down to my belly button. My arms stick out of the sleeves just below my elbows. I look like Chris Farley when he does "fat guy in a little coat" in *Tommy Boy*. I know it, but I've worn it anyways. It's made me feel close to her. I take it off now, fold it reverently, and change into a suit and tie.

It's cold and wet outside. The roads are icy, and on the way to St. Joseph's church we see cars sliding down the highway, wheels locked, like skiers on a mountain. I pray silently for them, that if anyone has to die on the road that day, it can be me.

St. Joseph has a modern feel, with the low, boxy look common among newer Catholic churches. The large cross adorning the steeply angled roof line is the only thing to differentiate it from a school or a library. It isn't far from where Laura grew up. Laura and I came here on Christmas and Easter to be with her family. Inside, the sanctuary is wide and open, angled toward the altar in the front. The altar is framed by exposed wooden beams that run up the walls and across the ceiling.

Before the service, I stand in the back of the church with Laura's aunt. She embraces me tightly and whispers in my ear.

"You know we love you very much, Mark," she says. "Laura is with us today, and she always will be."

When I open my mouth to whisper a response, a primal cry bursts out from deep inside me. I don't even realize the sound is coming from me at first. It startles some of the other people around us, and they turn and stare at me. I bet they're wondering how I could even show my face here at all. I still can't believe I could have been driving, but I know it's what everyone else thinks happened.

I'm surrounded by the smell of incense and candle wax and the sound of a hundred whispered conversations. I can just imagine what they must be saying. "I heard he was so drunk he didn't even remember being in the crash." "I can't believe her parents would even let him come to her funeral." "I can't believe *he* thinks it's okay to be here."

I walk over to David and give him a hug. I've never seen him like this. He's usually a life-of-the-party, take-care-of-everyone, all-around good guy. He's in his late forties or early fifties but looks like a fit thirty-something with a broad chest and Roman nose. Laura was in awe of her father. I've respected and, to a certain extent, feared him as all young men should fear the fathers of the girls they love. But if he was intimidating, he was also gregarious and welcoming to me, didactic and fatherly. His eyes, usually smiling, are sullen and dark now, weary.

I see my mom across the sanctuary and try to duck before she sees me too. I know I shouldn't avoid her, but the anguish on her face is making everything harder. She can't help how she feels, but the way she looks at me is a constant reminder of the pain I'm causing everyone.

❖

I sit in the front of the church with Laura's family. We're all crying, and I know I need to pull it together. I'll giving her eulogy along with her sister and a family friend in just a moment. When it's time, we walk together to the front of the church.

I tell the story of meeting Laura for the first time. It was at a party at Theresa's apartment. Laura was with Mike, her boyfriend who she lived with, and Mike and I were playing with their dog on the back porch. I thought Laura was cute, but she was taken. I don't say it during the eulogy, but I was into one of Theresa's other roommates at the time.

"After she and Mike broke up, and Laura moved in with Theresa, I got to know her, and I fell head over heels. I'm not sure I know how to go on without her. I can't believe the life we planned is over. I'll love and miss her forever."

*And, as you're all thinking, I did this.*

After the service, David and I step out on the porch together. I stand next to him, our arms resting on the cold, damp, metal railing.

"She loves you a lot, Mark. She wants you to be happy," he tells me.

"I love her too." We still don't know if we're supposed to talk about her in present or past tense.

"I know you do. I knew it the first time I met you, before you started dating. I could see it coming. You two were just right for each other."

"That doesn't happen twice in a life, does it?" The question feels inappropriate, but it's not that I'm asking if I'll ever find love again. What I mean is that I'm realizing that the rest of my life is going to be completely empty and devoid of love.

"I don't know, Mark. I don't know."

Laura, the best thing in my life, is gone, and I'm looking at a long, lonely, miserable journey to my own death. If I live to be eighty years old, that would be fifty-five more years. Fifty-five years times 365 days a year minus the seven days it's been since my birthday plus fourteen leap days. That's 20,080 days. 20,080 more days without her.

I pray to God that my life will be shorter. *I can't live that long without her.*

❖

Later that evening, I'm in Theresa's backyard listening to music and talking with a dozen of her friends. Theresa is, *was,* Laura's best friend. They've been inseparable since high school, two spunky little brunette party animal peas in a pod. Theresa's eyes are bright blue to Laura's green, and her hair is wavy to Laura's straight. They share a love for the beach and water and a fierce loyalty to their families and each other.

Theresa isn't the type to cry during a movie or really any other time for that matter. Her feelings are rarely on display. Like me, she uses humor and sarcasm as a defense against revealing too much. But now her puffy red eyes and slumped posture betray her grief.

Our group of college friends has dispersed around the country in the three years since we graduated. Some of us live on the west coast now, but they've all flown in to participate in the rituals of death and grief. The closest of our friends have taken up residence in Theresa's parents' basement. It's close to

Laura's family and to the church where we had the funeral today. We've needed to be together, and we've spent most of each day reminiscing about Laura, telling each other all the stories about her that we can recall, or just sitting in companionable silence and mutual understanding. Time has seemed to stand still here, none of us sure how exactly to move forward with our newly shattered innocence.

Tonight, a larger group is over, and we're all hanging out and sharing our best Laura mischief stories.

"She was so laid back."

"Unless you pissed her off."

"She was always down for a party."

"I've never seen such a little girl drink so much Captain."

"She was my best sneak-out-for-a-cigarette-between-classes friend in high school."

One of her high school friends who had trouble with drugs and occasionally stayed at Magothy Manor with me and Laura whenever his parents kicked him out tells me about how they used to skip school to hang out in their boats on the Magothy River. One time, there was a retaliatory boat burning incident against one of Laura's ex-boyfriends, but she was just a witness, not a participant, and the retaliation was for something that had nothing to do with her.

"I'll never forget how hard she would laugh when we told that story! So hard she'd start to cry, and her voice got so high you couldn't even understand her."

Laura and I both partied *a lot* in high school and college and made plenty of ill-advised choices when we did. The irony is that even though a tragedy like this happening in our group of friends was entirely predictable, maybe even inevitable, it didn't happen in the era when we were partying every weekend, sometimes every night. By the time our youthful bad decisions caught up to us, we'd already grown out of them. We were two home bodies finishing up school and leaning into the domestic bliss we envisioned for our future. My birthday party was meant to be as much a final farewell to frivolous young adulthood as it was a send off into that happy adult life.

The chatter is animated and almost joyful. Laughter comes as easily as tears, and a warm glow suffuses the evening. Time and the reality of our loss are suspended. Laura isn't quite gone, and it feels like if we never leave this place, then she will never leave us either.

Theresa talks about meeting Laura and becoming best friends when Theresa got kicked out of private school and transferred to Laura's public school— that was tied into the boat burning incident. We talk about the crazy nights we spent together in college, like the night we punched some dude in the hallway of Theresa and Laura's apartment building because he got handsy with Laura and the time the blizzard snowed us all in for three days with nothing but junk food and Jack Daniels.

"Ugh. I don't think I could ever have another Jack and Coke after that week," I say, then wonder if everyone's thinking that after what I did, I probably shouldn't drink at all. I look down at my feet and silently apologize to Laura.

Over the next few hours, the crowd begins to thin, and the small group of us staying at Theresa's parents' house is left alone. The sadness and silence slowly return, and we resign ourselves to finding the fleeting peace of slumber. We quietly put the chairs away, careful not to disturb the ghost among us, and walk inside making half-hearted jokes and gentle attempts to cheer each other up. "She'd want us to be happy," one of our friends declares solemnly, but I'm not sure she'd want me to be happy if I'm the one who killed her.

# CHAPTER 4

The shrink's office is in a typical suburban office building with a professional mix of lawyers, architects, consultants, dentists, and doctors. Unblemished business name plates are screwed into the brand new drywall by each door.

I open the door and walk in. The waiting room has a half dozen comfy wooden arm chairs, and after signing in, I observe the neatly hung nature prints of mountain and ocean scenes, their silver frames reflecting the shine of recessed lighting from above, and wait for the shrink to call me back.

Kara is a tall blonde psychologist who tells me she specializes in treating patients with complicated grief. She knows why I'm here but says she wants to learn more about me before we talk about Laura and the crash.

"Tell me a little about yourself. Where did you grow up?"

"Everywhere." That's the short answer. I'm on edge, and I run my hand through my hair compulsively as I avoid eye contact and explain that I grew up in a military family. Moving a lot was just part of the military life. "By the time I was thirteen, I'd already lived in seven different places."

My dad was in basic training while my mom was pregnant with me. He was a newly minted lieutenant when I was born: chin up, back straight, proud and solid. He didn't raise his voice; he expected to be listened to.

I was born in Connecticut, and we moved to Georgia pretty soon afterward. By the time I was one, we moved again.

The first home I remember is the single-story rectangular brick rancher with a two-car garage in Fort Sill, Oklahoma where we lived until I was four.

Then there was the apartment building in Augsburg, Germany. "It had an empty apartment on the top floor that the parents turned into a playroom for all the kids in our building," I tell her, staring blankly out the window to the parking lot surrounded by newly planted trees and the apartment complex across the street— I partied there a bunch in college. "When Desert Storm started, they checked for bombs under our school bus at each stop, and there were guards with machine guns posted at the front of our building."

When I was eight, we moved to Pennsylvania. My dad taught ROTC—the program for college students who plan to become military officers—and coached the rifle team at Penn State. It was our first civilian neighborhood. We lived around the corner from Joe Paterno in a little one-story rancher with a walkout basement and screened back porch. It was the first time I met kids who'd known each other for more than one or two years. Some of them even had parents who'd grown up together!

"It hurt more to leave there than the other places because I knew my friends would all get to stay together. On the bases, people coming and going was just a part of life."

After that was White Sands Missile Range in New Mexico. I was in fifth grade and loved disappearing into the desert with my friends for adventure, the missiles being tested screaming over our heads and into the mountains. We had two pecan trees in our yard and collected the nuts so my mom could make pie.

We finally settled in Maryland when we moved to Aberdeen Proving Grounds and lived in an old stone house across the street from the first hole of one of the base's golf courses. All the moving was hard for my mom and sisters.

"My dad always asked me to keep my feelings to myself so I wouldn't make it harder on them, so that's what I did. To be honest, I'm a little uncomfortable with the whole therapy thing. I tend to keep my drama to myself."

"It's not drama, Mark. You've been through a terrible tragedy," she says. "Let's just take it slowly and see if there are things we can work on together to manage what you're going through."

The momentary detour from my background toward a discussion of my loss sends a wave of grief washing over me, and I have to fight to stifle a sob.

"Growing up in a military family must have been very different from most people's childhoods," Kara says, redirecting me from the pain.

"Ha. Yeah you could say that," I say, recomposing myself.

All the men I knew were soldiers and officers. The culture was intensely patriotic. Liberty and justice weren't just words; they were ideals that were worth dying for. My dad taught me to live by a code: the strong protect the weak, men fulfill their duties, and there is no higher honor than to give your life for someone else. There is good, and there is evil. "Be one of the good guys," he'd say.

Lessons about duty, honor, and sacrifice were reinforced in Boy Scouts, also led by military officers and Army Rangers. We attended Catholic church religiously. I guess that's the only way to attend Catholic church, but you get my point; we did it every week.

"My upbringing gave me a very black and white perspective on right and wrong. I've always thought of myself as one of the good guys."

I was an altar boy and then a lector, reading the weekly message to the congregation each Sunday. I volunteered as a swim coach with the Special Olympics and worked at a school for kids with special needs. I was kind and learned to make friends quickly.

"My high school class voted me "Most Likely to Make You Smile," I tell her with a momentary grin. It's the thing I am most proud of.

So far, this isn't so bad. I thought I was going to be expected to lay on a couch and pour my heart out about Laura, but so far it's just talking about growing up.

"Would you feel comfortable telling me a little about Laura," Kara asks.

*I guess we couldn't avoid the topic forever.*

"She was my best friend. It's hard to explain, but we just fit together perfectly. I never felt so comfortable around somebody before. Being with her was exhilarating, but it was also comfortable and relaxing. I was never really myself until I was with Laura. I was just whoever I needed to be to fit in."

I tell her that Laura was incredibly loyal. "When she was

in your corner, you knew it. And she was *always* in my corner." She was playful and fun, laughed easily, and didn't take life too seriously. "She was just fun to be around."

I miss her so much, and I can't imagine having to live my whole life without her. "And on top of that, I feel like I let everyone down. I'm so embarrassed."

What I don't say because I'm not one to make a scene, and I'm not ready to be totally open with her, is that assuming the police are right, and I was driving, it's clear I'm not one of the good guys. I'm one of the bad guys. *Probably always was.* I broke the rules by driving drunk and putting other people's lives in danger. The night of the crash wasn't the first time. It was just the worst time. I didn't fulfill my duty to keep Laura safe. I put her life in danger, and because of me, she died.

The other part of the code I learned growing up was to never be a wimp who cries or doubts himself. If there was a challenge, it wasn't enough to overcome it. I needed to destroy it with overwhelming force. I was strong and stoic. My emotions were mine, and, unless my feelings were going to help you, I kept them to myself. I mostly followed the rules. And if someone messed with the people I loved, I'd go through a wall to protect them. But now I cry all the time, and I don't just doubt myself. I hate myself. I'm sitting in this chair, looking at my feet and rubbing my toes into the berber carpet, hoping this stranger can make all the pain go away. I'm an evil, rotten, no-good, failure who can't take care of himself. A loser. A killer. Probably a criminal. I'm not the son my parents raised. I don't know how they can even look at me now.

"I don't remember what happened, but the police told me I was driving. She was supposed to drive, but they say it was me. What if I killed her?" I ask desperately. "A few weeks ago, I thought I was this impressive guy, going to this great law school, about to graduate and start a big-time legal career. At night I would shop for big wedding rings and cars to buy when I had all that money. Now I'm embarrassed to be alive, and I know everyone thinks I'm a killer."

"I don't think people are thinking that. It seems like a lot of people are worried about you," she says. "Our time tonight is just about up, but I want to tell you how thankful I am that you let me get to know you a bit. I think it would be really good if we saw each other again in a week, and maybe we could talk more about Laura. Would that work for you?"

# CHAPTER 5

*"We had a plan," I tell her accusingly. "How could you change the plan?"*

*"You think this is my fault?" She's irate.*

*"I'm not the one who changed the plan. You were supposed to drive. I'm pretty sure we didn't get to the car, and I decided, 'what the hell, let me drive even though I'm wasted.'"*

*"So you do think this is my fault," she replies, challenging me to just come out and say it.*

*"Yes, dammit. It's your fault. You were the designated driver. The autopsy says you were drinking. Not as much as me, but you were! I was counting on you."*

*"What do you want me to say? I'm sorry? Fine, I'm sorry."*

*It's not just that she didn't do what she promised to do. It's that I'm the one left behind to deal with the pain of losing her and all the other fallout from her death. She's pleading with her eyes, but I won't give her the satisfaction.*

*"You have no idea what this is like. You should be here feeling this. Not me. Every day now is the worst day of my life. I hate, I hate, being around all these people either pitying me or judging me. And even worse is seeing your family. You turned me into a monster who did this horrible thing. And I miss you. I need you. And you're not here. You were supposed to always be here."*

*"I'm sorry. I don't know what else I can say. I'm sorry. I'm sorry. You're right."*

*"I wish I were dead, but you're the one who gets to be. Your dad told*

*me he thinks I had to survive because you wouldn't be able to pick yourself
up off the ground if it had been the other way around. But I don't feel like
I'm off the ground, and I don't want to be alive without you. It isn't fair
that you aren't suffering any of it."*

❖

I wake up ashamed of dreaming my anger and blaming
her in my sleep. When I'm awake and I start to blame her, I
can shut it down pretty quickly. She's dead, and I'm alive. She's
dead, and it's my fault. I walked away from the crash with barely a scratch. Her body was ripped apart and her life was ended.
It takes a lot of gall to get mad at the woman you loved, the
woman you killed.

But I can't hide it from my dreams. I'm mad at her. My
dad used to say "if you fail to plan, plan to fail" and "proper
prior planning prevents piss poor performance." Well, we had
a plan. And I wasn't the one who was supposed to be responsible for keeping us safe the night of the crash. I'm not just mad
at her for letting me drive, though. I'm mad at her for being
dead, for leaving me.

*How could she?*

I look over to Laura's side of the bed and shake my head
at the place where she should be laying. Her side is still made,
the bunny blanket her grandmother made her as a child spread
out for her to sleep with.

After Laura's funeral, I'd gone back to the house in Magothy Manor to finish moving out the rest of my belongings,

but I hadn't really done any of the work. Some of my friends had come to help. I wandered listlessly among them as they worked, too overwhelmed to know where to start. It felt like I wasn't even there, like everything was happening around me. Everyone was there *for me*, but nobody expected anything *from me*. I felt invisible, like a ghost. It wasn't the first or the last time I thought maybe I *had actually died* in the car too. I'm still stuck in my body on earth. The body breathes, and the blood flows, but the spark of life has left. By the end of the day, I'd been exhausted. The house was empty, and I knew I would never see the place again.

I stayed on my sister Courtney's couch for a couple of weeks, and then she invited me to move in for as long as I needed to stay.

Courtney and I look alike: round-faced, full lips, receding chin, and rosy cheeks. Unlike me, she is short and petite. She has spiky hair and a hip style. Courtney and her partner are new moms. My nephew is three months old. Their house is an old brick row home tucked away in the corner of the neighborhood, across the street from the train tracks.

I sit up and look around the room. I'm so grateful to have a place to stay, but my gratitude doesn't change the reality that the basement of this Baltimore row home is a big step down from the perfect little nest Laura and I created at our home on the Magothy River. It has a low ceiling with exposed pipes and wires running about. Not in the cool industrial way that modern places do. More in the this-place-isn't-really-meant-to-be-inhabited kind of way.

There's a laundry room with some storage space, a small living area, and the bedroom I'm in right now with a single square window about a foot above the outside ground level. It's still dark out, but even in the daytime not much natural light comes in, and the fluorescent lights are too bright. The wall of the bedroom is cinder blocks, and dust from the mortar falls in piles on the window ledge. The basement reminds me of a dungeon, and that's what I've decided to name it. *The dungeon.* It feels appropriate that this is where I live now.

Outside, the urban ambiance consists of the patter of scurrying rats, the stench of trash, and burning fuel from the trains on the tracks just across the street. At night, I fall asleep to the bickering of drunks stumbling through the alley that passes by the window to my dungeon.

Rocko has always had an old-man droopy face, but now he's got his head in my lap all the time, looking up at me questioningly. I can't tell if he misses Laura or his home or having his yard to run around. Probably all of it. Looking at him reminds me of how she used to hold his face in her hands and put her forehead affectionately on his, telling him, "you're such a good boy" in our silly Rocko voice.

I reach for the journal on her side of the bed. I've been so worried that my memories of Laura will fade. Scratch that. I know and agonize over the fact that my memories will fade. I understand from moving so much as a kid how hard it is to remember people and places after they're ripped from your life. Other people remember their childhood homes because they can drive by them as adults. They can picture times they shared with their best friend because they still know them. But when people and places are gone, the mind has a way of erasing them.

I've started a journal to write down everything I can about Laura. Her smell. The taste of her lips. The brown flecks in her blue eyes. The strange white imperfection on one of her teeth. The way she walked, her hips bouncing from side to side beneath her slender back. I have pictures, but they'll never be enough. I don't want to remember her as a still life. I want to remember her in motion. I regret that I don't have more videos of her, any videos really. I can't hear her voice or her laughter anymore, except in my memories. I don't even have any voicemails; I'm the type who deletes them as soon as I listen to them.

*That was dumb, but how could I have known?*

I don't want to forget a moment of our life together, and I feel like I should be the custodian of the stories her friends have shared with me since her death, obligated to keep them and retell them, the guardian of *her story*. As long as I have her story, she's not really gone.

So I write everything I remember as soon as I remember it. "She used to hold Rocko's face with her two hands under his chin and tell him what a good boy he was," I write.

Even more troubling than the idea of my memory fading is the strange sense that the private memories I shared with Laura no longer matter. If there's nobody to remember the Outer Banks trip we took, nobody can agree with me that it was the most serene and perfect time two people could experience. If the memory can't be shared and discussed, if nobody can vouch for it, were the yellow curtains and the cool breeze just my own construct around an event that may or may not have been as perfect as I remember it?

The somber realization heightens my grief: not only have I lost our future, but I've also lost our past. There's no longer anything tangible to it, no connection to something outside my own mind.

*It may as well be the Matrix.*

I brought plastic bags full of photos from the old house. At Magothy Manor, they'd decorated our whole house. Now I've placed them around the dungeon, surrounding me and Rocko in every direction with the best memories of our life with her. I'd made her a photo book with pictures of us as a gift. I flip through it every day now. I put our loose photos and mementos in a scrapbook, the physical remnants of our love that prove she was here.

When Laura's parents and I collected her belongings, I placed her clothes and our sheets in plastic trash bags and sealed them tightly. I've been removing one of her t-shirts at a time and quickly resealing the bag to keep her smell on the remaining pieces of fabric for as long as possible. It's not the smell of her shampoo or the cocoa butter lotion she rubbed on her skin each day. I could buy those in a store and be reminded of her. I've been savoring the smell of her skin on her clothes, of her in the morning before she got out of bed. For the rest of my life, I think I'd recognize her smell just as easily as I'd recognize her face or the sound of her laughter.

I wrap myself in the grief and guilt like a warm blanket. It feels good to feel miserable. I settle down inside the pain, surrounded by her, to suffer. The worse I feel, the closer she feels. And if I feel horrible and guilty enough, maybe I'm not the awful person I know I must be if I really did what the police say I did. When a little bit of humor or joy sneaks in, I force it out. There is no room for happiness in the dungeon.

❖

I've always tried to keep my feelings to myself, but there's no keeping my grief private. Anyone can see the distress plainly on my face, and Courtney has taken on the role of caregiver since I moved in, staying up late to comfort me with her company.

We're sitting on the Ikea sleeper sofa in her living room, talking about Laura while she nurses my baby nephew. When she's finished, she hands him to me. I hold him and love him, but I can't help thinking his life is some cosmic bargain the universe made for my family: one new life in, one old life out. And I'm ashamed that if the price of this new precious life is the loss of Laura's, I wouldn't have made the bargain. I begrudge him his existence, and I begrudge Courtney for her happy motherhood. At the same time, I'm so grateful to her for the care and welcome, the familiar affection of my oldest friend.

I don't understand grief, and I've been reading the grief books recommended by friends who've previously experienced the deaths of loved ones. There's a stack of them sitting on the ledge under the window in the dungeon. Laura's is the first death I've ever deeply grieved. People at the periphery of my life have died, and it saddened me. But this is the first loss to linger, to demand my full attention, to feel like a part of my life has been torn away. In losing her, the entire future I pictured collapsed. We will never marry, never have kids, and never grow old together.

"I don't think any of us can really understand what another person is going through. I mean, we can try," I explain to Courtney, telling her about one of the books I've been reading. "But there are just so many factors that affect a person's grief." Things like our relationship with the person who died, the things we wanted to say but never did, the futures we planned, the memories we shared, and the depth and kind of love between us all shape the way we grieve.

"We bring all our own shit to the grief too," I continue. Have we previously experienced the loss of a loved one? Are we introspective? Emotional? Do we have a history of depression? Are we stoic, not prone to display our sorrow? "And the way the person dies matters too." Grief can be complicated or relieved by the circumstances of the death. Did the person live what we consider to be a full life, and die peacefully? Did they suffer from a long illness? Were they cruelly taken from the world unexpectedly? Do we feel responsible for not doing more?

I pick up my nephew, Lucky, and blow raspberries on his little milk-full belly. "Or, you can be like me and actually be the horrible person who did it," I say to my nephew in one of those goofy voices people like to use when they talk to babies. Then, sighing, I look out the window and lose my train of thought.

I'm in the middle of *A Grief Observed* by C.S. Lewis, and I start to think about it now. It's about Lewis' experience grieving for his wife of four years after her death from cancer. Like me, he feels compelled to document, to remember, to ensure he won't forget. Reading it, the similarities to my own emotional experience stick out. But, I can't help feeling envious of Lewis. He got to marry his love. She was sick; he knew for years that he would lose her. He got to tell her how much he would miss her, how she had made his life a better one. They got to say a long goodbye and make the most of the time they had together. You had it easy, C.S. Lewis. Try waking up to find her gone out of nowhere.

*Try being the one who killed her.*

But I know others who've had to watch a loved one die slowly and wish their person could have gone more easily, that they didn't have to suffer, that they didn't have to dread the end.

My mind comes back to the living room, and I smile sheepishly at Courtney. "It's probably never easy. It's always just horrible."

The real agony is my separation from Laura and the knowledge that my path continues—that it will wind in unforeseen ways, with new adventures and sorrows, successes, failures, surprises, letdowns, and accomplishments—while hers has ended and fallen away from mine forever. My body feels different without Laura in the world, like a part of me is missing too.

"I think I might have died with her," I tell Courtney,

apropos of nothing and certain she can't possibly understand. There is still a Mark O'Brien. But he's just a body now. The spark of life is gone.

# CHAPTER 6

"What do you think about the police situation?" Kara leans back slightly as she settles into our session.

"I'm in pretty deep shit if I was driving."

I never imagined I would be the one in need of a criminal defense lawyer. When I started law school, I wanted to help people less fortunate than myself. A career of service to others would have matched the values I'd been raised with. I'd considered becoming a criminal defense lawyer or doing public interest work for people with disabilities or mental illness. Laura was going to be a social worker and help people addicted to drugs. We were two young idealists out to make the world a better place.

But after a year of law school, my plans changed. The money and power that would come with a job at a top law firm were so alluring. The plan became to work as a corporate tax attorney. I was at one of the top law schools in the country, excelling in my classes, and working at the United States Tax Court with a front-row seat for some of the biggest tax cases in the country. I thought I had it made.

I'm technically still in my final semester of law school, but I'm not attending any of my classes. The school dean said I can come back and finish the semester whenever I'm ready, but I don't think I'll ever be.

Now I've got three separate legal issues because of the crash, and I'm the one in need of legal assistance. Laura's family could sue me for causing her death. The motor vehicle administration is probably going to take my driver's license. And, worst of all, I could be charged with negligent manslaughter.

"I could go to prison for up to ten years, and there's no way they'll ever let me practice law with that kind of conviction." Despite the reputation of lawyers being unscrupulous, the bar doesn't look favorably on felons.

My mom knows I'm not just heartbroken but also in serious trouble. She's been doing everything she can to help. I'm trying to feel grateful, but I'm also feeling a little suffocated by it. It hurts so much to see her look at me with so much sadness. She's a strong lady. She lived the dutiful life of an army wife, making a new home for my sisters and me every few years, uprooting and restarting with friends and jobs, until my dad left her after eighteen years. She was a mess at first, but she met my stepfather, got remarried, and found happiness again. She's diminutive but energetic, with brown hair and green eyes, and wears her heart on her sleeve. Right after the crash, she called a family friend who's a lawyer and asked for advice. He told her he could handle the stuff with the driver's license, but the homicide charges were out of his realm.

"He told us to contact his friend, and I met with Harry, the lawyer he recommended, the other day."

I showed up at Harry's office in my best I-was-going-to-be-a-lawyer suit, thinking I should be as formal as a lawyer in court would be. He showed up in jeans and a sweater like a normal person.

My first impression was that Harry was young but not too

young, and his thick Irish brogue made him instantly likable. He was graying just enough to let you know he had experience. He was gregarious and animated, and he took the right amount of time to express his sympathy before diving into the case.

I told him about the accident and Laura's family's forgiveness. "They don't want me to suffer any more than I already have," I told him.

He's a lawyer, so he's always thinking about risk, and he warned me it might not stay that way.

"He said I should stay in touch with them to keep on their good side because if they get mad, my legal situation might get worse," I sneer. "I know it's his job, but that felt like a really slimy reason to be nice to them. I can't even believe they let me come to her funeral."

Kara nods her understanding, encouraging me to continue. I look down and rub the wood of the armrest with my thumb.

"I told him Laura was our designated driver, and I didn't remember the accident or have any idea how I wound up driving. He said I might not have been. Accident scenes are chaotic, and it's possible the police got it wrong. But the more I think about it, that seems a little far fetched to me," I tell her. "He's having an investigator interview everyone who was at the party to see if we can find out more, and he said he'll also get the police reports and autopsy if he can."

"Can we talk about the accident? *Do you* remember any of it?"

I thumb the armrest harder, trying to wipe away some

invisible stain on the wood. I look down at my feet still rubbing nervously against the carpeting and invite the bitter jumbled memory of the crash back into my consciousness.

"I don't remember a lot. I remember being at the bar with her. We had seats, and everyone was standing around us, toasting me and buying me shots. The next thing I know, I'm hanging upside down in my car."

I tell her about the paramedic who I thought said I was gone. "I thought he meant I was dying, like that scene in *Signs* where Mel Gibson's wife is pinned against the tree, and the cop tells him his wife is dying."

"I wanted to get out of the car, but I couldn't," I start to panic and take a deep breath to calm myself down. "I didn't know she was there. I don't know why I never turned to look, or maybe I couldn't see her for some reason."

"After that, I was in the hospital, and they were telling me Laura was dead," I continue. "I know this wasn't real—I promise I know—but it felt like I was floating out of my body in the hospital, just watching myself."

"Something like what you've been through can do that to a person. Trauma and grief can feel truly strange and disorienting." Kara says trauma is a completely normal psychological response to terrifying events where we fear for our life or safety or witness the death of someone we love.

"You had both those experiences wrapped up into one. Our brains go into a state of shock, and it's not uncommon for people to feel like they're out of their bodies. It's called disassociation, and it's one way your brain protects you from being overwhelmed in the moment."

"It probably did keep me from losing my mind in the hospital," I say. "I'm usually very sharp, but I've been so scatterbrained since the crash. I feel like I'm just stumbling through each day. It's so weird. How can I not remember the accident or seeing Laura in the car? I loved her so much, and she was hanging in the car dead next to me, and I don't even remember it." Not remembering feels like a betrayal on top of my guilt. Not only am I responsible for her death; I didn't care enough in the moment to even notice she was there.

"I just found out a few days ago from a newspaper article that they cut me out of the car with the jaws of life and flew me to shock trauma in a helicopter."

"You might not have seen her, Mark. Our brains do strange things when we're in shock. There was a lot happening at the scene, and your attention could have been on other things the whole time. You just said that *you thought you were dying.* And it's also possible that the memory is just too painful, so your brain is protecting you from it. You might never know, but at some point, the memory could come back to you. If it starts to come back, or you think it does, we should talk about that."

"I've never ridden in a helicopter. My brain could at least have let me remember that." I force a grin as I say it, trying to protect Kara from the pain I'm feeling. Humor is a good way to do that.

"Trauma can really mess with your memory," Kara explains.

Inquisitive by nature, I ask her why our memories would stop working.

"It seems like we'd evolve to remember something like this so we could learn from it," I say.

"That makes sense, but there's a trade-off. Your brain knows the situation is dangerous, so it's programmed to prioritize reacting over learning."

Perceiving serious danger, the primal parts of our brain disrupt our normal memory storage so we can react more quickly to the threat. Our memories aren't properly stored away and remain in the active parts of our brains. Experiences like this are difficult to describe because our brain hasn't shaped our memory coherently. The memories of danger remain active, so we stay on edge and alert.

"How is it going at your sister's house?" Kara asks, changing the subject.

I tell her the dungeon is less than optimal, but it's good to be around other people. I don't feel like taking care of myself, but I shower, brush my teeth, and wear clean clothes since I regularly see other humans.

Courtney spends a lot of time with me. She has a wonderful way of talking just the right amount about Laura and making me feel comfortable talking about her too. When the moment is right, Courtney brings up her memories of Laura and times Laura and I spent with her.

"When I don't want to talk about Laura, she gets it, and she doesn't push. Other people either don't want to talk about her at all, or they won't drop it when it's too much for me to handle," I explain.

Courtney doesn't judge how I'm grieving, but she's there to listen whenever I need her. Growing up, she was one of the only constants in my life, always right down the hall wherever in the world we moved, and she's there for me now.

My other sister doesn't know how to handle my grief. She is so uncomfortable with all the emotions involved, all the emotions I'm showing. "She's just like me. I wouldn't want to be around me either," I say. One afternoon she was supposed to visit me but canceled because she was going to see the Body Worlds exhibit that showcases dead people preserved in colored plastic. The colored plastics highlight various organs, muscles, bones, veins, and arteries.

"She invited me to go too." I laugh acerbically. "Like, why the hell would I want to see *that* right now?"

The fact that she was comfortable going to gawk at dead bodies and thought I would be too felt offensive. On the one hand, she didn't see my grief clearly enough to know how painful it would be for me to spend the day staring at corpses processed to be literal human spectacles. And on the other hand, she'd been so indifferent to Laura's death, the death of someone who was supposed to be like family to her, that the idea of staring at corpses was palatable for her.

"Part of me thinks she was doing something so morbid because she knew I wouldn't go. It was like a get-out-of-jail-free card for having to hang out with me. She's not the only one. I just think some people don't know how to be around me anymore. I shouldn't blame them, but I do." My eyes are burning, and I'm doing everything I can to hold in my tears. I hadn't realized until this moment how hurt I was by what I saw as my sister's rejection of me.

"It's not unusual for some people to be uncomfortable when they care about someone in such a tough situation," Kara tells me. "I don't think your sister would consciously try to avoid you like that. You told me you were close with both sisters. This might just be really hard for her. Is it something you could talk to her about?"

I look out the window and try to picture what the conversation would be like. I still can't look Kara in the eyes. It's hard to look anyone in the eyes. I know they'll see my pain and patheticness, and if I let them see me, I'll start to cry. I turn my attention back down to the floor before continuing. "I don't think so. I'm not into that kind of drama."

I'm as uncomfortable with conflict as my sister seems to be with me right now, and we don't talk about difficult things in my family. We shove them down and ignore them. It works for us.

"That's okay as long as there are people you feel are there for you now. Support from your friends and family is one of the most important things you can have."

Kara ends our appointment and tells me she'll see me again in a week. "Try to focus on who you can turn to for support between now and then."

I smile sheepishly and nod as I walk to the door she's holding open for me.

❖

Courtney is outside waiting to drive me to her house after the appointment. On the way home, I'm thinking about the end of my conversation with Kara and how all the people in my life have reacted so differently to Laura's death and my grief.

Some of them are so uneasy being around me now. I think my emotions are too heightened for them, and it's stressful because they don't know what to say. Maybe I remind them of their worst fears about losing a loved one or about their own mortality. Maybe some of them are selfish and don't want my sadness to bring down their own mood. Sometimes I can tell they want to be present with me, but they want to talk about anything at all besides Laura. But Laura is all I can think about right now. Everything else seems trivial.

Other people are willing to listen, but if they say the wrong thing about my grief, I hold it against them. It's an opportunity to redirect my anger at someone other than myself. People just don't always know the right thing to say. And in my grief, I'm not very charitable to them.

I've been so angry at Chris for something he said a few weeks ago, even though he's called or visited me every day since the crash. We were sitting on the couch at Courtney's house, and I was telling him overwhelmingly painful it was not having Laura with me.

"I know it's hard," he'd said. "But it might help to have some perspective about it."

He'd seen a story in the news about dozens of women and

children who were murdered in Kenya. "Imagine the pain their loved ones must be feeling after so much loss," he said. "Death is happening all the time. It's just a part of life."

It was the wrong thing to say to me. He only wanted to help. He didn't mean to be hurtful. But in my mind, I've been holding that one slip up against him since then. "How can he be so cold about my loss? How can he think I should keep it in perspective? Why should the deaths of people I don't know thousands of miles away matter at all to me when my entire world is collapsing?" I've thought. But now I'm thinking maybe I should just let it go and be grateful he's trying.

Then there are all the people who think they know how I should grieve: how long, how hard, and in what ways. Most of them have never been through anything as painful as this, but they offer their advice and insight anyway.

"I've heard you'll get over it in about a year."

"You just have to keep living your life."

"If I were you, I wouldn't even be able to leave the house."

"You just have to learn to accept it. You can't change the past."

I wish they'd just listen and keep their opinions to themselves, but I realize now that I'm also guilty of thinking I know best how others should grieve. I'm mad at my sister for not grieving Laura the way I think she should. Who am I to say she isn't grieving right? Who am I to say that in her grief over Laura, she should have no interest in seeing an exhibit so many people are interested in? Maybe it's her way of better understanding that bodies are just physical vessels, or maybe for her, it has no relationship at all to Laura's death. Laura undoubtedly meant more to me than she did to my sister, and my pain is heightened because I'm also the one who caused Laura's death. Why should I think my sister's grief would be as intense as mine or that she would express it in the same ways that I do? It's fair to be upset that she canceled her plans with me when I needed her, but it's not fair to be angry with her for how she grieves. If I want people to be comfortable around me, I should probably cut them all some slack.

# CHAPTER 7

Two weeks later, I'm sitting on the couch in the dungeon, reading a book about the stages of grief by Elisabeth Kubler-Ross and David Kessler. The stages are denial, anger, bargaining, depression, and acceptance. They don't always happen in order, and people move back and forth into and out of them. I feel like I'm cycling between denial, bargaining, depression, and anger every day, sometimes every hour. I haven't had any moments of acceptance.

I think about how each of the stages feels. In my moments of denial, it's not that intellectually I don't know that Laura has died. It's just that I'm not ready to acknowledge the reality and finality of it, and denial keeps me from experiencing all at once what it means for her to be gone. For that brief moment when I forget she's gone, everything is normal. *Denial is the absolute best.*

When I'm in the bargaining phase, I try to make deals that will somehow bring her back or make the pain more bearable. I beg God to make the pain stop or let me wake up and find out the loss is only a nightmare. I promise if I can just wake up from this horror, I'll dedicate my life to helping others. I ask for God to swap me out, return Laura to her family and have me instead. I wish I could trade places with her, or at least know I'll see her when I die.

Depression is the worst and the best. It hurts the most, but it's also when I feel most connected to her. The pain of the loss focuses my mind entirely on her. I don't feel like getting out of bed or going on with my life at all. That's because there is no point to life anymore, besides suffering. *I guess suffering could be the point.*

The book warns that our loved ones will try to shake us out of our depression prematurely, but if we want to heal, the experts say we have to spend time with these feelings and process them in our own time. Some of the people who try to cheer us up when we're depressed are waiting for us to reach acceptance and hoping we can quickly "get over" what has happened. They're the people I've noticed being so uncomfortable around me. They mean well; they just don't understand how grief works. They don't know what acceptance means. There is no "getting over" a great loss.

The book says that when I find acceptance, it won't mean I'm okay with what happened, only that I understand that the loss is a permanent fact of my life. I'll learn to live in a world that doesn't include Laura. I may want my life to be the same as when she was alive, but I'll accept that it cannot go back to the way it was. It doesn't sound like a place I'll ever reach.

❖

I put the book down and pull one of Laura's shirts from the plastic bag that's been keeping her smell from fading away. Every time I've pulled out a new piece of fabric, it's kept its scent for a little less time than the last one. And now this one doesn't smell like her at all. None of them do.

I feel like I'm losing her all over again. At first, I want to crumble into a ball on the floor and weep, but then a wave of heat sweeps over me, and I'm cursing God for what I'm going through and for taking Laura from me, from her family, from the world. This is the anger phase.

These days, my anger comes in many forms. I'm mad at Laura for being gone and the universe for taking her from me. I'm angry that I didn't have more time with her, and I'm angry that my life has been so completely turned upside down. I'm especially angry at the bastard who caused all this, myself.

One of my favorite targets for anger is God. I wonder how a loving God, a God who is supposed to be good, could so cruelly take my love and happiness, could so unfairly allow the death of a girl with so much life in her and ahead of her. Is all this punishment for something I did? For something she did? A shot across the bow to remind me he's there? Can the idea of a loving and good God be reconciled with that kind of viciousness?

"How can you do this to me? How can you do this to her? I'm supposed to believe you're good? You? You let this happen," I say out loud, my voice dripping with disdain. "You're either not real, or you're a real asshole."

Growing up, my family attended Catholic mass every weekend. We volunteered and participated in all the rituals and events of our church. That all changed when my parents got divorced. I was in high school, and my dad was the driving force behind my faith. He was the one whose values I'd always strived to model. His was the only way I knew to think about the world.

I believed the best way to live was with duty, honor, patriotism, and a firm understanding of good and evil. But I also saw his leaving as a hypocritical failure to live up to the values he preached. He taught me to see the world without shades of gray, and divorcing my mom and leaving us was a clear violation of the code. I gave him no benefit of the doubt. So, I kept the values, but I refused to acknowledge any authority in my life. I rebelled. I drank. I did drugs. I fought. And I stopped going to church.

By the time I met Laura, I wasn't in full rebellion against the church anymore; I was just indifferent. Laura and I were both "Catholic," but we weren't really practicing. We attended mass occasionally with her family. If someone asked, I would have said I was Catholic *but not really Catholic*. I believed in God but didn't spend much time thinking about it.

But losing Laura has forced me to rethink my relationship with God. I desperately need a connection to the spiritual world. It's the only way I see to connect with her. My internal monologue is increasingly with God or with Laura. I feel like I have a phone line in my brain that connects me directly to them. My self-talk is no longer with myself but with them.

Sometimes, I beg God to care for her and reunite me with her when I die. I want to believe, I need to believe, that there is something after this life. Sometimes at night, I swear I see her at the foot of my bed. She looks at me so lovingly, so serenely, but there's a touch of melancholy in her eyes. She's not sad for herself. She's sad for me. She wants me to know she's at peace, and she wants peace for me too. I wake up more convinced that there's an afterlife, that there's something more than our physical existence. I believe she is still somewhere.

In that moment, I experience pure joy. All the anxiety of my loss disappears like fog burning off in the morning sun. All the anxiety of not knowing what comes after death, for Laura, for all of us, vanishes.

Praying isn't just a way to connect to Laura. It also seems like the best way to earn an afterlife with her. I pray constantly. Not daily. Not hourly. All the time. I beg God for forgiveness for the crash and for every other rotten thing I've ever done. I feel so much more connected spiritually, but my constant prayers for forgiveness and efforts to get back in God's good graces, are also part of the bargaining phase of grief. I'm playing *Let's Make a Deal: God and Death Edition.* I'll pray more, and in exchange, you promise to let me be with Laura after I die.

Even though most of the praying I'm doing is just bargaining with God over the terms of Laura's death, some of it is actually increasing my spiritual satisfaction. But that's not the case with the conversation I'm having right now. Right now, in the dungeon, I'm not trying to earn my place in heaven or connect with a loving God. I'm pissed.

"Why would anyone praise you? You don't deserve that. I'm glad I turned my back on you. You're just a bunch of bullshit."

My interactions with God have never been more authentic than this. Even in my anger, the feeling of closeness is uncanny. I have no doubt God is there. I know he's hearing me. I know that he knows I'm pissed.

I'm not distracted. I'm not saying some formulaic, rote prayer. This conversation is intimate, honest. I think maybe God appreciates the real talk, but I also don't care what he thinks right now. He's an asshole.

As my tirade reaches a crescendo, I feel the floor beneath my feet become wet and look down. The basement is flooding. Some of my stuff is already ruined. Is God now giving me a piece of *his* mind?

*I better watch myself. I've seen what this jerk can do when he's mad.*

❖

But honestly, I'm not sure I even care. What's he going to do at this point? He's taken everything that matters.

Losing Laura is making me insane. Even though I know she's died, my heart refuses to accept it. I'm starting to see things that aren't there, like her walking ahead of me on the street or in the train station. I enjoy the delusion, and once I remember she's gone, I squint my eyes so I can pretend it's her for just a little longer. Or I think I hear her voice. Or I pull out my phone to call her. In the moment before I realize what I'm doing, that she isn't going to answer, for just a second, life feels normal.

For as long as I can remember, I'd struggled with insomnia, even as a kid. I've read that some people have a hard time falling asleep after a traumatic event. But I am so emotionally exhausted every day, that for the first time in my life, I fall asleep easily. I lay down to sleep and talk to Laura. I ask her—beg her actually—to visit me. Sometimes it seems like she's there with me. Like I can feel her holding me. Like the softness and warmth of her love is surrounding me. Those nights, I sleep so peacefully.

On other nights, I have nightmares. In one, I see Laura, and she is terrified. I go to comfort her and realize *she's afraid of me.* She turns, horrified, and sprints away from the monster who hurt her. I chase her, begging for her to stop, telling her I would never hurt her, but she knows I'm dangerous. In another, I find out Laura is still alive. I see her on an airplane returning home. I'm overjoyed and throw my arms around her. She backs away and explains that she faked her death to get away from me. She never really loved me, but she didn't know how to end it.

Some nights, I don't remember my dreams, but I wake up sure I was about to die. At first, I think the wetness is just my sweat, but then I realize I've peed myself in fear.

When I'm awake, I sometimes don't believe she's really dead. I know it's insane. *I promise.* I really do know it's insane. I concoct extraordinarily far-fetched scenarios to explain what happened. I wonder if she really did fake her death to get away from me. Or maybe we are part of some despicable CIA study where they're trying to find out how much of someone's life you have to take away to destroy them. *Does Laura know we're in the study? Is she impressed with how I'm handling myself so far? At what point in the study do I get her back?*

I know it's crazy, but it doesn't seem as crazy as what's actually happened. How can everything change so quickly? One second you're going out to celebrate a birthday with the woman you love, and the next second you're packing up her things because she's dead. There has to be a bigger explanation. There has to.

I've kept her toothbrush and her hairbrush since we cleaned out Magothy Manor. I think maybe someday we'll be able to clone people, and if I have her DNA, I'll be able to have her back. They've cloned a sheep. Surely there will be people clones soon. Of course, the clone Laura will be different from the real Laura. But, she'll also be the same in many ways. I'll get to see her again. It probably won't be appropriate for me to date her—I'll be so much older—but I could be her friend, and have her in my life again.

I'm in so much pain. Relentless pain. I can't explain what has happened. I just know that a horrible mistake has been made. Laura is not supposed to be gone, and I am not supposed to be without her. I know there must be some explanation and some way for me to get her back. I think about her all day every day. I count down the years, hours, and minutes I have left to live without her. If this is real and permanent, it feels like death will be the only release from the hurt.

I'm reluctant to put more people through the pain I'm feeling, but I think often of taking my own life. My Catholic upbringing makes me believe suicide might cost me my chance to be with Laura again; she is definitely in heaven. But I think I've found a loophole in the heaven rule when I decide that if I can run hard enough to give myself a heart attack, it's not really suicide because I'm just exercising. I try it, but it doesn't work. I run out of steam before my heart breaks. I mean, it's broken already, but not enough to kill me. Instead, dozens of times a day, I fantasize about a gun floating in the air. Nobody is holding it, absolving me of responsibility, but it's placed against my head. The trigger squeezes.

*Click. Bang. Oblivion.*
*It's my fault she is dead.*
*Click. Bang. Oblivion.*
*I'm not the person I thought I was.*
*Click. Bang. Oblivion.*
*This pain will never end.*
*Click. Bang. Oblivion.*

God has taken everything from me. So what if he's mad I'm yelling at him. He took Laura. He took my future. He took my sanity. And I don't even want to be alive. What else could he possibly do?

I stand up, pick up some towels to dry the floor, and stick my middle finger up to the sky.

# CHAPTER 8

*"I just wish I'd gotten to marry you," I tell her.*

*"You did. Well, sort of. Don't you remember Vegas?" As she says it, we're transported there, and the lights of the Strip emerge around us.*

*Last year, Laura and I took a trip to Las Vegas and stayed at the Stratosphere. We drank in the lights, the sounds, the free drinks, and each other.*

*"Remember we walked down there and stopped at all the hotels?" She points down the Strip and the path we'd taken that night. We'd gone to The Mirage, Caesar's Palace, Treasure Island. It was a long walk, and we didn't quite make it down to the Luxor.*

*"That pink dress you were wearing made me want to make it a short trip out and get you back to the hotel room." After just a couple hours on the town, I suggested we head back.*

*"Do you remember the cab driver?"*

*"I do now." He was jovial and buoyant, like our moods, and had a warm Caribbean accent.*

*"Remember what happened after he asked if we were married?"*

*"We told him we weren't and he asked if we loved each other."*

*"Yes," we said in unison.*

*"Then what's the holdup? Marry the girl, my man," he said back, grinning in the rearview mirror.*

*"We laughed so hard, and you told him our whole life plan. Finish law school. Ask my dad's permission. Get a big lawyer job so you could get the big ring you thought I deserved." She says "big lawyer job" with playful teasing in her voice.*

"Nah, man. If it's love, you just do it," he said. "You're in Vegas. I can take you somewhere right now."

We were both tipsy and blissful, laughing and enjoying the conversation.

"My dad would kill me if we did it without him," Laura told him.

"It's easy. Let's just do it here. What are your names?"

"Laura and Mark."

"Do you, Mark, take Laura to be your wife?"

"Ha. Yes, of course, I do."

"Good. Do you, Laura, take Mark to be your husband."

"Forever, yes. I do."

"Kiss her, man. That's it!"

I look at Laura and start to cry." He was right, you know? 'If it's love, you just do it.' I was so stupid to think I needed more money to get you the best ring before we could start our life together."

"We did start our life together, Mark. I knew it was forever then, and I still do," she says, and I touch my chest where I got the tattoo the week after she died. I had the tattoo artist trace her handwriting on my heart. It says "forever."

"I just wish we'd gotten to have all the big moments and the big day. I never got the chance to ask you. You never got the chance to say yes. We never got the marriage license. We never got to have children. Or grow old together," I tell her.

"But we did get to say 'I do.'"

"I guess that's something. I love you." I kiss her forehead.

"I love you too. Forever."

❖

I wake up thinking about Las Vegas and some of the other wild times I spent with Laura. I partied a lot in college, less so in law school, and by the time of the crash, I was so busy with classes, preparing for the bar exam, working at the court, and applying for law firm jobs and judicial clerkships that I barely drank at all.

You might think I'd never drink another drop after the crash. Instead, I've been drinking all the time. I have plenty of time to drink. I'm not going to classes anymore. My job at the court is part-time. I've stopped looking for a job or preparing for the bar exam since the bar probably won't accept me with homicide charges hanging over my head, and I don't have the energy or focus for it anyway. I'm probably going to prison, and I have plenty of sorrows to drown. I've lost everything that matters, so hey, *what do I have to lose by having a few drinks?*

I went out to the bar last night and ran into some of my high school friends. Like most of the people I see these days, they knew about Laura, but they didn't talk about it. There were some guys about our age glaring at us at the bar. I think they were just looking for whatever trouble they could find. When the bar closed, and my friends and I started walking home, they were walking behind us, talking shit. I was trying to ignore them.

"You're going to make me break my promise," I thought to myself.

I used to get in fights, but it was usually because I was

defending someone else, protecting someone I cared about. Occasionally, I was just being stupid. It's been a couple years since the last brawl. It was St. Patrick's Day, and I was off work, so Laura and I had walked to the Irish pub by her house, the Irish pub I worked at. I got wasted that night, and on the way home, some guys had whistled at her from their car, then rolled up their window and drove away. It was disrespectful to Laura, and I felt it was my job to defend her. I chased the car down at the next red light, punched the passenger in the head through the window, and fought him and his three friends. The police broke it up before anyone got injured. But Laura made me promise I'd never fight again.

"We're getting too old for this," she'd said.

Now it was taking every bit of my self-control not to drop the guys walking behind me running their mouths.

"You promised. Don't disappoint her," I thought. "The last thing you need is to get arrested for fighting while you're hoping not to get arrested for killing her."

But then one of them kicked me. I had no idea why these guys were messing with us. I don't look like someone who's going to start a fight, but this was really uncalled for, even for a bunch of drunk guys.

"He hit me first, babe," I said to her silently. "I'm sorry."

I spun around and drilled the kicker right in his mouth. He fell on his back. Unleashing the rage was the best feeling I'd had in months. I hit him so hard that I lost my balance and started to fall forward. I got my footing and wheeled back around, hoping his two buddies would try to defend him and give me the chance to feel even better by hitting them too. My friends stepped back, amused—they knew I could handle myself.

"Whoa. Sorry man," one of the kicker's friends said. "It was all him." They grabbed the kicker, but he tried to step toward me.

"You wanna end up on your back again?" I mocked him, but I wanted him to keep coming. His friends convinced him it was a bad idea and pulled him away.

The two cops watching from across the street seemed to think my punch was justified, and they turned away as the kicker walked off. I thought about the promise to Laura I'd just broken.

"I hope you think it was justified too. I'm sorry, babe." *For everything.*

❖

I'm getting ready to go out drinking again. Chris and I are going to spend the night in DC and go out to the bars. I throw on a preppy outfit— khakis, white button-down shirt, and a blue blazer— thinking if I dress nicely I might feel better about myself and not be a complete drag all night. My knuckles are a little bruised from the short brawl last night. But I'm no worse for wear, and the other guy is probably fine too.

David texts me to see how things are going, and I tell him I'm doing okay. Laura's family continues to be unbelievably loving. They returned to Florida the week after the funeral, but I continue to talk to David regularly. I know he's asked the state's attorney not to charge me in her death. *This was a terrible accident. He's suffered enough. We've suffered enough. This will only make it worse.* The state won't say one way or the other whether they plan to file charges, so as far as I know, I'm still facing up to ten years in prison. I can't begin to heal because I don't yet know the extent of everything I've lost. The accident and its aftermath are still unfolding; the crash is nowhere near over.

Every day is so intense, and everything in my life seems to have taken on an added significance. Everything feels like it's tied into my grief over Laura and relevant to how I should understand her death and my loss. Losing her is the only subject my mind can focus on; the only lens through which I can interpret my thoughts and experiences is her death and my role in causing it. I pray to God and ask for his comfort, and in that moment the sun breaks through the clouds and shines on my face. *A sign.* Or I'm watching TV, and a wife tells a husband that when she's gone, she wants him to find happiness. *Is she talking to me? Is Laura sending me a message?*

Small coincidences become signs from God, from the universe, from Laura. I remember that Laura and I discussed our deaths the night before she died. *Did she know it was coming?* I see a purple Honda Civic, the car she had when we met, drive by just as I'm thinking of her. *Is she saying hi? Hi, Laura, hi!* Every little coincidence has taken on this mystic significance. I know it's irrational, but my brain is on high alert for anything it can assign meaning to, anything that can make sense of what is happening in my life.

I leave the dungeon and start walking towards Chris's

house. It will be the first time I've been in his house since the night of the crash. My last clear memory of Laura is of her sitting in my lap in his living room. I walk through his front door and sit down in the same living room, in the same chair— I can picture her right here with my arms around her waist— to wait for Chris to finish getting ready.

Chris is a lady's man, a bit of a player. Girls love him because he's a good-looking guy, but also because he is genuinely caring. He's called or visited me every single day since Laura died, and even when I haven't been in the mood to talk, he's done his best to get me out of the house and out of my head. As I sit in the chair where I last held Laura, Chris's roommate and a few of his friends walk in.

One of the girls has an athletic build, with eyes that are a deep, dark blue, coy and mysterious. She has an exotic and stunning beauty, her long curls falling gently over her shoulders, and she exudes confidence. *Who is that?*

I quickly sit back in the chair and look away, embarrassed that she might have seen me watching her, or that Laura might have.

I can't look at girls who remind me of Laura anymore. But this girl is taller, her hair curly instead of straight, with larger eyes and a squarer jaw. It doesn't hurt to look at her because she doesn't look at all like Laura. But at the same time, I'm ashamed to even think about another woman so soon after Laura's death. I assure myself I have no interest in getting to know her. It's natural to see an attractive woman and be attracted. It doesn't *mean* anything.

"Hey, Mark. This is Maria. Maria, this is Mark," Chris's roommate introduces us.

"Hey. It's nice to meet you," I say, as the blood rushes to my face, and I'm sure I'm blushing.

"You guys should just come out with us instead of going to DC," she says, and Chris and I decide to join them, which means going back to the neighborhood where my sister lives, where I now live in her basement.

We get to the bar, and the other guys flirt with Maria. I convince myself to move on quickly from my initial interest. I don't just miss Laura. I'm still very much in love with her. Maria is pretty, but I'm already taken.

As the night goes on, our friends mingle around the bar, and Maria and I find ourselves alone. I try to make the normal small talk and act like a normal person. *Where did you go to school? How do you know Chris? What do you do for work?*

"So, what are you going to do after law school?" she asks.

"I have no idea. My life is kind of a mess," I look down at my shoes, embarrassed.

"What do you mean?" she asks.

"I was in a car accident a couple months ago. My girlfriend died in the crash." I feel the tears accumulating in the corners of my eyes and look away toward the bar, hoping the air will dry them out before they run down my face.

I don't know it, but Maria already knows about the accident. One of my friends mentioned it to her, but she doesn't let on. She tells me she is also grieving.

"My dad died last year from pancreatic cancer. We found

out five years ago, but he was pretty much fine for four years. He was in a study up in Boston. My mom would drive with him, back and forth, every month. Out of everybody in the study, he had the best results. But nobody ever survives the type of cancer he had. We called it 'small c cancer,' because it's not the worst kind of pancreatic cancer. There's another kind that kills you really fast."

It's complete word vomit. She tells me her whole life story in about five minutes. And I'm captivated. I know I miss Laura terribly, but what I haven't realized until this moment is that I am also incredibly lonely. I'm overwhelmed with powerful emotions every day, but I don't have anyone to share them with. My sister, mom, Chris, and other friends are always there and constantly checking on me, but I want to protect them from the worst of what I'm feeling. I put on a brave face for them. I don't want to add to the burden of pain they already have from Laura's death, but I long for a person to connect with and talk about my despair.

"I'm sorry about Laura." I don't know why, but I don't like hearing her say Laura's name. "I think she would still want you to finish school and start the career you planned though." *How would you know what she'd want?*

I half grunt, half laugh bitterly. "Well, the other part of it is that the police say I was driving. I don't remember it, and Laura was supposed to drive us home. I'm not even sure I *was* driving, but I might be going to prison and have no idea if I'll ever be able to practice law. Everything I built and planned is gone. Just like that."

*Nice to meet you.*

Maria puts her hand on my arm, and I feel a jolt of electricity. I look down at her. I think it's the first time I've been able to look anyone in the eyes since the crash, and she gazes back, her eyes full of understanding and care.

"I'm going to hit the bathroom," I tell her, breaking the moment awkwardly.

*What the hell am I thinking?*

As I walk to the bathroom, my mind turns to Laura. I think about all the holes losing her has created in my life. When I lost her, I lost all of the roles she played in my life too. I guess that's true for everyone who loses someone they love, and Maria must have holes in her life from the loss of her father. When Laura was alive, I knew I loved her, but I wasn't introspective enough to truly reflect on all the ways she enriched my life. Now I am keenly aware of her absence from so many parts of my day-to-day existence. The entire way I went through each day, all my habits, involved her.

She was my best friend, the person I could talk to about my day without having to fill in all the background details. She already knew everything about me, and I already knew everything about her.

She was the companion I could count on having every night when I got home. She was the one who shared the responsibility of taking care of our pets together. She made our home smell good, like cocoa butter in the morning and sweet pea spray in the afternoon. We made dinner together. Our kitchen was small, but when we cooked together we moved like a choreographed dance, spinning around each other and handling the work as if all four of our arms were controlled by one mind. Every morning, we had coffee together unless I had to leave too early for school, and she always laughed at the corny jokes I love to make.

She was the person who knew all my important memories from childhood, my truest feelings about all the big events in my life— the pain of moving around as a kid, the devastation of my parents' divorce, my excitement about becoming a lawyer— how I became who I was, and what I wished for our future. Laura was the one who encouraged me to follow my dreams.

She made me a part of the big, close-knit extended family I'd always longed for. Growing up on the move, I never got to spend much time with aunts, uncles, grandparents, and cousins. Her family was together all the time; one uncle, two aunts, her grandma and great aunt all lived in the same house a few miles from us. She made my favorite cake the best and introduced me to homemade manicotti.

*God, I miss the manicotti!*

I've lost her, and I've also lost all the rituals and traditions that were a part of our love, like going to Fishpaws for chicken tender sandwiches and sitting quietly on the bench at our neighborhood beach overlooking the Magothy River. She knew my order at every restaurant, and she also knew the things I wouldn't eat no matter how hungry I was. *Asparagus? No way!* She fit so perfectly under my arm on our couch. When we saw a Volkswagen Beetle, we'd yell in unison the color of the car and then "punch buggy no punch backs." Then, since we said it at the same time, we'd continue in unison: "Jinx, personal jinx, infinity jinx. You owe me two sodas," always in unison.

*Who else can jinx like that?*

We called each other "vu" instead of "you" when we wrote each other notes or said I love you because we thought it was funny and cute to use romantic French with each other, and by the time we figured out that "vu" means "see" in French while "vous" means "you" but indicates a formal relationship rather than an intimate one, it was our thing so we kept doing it. "I love vu, mister." "I love vu, princess."

*Where are vu now? I need vu here.*

I don't want to be at the bar fumbling my way through what is starting to feel like an impromptu first date, feeling the butterflies in my stomach wondering if this other girl senses the chemistry between us too. I want to be with the familiar comfort of Laura.

I look at myself in the mirror as I wash my hands. I reach up and fix my hair where it's fallen down in my face.

*I'm already in love with Laura. I can't be into this girl. How can I even think about being with another girl?*

Yet, in the strange superstitious world of my grief, meeting Maria while sitting in the chair where Laura and I shared one of our last moments together seems significant. That Maria can relate to my feelings of loss and that I'm meeting her at my lowest point, a point where I'm begging Laura every night to comfort me, makes me think it is more than a coincidence.

*Did Laura want me to meet this woman? Is she coming into my life for a reason? What are vu doing?*

# CHAPTER 9

When the bar is closing, Maria and I realize we're walking in the same direction. *What a coincidence.* As we approach her friend's house, she asks if I want to come up to the party her friends are having. I don't know anyone else and don't feel very outgoing, but she stays by my side talking my ear off for the rest of the night. She tells me everything there is to know about everyone in the room. Who dated who in college. Who cheated on who in college. Who she made out with at which party. Where they're from, and what sports they played. What everyone does for a living. Who is kind of a screw up.

We make a great beer-pong team. She's a better shot at getting the ball into the red solo cups at the other end of the table, but I don't make a bad showing either. The winning team gets to keep playing, and we dispatch a few teams before we're finally beaten and pushed off the table.

"Not bad," she tells me, smiling and flushed from the alcohol. She really is very cute.

"You either," I smile back, the alcohol easing the stress of unfamiliarity and numbing the feelings of betrayal that had been creeping up on me at the bar.

"So how long do you have to wait to find out if they're going to charge you?" she asks.

"I talked to a lawyer, and he said the state would take their time to decide whether to press charges and what charges to file," I tell her. "If I make it eight months without charges, there's a good chance they won't ever charge me."

"You might not have even been driving, right?"

"I mean, I don't remember driving, and I can't think of any reason I would have been. Laura was our designated driver. Harry— he's my lawyer— did some kind of investigation to see what he could find out."

Harry got what he could from the police. They say the evidence shows I was driving, but my friends all insist I wasn't.

Chris told Harry that we went back to his house after the bars closed and stayed up drinking for another hour or so. We were out back, and people were smoking cigarettes and a little weed.

"Most of our friends who didn't live close by were staying the night, and Chris offered for us to stay too," I tell Maria. "He knew I was drunk and shouldn't be driving."

Laura had dangled the keys from her finger and told Chris, "I'm driving. I barely drank anything." I'd always been a homebody, and if given the option, I'd always have preferred to sleep at home. Laura is, was, the same way, and she said she was okay to drive.

"I could see us deciding that if she only had a bit to drink over a seven-hour night, she was fine, that the little bit of risk was worth it to be home in our bed." The risk we would've considered, of course, was of getting pulled over, getting a DUI; not of crashing, not of one of us losing their life.

I have no idea what happened between leaving Chris's front porch and the paramedics finding my car upside down on the guardrail. "But I guess something changed in our plan.

Or maybe nothing changed, Laura was driving, and the police are wrong."

Harry said the confusion of an accident scene in the dark with sirens all around, the need to cut me from the car while the paramedics pronounced Laura dead at the scene, could have led to an error in the investigation. The police are the pros, but mistakes happen. I don't remember, and Laura isn't here to tell me.

"The truth is, I doubt they'd make a mistake like that. My guess is that Laura driving was the plan when we left Chris's house, but something must have changed on the way to the car. I don't know what it could have been, but really, could the police really get it *that wrong?*"

"Was the accident bad?" she asks.

*My girlfriend died. How could it not be bad?*

"The car flipped upside down and slid down a guardrail. My dad and I went to the police impound lot and saw the car." The car was evidence, and it was totaled anyway, but the police said I could pick up the embossed leather wallet Laura bought for me, some Sublime and Slightly Stoopid CDs we were listening to, and some other random possessions found at the crash scene.

"It looked like a bomb went off in the car. Everything was destroyed: the roof, hood, trunk, and the entire driver's side were shredded. After I saw it, I couldn't believe I walked away," I tell Maria the details of the accident like it's some impressively macabre detail of my life.

There was so much dirt caked into the driver's side panels that it looked like the car must have been buried. The tires were on the rims, but the driver's side front tire was blown out.

"I told Harry I'd been having trouble with that tire before the accident. It had a slow leak and kept deflating. Instead of replacing it, I just kept re-inflating it. I blew it up that morning before heading to DC for work and school." The tire should have been replaced, but I didn't have a lot of extra money, and I thought inflating it every few days was good enough.

"Harry said the tire might have blown and caused the crash," I tell Maria.

*Would Laura be dead even if I were sober? Even if she were?*

The front passenger seat where they say Laura was sitting had deep gouges in the top. The car had spun around so it was traveling backwards on the guardrail, and the top of the seat was bent forward where the guardrail came through the roof. The headrest was ripped away from the seatback and cut to pieces.

The guardrail went through the rear seats too, and they were ripped and bent forward at the top. "The area above the passenger side doors was all jagged metal." I wasn't sure if that was from the collision or the paramedics tearing the roof off to get me out. "The hood was gouged and dented from riding on the guardrail, and the trunk was crushed in the middle."

I don't tell Maria, but in the telling of it, I can see the blood, skin, and flesh that were all over the car and especially around the top of the driver's side door, passenger door, and front seats.

*That was her on the door and the seats. That was what I did to her.*

Maria looks captivated by all the details, but talking about the crash is starting to take me to a dark place. I grab us another round of beers, and we sit on the kitchen counter. I change the subject and ask her about her family and childhood. She has two sisters. They grew up in Lutherville just a few miles away from where she went to college. She tells me she went to Loyola University, just like one of her sisters, her parents, and her grandfather before her. I tell her I used to be a bartender at the Irish pub where all the Loyola students liked to drink, and we play "who do you know?" until we identify a few of my regulars who were also her friends in college.

We continue talking and drinking as people slowly trickle out of the party or find beds and couches to fall asleep on. The sky is starting to lighten, and I realize the sun will be up soon. I'm not sure what I'm thinking, but I lean in to kiss her.

She turns away, but she keeps on talking like nothing happened. She tells me how when she was in high school, and she had her first phone call with a boy, her sisters told her to prepare a list of questions and topics to discuss so that they wouldn't run out of things to talk about.

"I went through the whole list in like two minutes. I remember asking him if he collected anything. And he was like 'like baseball cards?' And I told him I collect spoons." I can't imagine her ever running out of things to talk about.

Even though she turned away before, I still want to kiss her, and she seems like she wants me to too. I lean in again, and she doesn't stop me. After having been with one woman for so long, I unconsciously expect her mouth to taste the same as

Laura's, to taste like the kisses I'm familiar with. I expect her to kiss like Laura too. But this is different. It feels good though, and I put my hands in her curls to kiss her more firmly. She slides her hand up my neck and kisses back. It's the first time in months I'm not thinking about Laura, and I'm completely aroused in seconds. We make out for another hour until the sun is all the way up.

# CHAPTER 10

Maria has work later in the morning. She's a photographer with her own business. We're in our mid-twenties, and most of our friends are just getting started in their careers. Nobody has their own successful business, and I'm impressed by her. Plus, her job is to capture people in their happiest moments: weddings, engagements, new babies, and sunny days on the beach. Photos and memories are all I have left of Laura, and it feels appropriate to be bonding with someone who makes a living ensuring memories last. This is a person who understands the value of memories.

I ask her what time she'll be done with work and if I can call her later.

"I'll be done at 6:00," she tells me after I put her phone number into my contacts. I call her at 6:02 that evening—I don't want to come on too strongly—and ask if she'll go to dinner with me. We go to Mother's Grill, a popular bar near my sister's house with plenty of tables and good food.

The conversation is easy and natural. The middle-class Catholic-school community in the Baltimore area is notoriously incestuous—nobody cares where you work or went to college; we ask where you went to high school—and we find that we have several common friends from growing up in the area.

"I can't believe we've never met," she says.

"I bet we've been at a few parties together without ever knowing it," I reply, suddenly aware that I'm actually having fun.

After dinner, we walk back to my sister's house, and we make out in the dungeon. Maria spends the night, and it's nice to have her with me. I'm still not used to sleeping alone, and it's a relief to be around someone who can relate to the pain I'm feeling and provide some of the companionship I've been missing. I wonder if Laura wants me to be with Maria. At the same time, I find myself feeling horrible about Maria sleeping on Laura's side of the bed. I feel guilty for taking an interest in her so soon after Laura's death. It feels like I'm cheating on Laura, and I worry it cheapens what I had with her. Then I think that if she didn't want another woman sleeping on her side of the bed, she shouldn't have abandoned me by dying. "You can't think that!" I silently castigate myself.

Maria's business gives her a lot of flexibility with how she spends her time. I'm not going to classes, and I only work two days a week, so I have all the time in the world. After a handful of dates, we start hanging out regularly, almost every day. I'm so used to always being with a girl that it feels normal to always have Maria around. I don't need to play games, waiting a few days after each date before calling her again. Courtney was surprised the first time Maria spent the night, but she quickly adjusts and accepts Maria as a new part of our life. I think she's just happy to see me doing something more than staring off into space.

I talk to David often, and when we speak a month into my hanging out with Maria, I decide not to tell him about her. David's dad died when David was a teenager, and his mom never dated or remarried. I think he will think that's how it's supposed to be. You get one love of your life, and when they're gone, you find other things to bring you joy. Romantic love is off limits. Maybe that's what I think too. And now I'm just failing to live up to my own standards once again.

I wonder if there's anything more complicated and confusing than the loss of a romantic partner. Nobody cares if you lose a friend and have other friends. Nobody cares if you lose a child and love your other children that much harder. Nobody cares if you lose any other kind of person in your life and use sex or romance to ease the pain. But when you lose romantic love, there is so much self-judgment and judgment from others. Or maybe I'm just assuming they're judging me. As I become more and more attracted and connected to Maria, I become more and more ashamed of how I'm feeling. "How can I betray Laura like this?" I wonder.

I expect my friends to judge me and hate Maria. They're a bunch of hippie party animals. Maria is a good girl. She's never smoked a cigarette or weed, and she never drank until she was twenty-one. I'm worried Maria couldn't fit in with the group even under the best of circumstances. And these are not the best of circumstances. I especially expect Theresa to hate her.

"This is Maria. Maria, this is Theresa." They've both heard about each other, but it's the first time they've met.

"Hey," Theresa says, drawing it out a little hesitantly but not unkindly.

"Mark talks about you all the time. It's so nice to get to meet some of his friends," Maria replies, and even though it's nice I cringe when she says "all the time" because I'm not sure how Theresa will feel about Maria and me talking "all the time."

Theresa is reserved, but it's not unusual for her to be skeptical of new people in our group. The introduction and time together go as well as I could have expected. I think Theresa wants to hate Maria but understands that I need Maria. Theresa has always been wise beyond her years, a little world-weary and cynical. She isn't a romantic and doesn't have any illusions about human nature. She gets why Maria helps me survive. And she doesn't make me feel bad about the betrayal of Laura, about making her participate in the betrayal.

I imagine what it would be like if the accident had turned out differently, if I'd been the one to die. What would my friends think if Laura had a new guy? How would I feel, looking down from heaven or wherever, seeing Laura with another guy so soon after my death? I think I'd be pissed. Maybe death would give me a different, more understanding, perspective, and I'd just be happy she found someone to ease her suffering a bit. I was always the jealous one in our relationship. I think even dead I'd be mad, and I'd worry she liked the new guy better than she liked me. Laura wasn't the jealous type. I don't think she'd even worry about who I liked better. She'd probably tell me to do what I needed to do to survive. And right now, it feels like being with Maria is what I need to survive.

❖

Later that week, I'm on the phone with Theresa, talking about the introduction.

"I think she's nice," she says of Maria. "Are you going to tell David about her?"

"Not yet," I say nervously, hoping she can keep the secret too.

I want to believe that hiding Maria from Laura's family is about protecting them, but it could be I'm just protecting myself. Being with her feels like cheating, but the feelings I have for Maria are nothing like the love I have for Laura. I'm not even sure I could ever fall in love again. There's the singular, unique love I have for Laura. And the singular, unique *whatever this is* I'm developing for Maria.

I rationalize my secrecy. It's too soon to tell Laura's family. It'll just hurt them more. Plus, it isn't serious with Maria anyways. It isn't going to get serious. I'm a mess, and I'm probably going to prison for a very long time. I'm not looking for a new girlfriend. Laura can't be replaced, and nobody could ever live up to the love we shared.

I keep Maria at a distance in my head. I'm nonchalant about our relationship, about her ongoing close relationship with her ex-boyfriend. I don't love her, so who cares if they still hang out? Love is only for Laura. Any other love is to be avoided, maybe forever. Because when you fall in love, loss hurts more. Loss matters. Loss makes you want to die.

Maria doesn't make the pain go away, but she makes it feel more bearable. She doesn't make the loneliness stop, but at least I'm not alone. Whatever is happening between us, it's not like other early relationships I remember. It's not all fluttery butterflies in my stomach. There's no anxiety, no nervous excitement about the possibilities. I'm not waiting by the phone for her to call or text, analyzing conversations for clues about her feelings, trying to figure out if this could be *the one*. I'm too much of a wreck over Laura for that. I don't worry about it not working out. I haven't had any other serious relationships besides my relationship with Laura, so I haven't had any devastating breakups, but I guess maybe this is what it's like to have a rebound girlfriend. She's good for the time, temporary, a small reprieve from my suffering. She'll be out of my life as suddenly as she's come into it. But for now, I'm happy she's in it.

❖

We usually spend the night in the dungeon, but tonight we're staying at Maria's house. She lives with her mom, and we're making out in the bed she's slept in since she was a child. The physical chemistry between us is strong, and I've found myself wanting her more and more. I want her now, and when she pulls her head back, looking down at me, I can see in her eyes that she wants me too. She steps down from the bed and gently reaches for my hand, pulling me to stand with her in the middle of the room.

"I think the bed will be too loud," she whispers, wrapping her hands around the back of my head and drawing me into a kiss. We undress each other, clumsy in our urgency and comfortable enough to laugh about it.

I haven't had sex with anyone but Laura in over three years. It's exciting, and like my first kiss with Maria, I notice it's different. My body was used to being with Laura. Maria moves differently. We fit together differently.

I'd love to say that it's the greatest performance of my life, that we're like Richard Gere and Julia Roberts in *Pretty Woman*, and that I doubt doing it on the floor keeps her mom from hearing. But that would be a lie. It's over more quickly than it should be, and I'm embarrassed by the performance and worried Laura is watching and now mad at me for cheating on her. When Maria returns from the bathroom, she lays down in the crook of my arm. Eventually, we get up and slide back into bed.

The next morning, Maria's mom sits down next to me while I'm naked under the covers. It's a little awkward, but she doesn't seem to be bothered by it. She looks like she's been crying, and Maria asks if she's okay.

"Just riding a wave," she replies and Maria looks at her knowingly, resting a hand on her mom's in a comforting gesture.

After she leaves, I ask Maria what her mom meant.

She tells me her family describes grieving as riding waves. They'd all been riding waves of grief since her father died. Sometimes, you're fine. The emotions are manageable. You might even have moments where you enjoy yourself, and you think, "I'm going to be okay. This is going to be okay."

But then the grief hits, the memories of your loved one, the savage awareness that you'll never see them again. It hits you like ocean waves before a hurricane. Sometimes the waves come so close together, you barely catch your breath before the next one hits. Sometimes, between swells, you feel nothing. You're so exhausted that you don't feel anything. "You're not even sure if you have any feelings left. But then another wave hits, and the pain is inescapable."

"This is exactly how I feel," I think as Maria is describing it. It's a relief to talk to someone who gets it, who understands what this is like, without needing to try to explain what I'm going through.

"You'll get better at riding them. You'll learn to hold the waves off when you need to and give into them when it's a better time. But you can't push them off forever. Eventually, they always come." Surviving this is about living with the waves, without them overcoming you.

Maria has ten months of practice riding the waves. I have just three. I'm not as advanced as her yet. She's like a level six wave rider. I'm still on level one. The waves mostly just crush me, and what I'm experiencing feels like waves that are so much more crippling than what Maria describes.

*Am I just weaker than she is? Maybe I'm a weak person and just need to get over it.*

But on my best days, *I am* learning to live with them. I'm learning to ride them. And I'm learning to use them to reconsider everything I believe and access a deeper level of self-awareness and empathy, a better understanding of what it would mean to live a life of meaning and happiness.

*On my best days.*

I'm also learning from Kara more about grief, trauma and their impact on our brains and bodies. I'm not weak, I remind myself. Much of what I'm feeling are normal responses to trauma that many others also experience when they've been through something this painful and life changing. Maria and I share the experience of grief, but my grief is complicated by the trauma of the crash.

Kara has told me that after a traumatic event, images of the experience, acute feelings of loss, memories of the fear and other feelings we experienced in the moment can overwhelm our consciousness. We aren't experiencing only the grief of loss, which is painful enough. We are also re-experiencing the panic and helplessness of our traumatic experience. Our fight or flight response kicks in over and over, leaving us breathing heavily, heart racing, and mind overcome with anxiety.

Then, just as quickly as we feel we're drowning in the swirl, we go numb. The wave passes. We feel detached and alone, even when we're around others. We don't feel the pain, but we also can't feel joy or love. We lose interest in things that used to make us happy. This can happen even if we don't remember the traumatic experience, or we only remember it in bits and pieces.

*Those are the waves I know.*

❖

"I mean, what does it say about me that I'm already seeing somebody new?"

"It says you're human, Mark. Everyone deals with grief in different ways. I'm glad you have her. Why do you feel guilty?" Kara asks. I'm at a therapy appointment and talking about Maria.

"I survived and got a chance to move on. She die doesn't ever get to experience anything ever again. And I't reason she's dead!"

"That's a lot to unpack, Mark. Do you really think you moved on?"

"You know what I mean." I haven't moved on, but *I am* feeling better sometimes.

She tells me it's understandable that I would feel guilt and shame after what happened. She knows I blame myself for what happened. "But Laura isn't blameless either. It was an accident, Mark. You didn't mean for this to happen."

Every time somebody tries to excuse my actions by saying I didn't mean for it to happen, I think back to my criminal law classes. They call your mental state *mens rea* in criminal law. Intent to do something, doing something on purpose and getting the desired outcome, is considered the worst kind of criminal *mens rea*. Intentional homicide is murder. I didn't intend for Laura to die, but my actions were probably reckless. I recite the definition of recklessness in my head without much thought: conscience disregard of a substantial and unjustifiable risk. Reckless homicide is manslaughter. Well, driving drunk was a substantial and unjustifiable risk. I put myself and Laura at risk along with everyone else on the road. But was I conscious about it? Maybe not. But I'm at least criminally negligent. That's negligent manslaughter, and it's not the same as "not your fault."

"It doesn't matter if I meant for it to happen. I created the risk, and that's why she's dead. It's not as bad as if I did it

on purpose, but it's still pretty bad."

Layered on top of the shame over feelings I have for Maria is guilt over surviving the accident. I'm the one with a chance to continue, to have new feelings, to have a life. On the night of the accident, either one of us could have died. After my car flipped upside down, the guardrail could have easily hit either of us. But it missed me, and it hit her. She died, and I walked away.

*She's dead, and I'm just out hooking up with some girl, living my life.*

It doesn't seem fair that she died, and I walked away. Kara tells me it's called survivor's guilt, and it's a common experience of people who live through events that result in death. I've heard of it before, but I'm not sure it applies here.

When I think of survivors guilt, I think of people who feel guilty even though they weren't at fault. They blame themselves or feel like they put their own safety first or that they could have done more to save the person who died.

Most of the time when accidents happen, circumstances come together in a perfectly awful way. So many small factors align for an event to happen that assigning blame is impossible. Death is just a fact of life. But with Laura, there is a very definite line between my actions and her death. I've become more convinced in the last few weeks that the police must be right. I must have been driving. They just couldn't get it that wrong. And believing I'm responsible is intensifying the trauma, the guilt, and the shame I'm feeling.

*Maybe Maria should just run now while she's still safe from me.*

# CHAPTER 11

*The wind blowing through her chestnut hair and rippling her swimsuit coverup makes her look like some kind of beach goddess, and I stare admiringly at the gentle curve of her neck and shoulders.*

*Laura is walking ahead of me in the parking lot at the beach on Ana Maria Island. We're visiting her parents and sister for the week, and the beach is close to their house. Last night, we had dinner with her family, Captain and Cokes with her dad. Whenever we visit, we always have Captain and Cokes with limes from the tree Laura bought for her dad. Her parents are at work, and her sister is at school today, so it's just the two of us.*

*We've been to the island before— for days on the beach, evenings watching the sunset, and cocktails at the beach bar— but today we're exploring a new part of the beach that her dad recommended. It's farther down the island, away from the bridges that provide entrance from the mainland, so it's more secluded and less busy than the parts of the beach we've been to before.*

*We walk across the boardwalk that traverses the small section of vegetation between the beach and parking lot, and we're rewarded with a stunning view of the gulf and a nearly empty stretch of sand. The public part of the beach extends just a few hundred yards to our left and ends at a pink wall surrounding a gated community of beachfront manses.*

*The sand is snowy white and as fine as flour. There are seashells, millions of them, fully intact because nobody walks down to this part of the beach. The sun is high, and the Florida heat makes Laura's skin glisten dazzlingly. We find a little nook at the top of the beach, where scattered beach grass has formed a semicircle nest for our towels, swelling our sense of privacy.*

*Laura pulls out a bottle of suntan lotion, and I reach to take it from her. She offers it without question, and I begin rubbing it into the supple skin of her shoulders and chest, watching the slow rise and fall of her breasts as she breathes contentedly and leans into my arms. I want her so badly and can't believe she's mine.*

*We lay down on the towel, and I light a joint and pass it to her. She puts her leg over mine as she inhales, and I run my hand delicately over her thigh, pulling her toward me. She exhales, and I lean in to kiss her.*

❖

"Earth to Mark. Are you in there?" Theresa asks me.

"Sorry," I tell her. "I was just thinking about last year when Laura and I came down to visit."

"It feels weird flying to Florida without her," Theresa says, and I nod.

Theresa and I are on our way to visit Laura's family in Bradenton, Florida, about an hour south of Tampa. Laura and I had planned to visit her family for her teenage sister's birthday the week after I finished law school. Her family lives on the Gulf coast, so the sun sets over the water. I was going to ask David if I could marry her and then propose on the beach at sunset. We would have gotten married and moved somewhere

warm and dry, like Phoenix or Texas. We would have started our very own brand-new lives together. Actually, we would
have started our very own brand new *life*, one life we would
share, *our life*.

But instead, I'm taking the trip with Theresa, and I'm full
of anxiety about going to Florida without Laura, to be with her
parents for the first time since the week of her funeral. I want
to see them. I miss them, and, along with Theresa, they're the
only people in the world who miss Laura as much as I do. But
I'm also worried about how they'll react to spending so much
time with me, the man who took her from them.

*Will they finally snap and treat me the way I deserve? How can they
want to be around me?*

I graduated from law school last week. As the end of the
semester was approaching, my family and friends encouraged
me to return to school. I hadn't been to class in three months.
I tried a couple times in the weeks after Laura's death, but I
couldn't focus, and it seemed pointless to be there.

I wanted to make Laura proud of me, so I started studying
with just a few weeks to go before exams. The studying turned
out to be a welcome distraction from my constant thoughts
about her— from missing her and dwelling on my responsibility for her death, from wanting to be with her, from wanting to
be dead with her— as well as my feelings of guilt over looking
forward to seeing Maria again.

I hoped I would somehow pass my classes and graduate.
I waited anxiously for my grades to post on the school's online
dashboard, and when they did, to my surprise, I'd actually done

pretty well.

"We did it, Laura," I thought. "We did it."

"What are you reading?" Theresa asks, gesturing toward the book I have shoved in the netting in the back of the seat in front of me.

I've always loved to read, but during law school, I had so little time to read anything but textbooks. When I stopped going to classes and thinking about school after Laura died, I had plenty of time to read other things. I used to enjoy mysteries and thrillers, but I don't feel like reading about fictional homicides. I'm still living through my own real-life homicide.

In place of the mysteries and thrillers, I've been reading more books about grief, spirituality, and the afterlife. My mom gave me *Don't Take My Grief Away from Me,* and other friends have given me books they thought would be helpful. I've been reading inspiring stories about meaning, purpose, and healing. I know I don't deserve happiness, but I sometimes hope that maybe, *maybe,* one day I'll have a life that doesn't hurt so much, that is full of meaning and purpose, that is healed.

"It's *Tuesdays with Morrie* by Mitch Albom," I tell her. "It's a memoir about this guy's weekly visits with his old college professor who was dying from ALS."

"Is it any good?" she asks dubiously.

"I like it. I've only been reading it for a couple hours, and I'm almost done. You're welcome to it once I finish."

Morrie, who has a terminal illness, talks about the day he found out he was dying and how shocked he was that the world didn't seem to care. "Shouldn't the world stop? Don't they know what has happened to me? But the world did not stop, it took no notice at all." I can relate. It feels so strange that the world just seems to go on without Laura in it. I see people going about their business, enjoying their lives, as if they don't know that the world is over. My world is over. Her world is over.

The plane lands, and Theresa and I grab our bags. Laura's family is waiting to greet us when we get past the security checkpoints, and they're as kind and welcoming as always. Laura's sister looks just like her but twelve years younger, and looking at her is like seeing Laura again. I wonder if the sadness and longing for Laura that it stirs in me is what David experiences every time he looks at his youngest daughter.

*How can he not hate me for what I've taken from him?*

I try to hide it, but I wonder if they can tell I can't relax. If they can, they don't lead on. The conversation is casual, almost normal.

"How was the flight?"

"Not bad. Just glad to see you guys."

"Congrats on graduation, Mr. Lawyer."

I wonder if they're play-acting the normalcy as much as I am. Maybe if we pretend it's normal for long enough, it will actually feel normal.

We get to the house, and David makes everyone Captain and Cokes while Theresa and I sit our bags out of the way in the living room.

"Tell us about graduation," Laura's mom says.

"Oh, man. It was hot as hell," I say, then remember Laura's sister is in the room, and not only might the saying be inappropriate for her young ears, it's probably where she thinks I deserve to be. "I mean, it was hot. We waited in line to process into the auditorium for like forty minutes, and I was sweating like crazy." The heavy robes we wore for the ceremony were dark purple and gray, and the synthetic fabric was sticky against my body. Graduation was on the main campus of Georgetown, miles away from the law school. My parents, sisters, and some other family and friends came.

I think that maybe Laura was there in spirit; Maria wasn't there at all. We've been spending more and more time together. She would have loved to come if I'd asked, but I've still been keeping her a secret from almost everybody, too ashamed to acknowledge her and the small amount of happiness I've allowed to creep into my life. The night before graduation, she took me out for a big celebratory steak dinner. We brought the bone from the steak home for Rocko to eat. Rocko has taken to Maria too, and I've at least stopped worrying that he's judging me for my disloyalty, though sometimes I still judge him for his.

"We finally walked into the auditorium, and the speakers made their usual inspirational graduation speeches challenging us to *legal careers full of meaning and impact*," I tell them, and we all chuckle as if we don't know my legal career is probably over before it even begins.

My thoughts wander back to the start of law school, so full of hope and excitement for the future, falling in love with Laura and agonizing over the few days a week I was at school in Virginia. Then transferring to Georgetown and sharing a home with her, building our little Laura, Mark, Rocko, Boots family. The unimaginable horror of losing her in the blink of an eye. Finding the strength to return to school and finish what we started together. And finally arriving at that moment.

"It really hurt to be there without her." I'm the first to drop the facade of normalcy. "At the end of the ceremony, all the graduates stood up to cheer for each other and receive applause from their family and friends in attendance, so full of pride in their accomplishment, ready to conquer the world. But it just felt wrong, and I couldn't."

I stayed seated in the auditorium and began to weep, a confusing mix of emotions sweeping over me: pride and relief were a part of it, but so were sadness, grief, regret, and loneliness. I was surrounded by a thousand people, but I'd never felt more alone.

"It must have been hard, Mark," David tells me reassuringly. "But we're proud of you. Laura is proud of you."

I'm proud to have graduated too, but I also know I might not be able to use my degree if I go to prison. I'm not even sure I want to be a lawyer anymore. The plan was for me to be a lawyer, making the money to support us, and Laura to be a social worker, helping young people struggling with drugs. But the life plan has gone out the window, and now I have no idea what to do with my life, besides sometimes hoping that it's over soon. I lost my job at the tax court the day after graduation. It was a clerkship for law students; by definition, I no longer qualified.

So now I have a law degree from one of the top law schools

in the country, but I don't know if I have any future, and all I really want to do is go back to my past.

"I went out for steak the night before the graduation and gave Rocko the leftover bone when I got home," I tell them half the truth, leaving out that I was there with my new girl-friend. "After graduation, we, Courtney and I, found Rocko upstairs with doggy diarrhea all over the floor. He'd eaten a hole through the basement door and escaped to the main floor. I think the bone must not have agreed with his stomach, and he tried to get out of the basement and get outside to do his business like a good dog."

*Or maybe he just wanted out of the dungeon as badly as I do.*

We have a few more rounds of drinks, and then everyone starts heading off to bed. David and I stay up drinking and talking about Laura. He tells me more about her childhood, how she wasn't always a chatter-box. As a child, she was what they called a voluntary mute. She barely spoke at all. I already knew, but I liked hearing him tell it.

"The first time her elementary school called to tell us she was disrupting class with all her talking, they thought we would reprimand her, but we were overjoyed!" Laura was a chatterbox once you got to know her, but she always had a wariness about her too. You had to earn her trust before she opened up, and I think it must have just taken a little longer to gain her trust when she was a kid.

I tell David about *Tuesdays with Morrie* and a concept Mor-rie calls the "tension of opposites."

"It's like how life is full of all these contradictions between what we want and what we have to do, between how we act and how we believe and feel."

My tension of opposites is that I know I deserve to suffer, but I want it to stop. I can't imagine a happy and fulfilling life without Laura, but surviving the crash is making me think more about what a happy and fulfilling life even means. "I don't come up with a good answer though," I tell him. "Every time I try to picture it, it's just the life Laura and I were already planning, but now one of the most important pieces is missing."

"Mark, you have time to find a way to move on," he tells me. "Laura would want you to be happy. I know she wants you to be happy. We're not mad at you, and neither is she." David gets up to pour us another Captain and Coke, and for a moment I consider telling him about Maria but then decide it's not the right time. I don't know if it ever will be. As much as I'm enjoying hanging out with her, I also think it could end at any moment, and why hurt David over something likely so fleeting? I see an alert for a text message she sends me and quickly put my phone back in my pocket before David returns with our drinks.

The next morning, it really does feel somewhat normal when David makes me and Theresa his famous BECS, bacon egg and cheese sandwiches that are somehow better than any others I've ever had. On one of my trips here with Laura, he told me the secret was to cook the eggs in the bacon grease and have one runny yolk and one cooked yolk on a well-buttered English muffin. I've tried to make it myself, but it never turns out as good as when he makes it.

After breakfast, we pack a beach bag and head to Ana Maria Island. Walking onto the beach, a tide of longing washes over me. The sound of the waves breaking gently on the sand and the smell of salt in the air carry my best memories of Laura. The waters of the Gulf recall the emerald green of her eyes.

I still feel Laura in the world sometimes. I see something beautiful and know she means for me to see it, to know she's okay, to know she wants me to be okay too. A rainbow when I'm crying. A feather blowing in the wind while I'm wondering where her spirit has gone. I'm so grateful to her for these signs, these messages. But I feel her even more here. If her soul could pick somewhere to be, this would be it.

I take off my shirt and walk out into the water. It's crystal clear so you can see your toes even when the water is past your waist. I'm breathing deeply, floating contemplatively on the waves, imagining her with me when I see the dorsal fins breaking the surface. It's a pod of dolphins swimming north about a hundred yards off the beach. They're still south of us, and I'm a strong swimmer, so I decide to swim into their path and try to get close to them. But I don't get there in time. They're moving too fast, and they're gone before I can make it. Still, coming within such a short distance of them is thrilling. I resign myself to being grateful for having seen them at all, even though I wish I could have touched them and they didn't have to leave me so soon.

I go back onto the beach, dry off, and have a Captain and Coke with David, then wander around collecting seashells with

Laura's sister.

A couple hours later, I get back in the water. I look out across the Gulf again, and the pod of dolphins is swimming south, returning from wherever they'd gone. Twenty or thirty bottle-nosed dolphins. I dive into the water and sprint toward their path, reaching and pulling with everything I have. I aim myself for a point in the water that is far in front of them, hoping the angle will give me time to intersect their path before they pass again.

I'm starting to run out of steam, my arms aching and protesting the strenuous effort as I stream through the waves. I take one final gulp of air and dive beneath the surface, and just like that I'm surrounded by dozens of dolphins as they swim around me. I open my eyes, amazed by their incredible speed and agility. Their graceful beauty combines with the quiet of being underwater to create a moment that is simultaneously exhilarating and calming. I lose my sense of myself as something separate from nature and feel completely unified with the universe around me. I feel great peace and have no fear. I am not sad or happy or grieving or longing or ashamed. I am part of them, and we are connected by the water that surrounds us to every other thing, to every other time. I'm exhausted and underwater, but, strangely, it feels like I can breathe for the first time in months. The transcendence of the moment erases even the distance between me and her.

The dolphins begin to swim away, but the feeling of completeness, of wholeness, of spiritual union, remains. Laura knows how much I love dolphins, but more than that, I think she knows I needed to be jolted from my wallowing. I look up to the cloudless blue sky and thank her for sending them to me.

*She wants me to be okay.*

# CHAPTER 12

My nephew just finished his nap and ate his lunch, and I'm getting him ready for our afternoon walk around the neighborhood. I've been watching him— serving as what my sister affectionately calls his "manny"—since earlier in the summer.

Courtney teaches at a residential school for students with disabilities that has classes all year round. Before I became the male nanny, Courtney's friend Mary had been watching my nephew since the end of Courtney's maternity leave. Mary's child had special needs and was one of my sister's students. They became close, and I got to know her family too. After the crash, she sent me a book based on the poem "Footprints in the Sand" about a person who looks back on his life and sees his footprints in the sand and Jesus' footprints beside them. The man sees that at the hardest times in his life, there was only one set of footprints, and he wonders why Jesus seems to have left him when he needed help the most. Jesus replies that at those times there was only one set of footprints because "I was carrying you."

Mary's son had been very sick for most of his life. Death had been stalking him since he was an infant, and it had finally caught him. Mary asked if I would read the eulogy they wrote for his funeral. I felt so honored when she asked, but it also brought back difficult memories of Laura's funeral. It hurt, and I was aware of the anguish Mary and her family must have been experiencing in a way vividly uncomfortable, but it also felt good to return the care she'd shown me in sending me and honor this young boy who died much too soon yet showed everyone around him so much about living with grace.

After losing her son, Mary wasn't up to watching my nephew anymore. She needed time to heal, and I imagined that she also need time away from other people's healthy children. I thought I understood the feeling because it's been so painful to see other happy couples since Laura's death, even when that happy couple is me and Maria.

Courtney asked if I could take care of my nephew until I found a job, and I eagerly agreed, happy to have something to fill my days and a way to repay Courtney for everything she's done for me since Laura's death.

Visiting Laura's family, enjoying the beach, and experiencing the transcendence of being with the dolphins was a nice break from my life, but once I got back to Baltimore, the reality of being a law school graduate with no legal prospect except the prospect of being a defendant hit me right in the face. I was ashamed to be unemployed, broke, and relying on my family and friends for support. I hadn't relied so much on anyone since high school. My dad had gotten me my car— the car that was now totaled— but I paid for college, law school, and all my living expenses on my own. Now I was living for free in the dungeon, not even able to pay for my own food.

I felt useless. I wanted to take care of myself, but I couldn't concentrate, and even though I was applying for jobs here and there, my heart wasn't in it. I wasn't even sure I could start a job with prison hanging over my head. Or maybe that was just an excuse to stay stuck in my rut, smoking bowls and watching *Saved by the Bell* reruns in the dungeon all day.

My nephew's name is Lucky, which feels like a kick in my unlucky shins, but also maybe some kind of a good omen. Lucky is both my nephew and my godson, and I was excited to spend more time with him. He's a reminder that even though precious lives end, precious lives also begin. As his charming little personality developed in the months after Laura's death, I became so fond of his sweetness and stopped thinking of his life as the new life that was cosmically traded for the end of Laura's. His life was his life, and it was a blessing in all of ours.

It's been good to get back into having a daily routine that includes more than waking up and wandering listlessly through the day, killing time until Maria can hang out. It's forced me to replace my mourning routine with a morning routine. Lucky's schedule has become my schedule. I've finally had to stop going through the motions of life. I have to be present for him, and I'm grateful that he has no idea I'm a loser girlfriend killer with no job and no future. I'm just a person he can trust to take good care of him and make sure he has everything he needs.

Doing something that makes Lucky smile or laugh, having him lay his head on my shoulder when he's tired, and getting the pure affection that only the youngest of us seem capable of showing is so healing for me. He experiences the rawest happiness from the simplest of pleasures-- a silly face, a good meal, a tickle on his belly. He reminds me that there still can be great joy in life. Lucky makes me feel like I'm needed instead of worthless, like a contributor instead of a leech, like I can nurture life instead of just ending one.

I go up to Courtney's bedroom in the morning and lay down with Lucky when Courtney leaves for work. I watch the news while he sleeps another hour or so, and then I give him a bath, get him dressed, and do his hair with gel and a comb to get just the right upward swoop in his part. Courtney is *very* particular about his hairdo and style. Lucky has the hippest clothes of any baby I've ever met. Lucky Brand jeans (no relation), rock band t-shirts, and Vans on his soft round feet. I feed him a bottle and some cereal, and then we play on the floor of the living room. Lucky crawls, but he doesn't walk yet, so I try to challenge him with activities that get him moving. If he could talk, he might say that he tries to challenge me to get me moving, too.

Around 11:30, Lucky takes a nap, and I watch TV or read. I'm devouring inspirational books, books about grief or finding meaning in life, books I would never have picked up before the crash. After his nap, we have lunch together, and then we take our afternoon walk.

By the gate in the row home's tiny front yard, I place Lucky in his stroller and pull his hat down over his ears. We walk a block north on Race Street on the sidewalk across from the train tracks. Right on Ostend. One more block to Light Street, the main road through South Baltimore. I point out doggies and flowers to him and feel a tiny piece of myself subtly coming back to life as I'm introducing him to the world around us.

A twenty-something with shoulder-length brown hair

and a yoga mat under her arm bounces by, waving at Lucky and smiling up at me. I can tell she assumes I'm his dad. That happens a lot when I'm watching Lucky, and it always makes me think about being a father and what it would have been like if Laura and I had gotten to have our family. I don't allow myself to think about Maria like that; I don't know enough about what my future holds to risk envisioning her in it. But sometimes I see her watching me with Lucky and think she might be evaluating my potential.

"That girl was cute," I nod to Lucky, who looks at me and smiles widely.

It's been seven months since the crash. My lawyer Harry says that if we make it eight months, the state is probably not planning on charging me. That's just one more month. Whether because of David's pleading with the prosecutor to show mercy or because there isn't enough evidence to prove her death is my fault—I know from law school how high the burden of proving guilt beyond a reasonable doubt is supposed to be—or because I actually didn't do it, I'm beginning to consider the possibility that I won't be going to prison.

"It's so nice out today. Why don't we go a little farther?" I make a monkey face at Lucky, and he grins back up at me, giggling and reaching for my face. I reach down and tickle his little belly, eliciting still more life-giving baby laughter.

Maryland is beautiful in the fall. I appreciate the warm sun on my face. The temperature is just right. Summer's humidity is gone. And even though the leaves won't change color for another two months, September and October make the rest of the year worth it.

Baltimore's Inner Harbor is a charmingly planned and re-developed waterfront. Industry has been replaced by marinas, restaurants, stores, and a science center and aquarium, all along a lovely brick walking path that meanders gracefully along the shore. The pier on the other side of the water has been convert-ed into a concert venue, and water taxis ferry tourists back and forth to all the destinations.

We make our way down to the walking path, and Lucky is smiling and enjoying the warm weather. I'm thinking about Maria, which makes me think about Laura. Maria, Laura, Ma-ria, Laura. My mood is as good as it gets these days, which, compared to a few months ago, actually is pretty good. I've enjoyed the summer with Lucky, and spending time with Ma-ria has been nice too. I'm still conflicted about whether I'm cheating on Laura by being with Maria or cheating on Maria by obsessing over Laura, but more and more I'm thinking that Laura would want me to be happy.

I'm bordering on blissful as we pass the Maryland Sci-ence Center and begin to approach the Spirit of Baltimore cruise ship.

"Your Auntie Laura and I went on that big boat once," I explain to Lucky.

One night, I surprised Laura with a dinner cruise around the harbor. We got all dressed up, went downtown, and board-ed the ship for a few hours of eating, drinking, and taking in the views of the city from the middle of the harbor. It was May, and a high school class had reserved most of the tickets for that night as part of their senior trip. After a couple glasses of wine, Laura and I climbed up to the top deck of the ship and found the quietest place around. We held each other and stood by the railing, sipping wine and laughing about the good fortune of sharing our romantic cruise with a class of high school seniors. We jokingly reenacted the scene from *Titanic* where Kate Winslet stands on the bow of the ship with her arms outstretched and Leonard DiCaprio's arms wrapped around her waist, feeling like the king of the world.

As I reminisce about the cruise, Lucky and I approach the ship, and anxiety unexpectedly swells in my chest. I realize I don't want to be near it; I *can't* be near it. The boat is her. It's our love. It's our happiness. It's my loss, and it's her death. My heart is pounding, and I have to consciously slow my breathing.

"Let's just walk up here," I say passively to Lucky, hoping he won't notice my panic. I leave the brick path and turn toward the sidewalk on Light Street, putting more distance between myself and the boat.

It isn't the first time this has happened. Even as my life has improved, certain reminders of Laura have continued to bring an overpowering sense of foreboding and fresh waves of painful grief. The list of places I avoid includes the restaurant where we had our first date—I wouldn't even consider going to the neighborhood—the shopping center by the house where she lived before we moved in together, Anne Arundel County where Laura grew up and where we lived together, the street with the bar we ate at the night she died, and so many other places I don't always realize are off-limits now until I start to go near them and experience the heart-racing anxiety that just pushed me away from the Spirit of Baltimore.

I've fallen into a strange dance with Laura's memory. I seek out certain reminders of her and the love we shared, but I'm repelled by other situations and experiences that torment and sadden me. There's little logic to the dance. I've surrounded myself in the dungeon with photos of Laura and continued to inhale the smell of her lotion, but I've stopped listening to music altogether so that I won't be confronted with any song that reminds me of her. Since most of the songs I used to like remind me of her, I haven't listened to music in months, doing this strange dance without a tune.

Pepperoni pizza is bad because I ate it with Laura the night she died. Purple is good because it was her favorite color. Honda Civics can be good or bad. If they're purple like the one she drove when we met, they're good. If they're silver like the one I drove when she died, they're bad. Any time I meet someone named Laura or hear another person called by her name, I immediately feel a pang of loss, but I also experience a strange sense of connection with them. I knew her name was a common one, but I never realized quite *how common*.

My taste in entertainment has changed too, but there's more logic to that, I suppose. I used to love horror movies, but I haven't watched one since the accident. I don't need any more horror. I'm a light comedy guy all the way now, and I'm especially drawn to rom-coms with characters grieving lost love. Over and over, I watch *Failure to Launch,* the Matthew McConaughey and Sarah Jessica Parker flick about the guy who can't move out of his parents' house because he lost his fiancé, and *Over Her Dead Body,* the Paul Rudd and Eva Longoria movie where the ghost of a deceased girlfriend tries to sabotage the leading man's new relationship. Bonus: Laura and I used to watch *Sex and the City* together, so Sarah Jessica Parker's role in *Failure to Launch* reminds me even more of my life with Laura. I just saw the *Sex and the City* movie, too, so I can tell Laura about it when I see her again.

Lucky and I turn on Pratt Street and pass the National Aquarium, Hardrock Cafe, and Pier Six concert pavilion. Then right on President Street, left on Fleet Street, down to Aliceanna. A homeless man with a cup full of change looks up as Lucky and I approach the corner where he sits.

"Sorry to bother you and your boy," he looks at me pleadingly. "Can you help me out? Even a dollar would help."

"I don't have anything on me, man," I lie.

I want to help him, but I can't. The day of my birthday party, the day of the crash, I gave half of a sandwich to a man outside a shelter by the tax court. I'd done the same thing dozens of times before. But because Laura died that night, I've closely, if completely irrationally, associated giving food to someone in need with the outcome of Laura dying. The idea of giving money to this man feels the same. I know it makes no sense, but I just can't shake the apprehension that helping him would spell doom for someone I love—maybe even Lucky—even though I know the right thing is to help people who need it.

Lucky and I continue our walk toward Fells Point. The cobblestones are a little bumpy for the stroller, but the historic section of the city is quaint and inviting. Laura and I spent last New Year's at the Admiral Fell Inn. The landmark hotel is just ahead, and the memory stings, but I force myself to stroll on, to put the discomfort with the Spirit of Baltimore and the homeless man behind me and focus on the pleasant weather and delightful charm of the neighborhood.

The historic row homes have mostly been converted to bars and retail boutiques. I notice how the wood railings on the old homes have been worn smooth by the decades, how the cobblestones have stayed strong and firm through the generations, and how the neighborhood is now alive with music and laughter. The structures are timeless sentinels looking over the waters that, though constantly moving and changing, are remarkably the same as they've been for centuries.

Laura would have loved to walk around here on a day like this. I find myself thinking about that more and more when I encounter things she would appreciate. I have a sense of responsibility for finding meaning and beauty in life. I want to honor Laura, and I need to make the most of the time I have. Because my life was spared, I owe it to her to witness the good things she cannot.

I slow down and take notice of nature unfolding: mums bursting with fall color, bees working urgently as the cool of late fall approaches, squirrels fattening themselves in anticipation of the cold months ahead. Some days, Lucky falls asleep in his stroller at the park by our house, and I lose myself in quiet observation. I wonder now why I never spent time looking at these things or contemplating the wonder of it all. Do we have to face death to fully appreciate life?

"What do you think?" I ask Lucky. He smiles at me and sticks out his tongue.

"Gah yee ana," he babbles back at me. I lean down and kiss his sweet little forehead.

*This kid has it all figured out.*

# CHAPTER 13

I stroll casually into Kara's office for our weekly appointment and sit comfortably in one of the two chairs facing the windows. It's another bright October afternoon. The sun will set in a few hours, and the world outside has taken on the vivid sharpness that only the perfect golden-hour fall light can offer.

"How are you feeling?"

"I'm actually feeling pretty good."

It's a relative term. I'm still grieving deeply and feeling guilty about my deepening relationship with Maria and embarrassed by my lack of a *real job*. But compared to a few months ago when I wanted nothing more than to be dead, I *am* feeling pretty good. I'm learning to live in the world without Laura even as I continue to miss her terribly. It's not quite happiness, but I might be approaching *acceptance*.

It's been eight months since the crash, and I just signed a lease for a row home in Hampden, a hipster neighborhood in North Baltimore. Laura and I had our first date at Cafe Hon up the street, and whenever I pass the restaurant, I feel a twinge of pain, but I've also noticed that these reminders seem to lose their power the more I'm forced to confront them. The row home looks like all the other ones on the block, two stories with red brick and a red awning over a small front porch. The basement walks out to a large-for-the-city backyard. Rocko will love having more space, and I'll love getting natural light in my bedroom.

"I'll be living with a friend from college," I tell her. "The lease starts in three weeks."

I've started working at a seafood restaurant downtown. Waiting tables after finishing law school isn't quite how I envisioned my life. But it's low-stress, and it will pay the rent. I've even been able to pay for the occasional date with Maria.

"That's good, Mark," Kara replies. "Renting a new place is a big step. Does this mean you aren't worried about the criminal charges anymore?" Kara knows the potential charges have been one of the reasons, or excuses, that I've used to justify not taking any significant steps forward in my life.

"It's been eight months since the crash. I don't know if it's because of everything David has done to try to stop the state's attorney from filing charges, or if they figured out the crash wasn't my fault, but I don't think they're going to charge me at this point."

"That must feel like a huge relief. How are things going with Maria? This must be a big relief for her too."

I smile and look up to Kara's eyes at the mention of Maria. I'm starting to picture an actual future with her. We're together all the time now, two little grieving peas in a pod. Some days it even feels like we're just another regular couple, not a mutual grief support group of two.

I didn't care too much before because I figured Maria was just a short-term pre-prison distraction, but for most of the spring and summer, I wondered why Maria had any interest in me at all. She had to pay every time we went out. Her mom, sisters, and friends warned her against getting attached.

"He seems like a nice guy, but that's way too much baggage… Maybe you should just be friends." Maria's an open book, and she told me what they said. It hurt, a lot. I'd never felt so undesirable before. I was used to being more than just a nice guy. I'd always been the kind of guy parents wanted their daughters to date.

Maria knew I might go to prison but said we'd figure out what to do when the time came, if the time came. "Let's not worry about that now," she'd say. "We don't even know what's going to happen." I thought maybe knowing this fling, or whatever it was, had no chance of lasting helped her not to worry too.

"Things are good," I tell Kara now. "I still don't know if there's a chance it will last, but I think I'm willing to find out."

"A lot has changed since we first met, Mark," Kara says. "You look different. You're sitting up. Your affect is completely changed. I'm really proud of all the progress you've made, and I know it hasn't been easy."

"I can feel the difference. It's nice to hear that you can see it too," I tell her. "I guess I'm learning to manage the waves as they come."

Kara nods knowingly, recalling the wave analogy Maria's family uses to describe their grief and how I've described feeling completely tossed about by them.

"What are you finding that works for you?" she asks.

I pause a moment to consider her question.

"It's partially that the waves have gotten smaller when they do come, and it's partially that I've figured out what usually causes them. Sometimes I want to feel it. I feel closer to her when I grieve. But other times, I know what I need to stay away from to keep my emotions at bay."

"Tell me more about that."

"Okay. But it's kind of weird, and maybe it's not as healthy as I make it sound."

I tell her about the dance I've been doing with reminders of Laura and the crash. Trying to avoid the wrong reminders of Laura controls where I can go, what I can listen to and watch, and even actions that are totally unrelated to Laura or the crash in any rational way at all.

"It's like I'm walking around trying to pretend to be a normal guy but have this secret dictating every move I make."

"I know it must feel strange, but it's a totally normal response to post-traumatic stress," Kara says. "You've been through an incredibly distressing event, and people can be traumatized even when they don't remember what happened. Not remembering might even be a part of the trauma."

All kinds of reminders can trigger intense memories of what happened or intense re-experiencing of the emotions associated with it. Sights, sounds, smells, and locations can all bring the traumatic event back to mind. Thoughts, feelings, people, and conversations can all remind us of what we've been through. And it's understandable to want to avoid those things.

"It's part of the way our brain has developed to avoid dangerous situations," she tells me. "In nature, we had to learn to avoid behaviors that resulted in injury and death. Our brains are programmed to make connections between causes and effects and learn to avoid actions that threaten our survival."

Psychologists call it avoidance, and in severe cases, avoidance can make it impossible for a person to engage in the normal activities of life. The list of things to avoid becomes so big that they can't do anything or go anywhere at all. I can see how easily someone could shut themselves off completely. If it weren't for taking care of Lucky and spending time with Maria, there were times I might never have left my dungeon at all.

"That's when it becomes a cause for real concern. But what you're describing isn't out of the ordinary at all. If you don't feel like it's keeping you from doing the things you need to do in your life, I wouldn't worry too much about it. Those reminders may lose some of their grasp on you over time."

❖

Later that week, Maria and I are in the dungeon getting ready for a kickball game. We joined a team with a group of Maria's college friends and other twenty-somethings from the neighborhood. We play our games right up the street from my sister's house, and I look forward to it every week.

After my appointment with Kara, I vowed to stop letting reminders of Laura control me. Laura wouldn't want my memories of her to be a source of stress and pain. They're all I have left of her, and they should be a source of strength and gratitude. I know it won't be easy, and reminders of the crash will always be painful, but I have to learn to take pleasure in her memory.

"Everyone's going to the bar after the game," Maria tells me.

"Awesome. We should go too."

I pull on my shorts and put on my team shirt. Maria's still in her underwear, and I pat her playfully on her butt. She turns around and smacks me on mine, then plants a big kiss right on my mouth.

I take a hit of weed from the bowl sitting on the window ledge, and Maria rolls her eyes at me.

"Do you have to?"

"No. But I want to. Relax." *I am.* I'm feeling the most relaxed I've felt since the crash. My phone buzzes on the window sill. I pick it up and read the caller ID. Harry. My lawyer.

*Shit.*

Maria sees the look on my face and knows something is wrong. She crosses the room and puts her hand reassuringly on my arm.

"Hey, Mark. I have some bad news," Harry says in his usually charming Irish accent. "The state's attorney's office let me know they are charging you with Laura's death. They got an indictment about a week ago. They don't want you to have to sit in jail all weekend, so they're going to let me drive you to the station on Sunday to surrender yourself."

My mind and the room start to spin.

"It sounds like they're using kid gloves on you because of Laura's dad," he tells me. "You'll see a judge Monday morning. I'm hoping they'll let you go without bail, or at least without a high bail. With any luck, you'll be home by Monday night."

I'm crushed by the news but relieved about the gentle approach the prosecutor seems to be taking. I know this is not the norm, that most defendants are not given any of these considerations and suspect I might be getting kid gloves not only because of David but also because of my middle-class upbringing, good lawyer, and the color of my skin.

"I'm sorry, Mark."

"It's not your fault. Thanks, Harry."

I hang up the phone and tell Maria. She puts her arms around me, and we both start to cry.

# CHAPTER 14

*I'm standing out front of my high school, underneath the awning, depositing a coin into the payphone so I can call my mom to come pick me up from school.*

*I hear the sound of footsteps around the corner and look up. I can't believe my eyes as Laura strolls casually around the lush garden adorning the entryway to the school.*

*"What is she doing at my high school?" I wonder. "What is she doing alive?"*

*Laura is breezy and composed as she turns the corner and begins walking toward me. She doesn't even seem to notice I'm here.*

*"Laura," I whisper.*

*She looks up, and in an instant, her calm tranquility melts into panic and terror.*

*She turns to run, and before I know what's happening, I'm running too. I'm getting closer, begging her to stop running and talk to me.*

*"Why are you afraid?" I yell. But she only runs faster.*

*"It's me, Laura," I try to get through to her. "It's okay. It's me. You're safe."*

*She looks back and screams in terror as something hits me in the back. I don't look back to see what it is. I just keep chasing her.*

*But then it hits me again, and again, and again.*

❖

My eyes fly open, and I'm covered in sweat, lying on the top bunk in the two-person jail cell I'm sharing with a stranger.

"Cut out the snoring," he demands. "People are trying to sleep."

The weekend had been a blur. I stopped by the restaurant where I worked to tell the managers I was being arrested. I wasn't sure if I'd be back at all, but I promised to let them know the outcome of my bail hearing if I could. They already knew about the accident, but I think, like me, they'd expected that since I hadn't been arrested yet, I never would be.

"If you get bail, you can keep working here until your trial. But if not, we'll be here when you get out."

My coworkers hugged me and shared words of encouragement.

After that, I made the rounds to say goodbye to friends and family, not knowing if it would be the last time I would see them outside a prison visiting room for a decade. I told Maria there'd be no hard feelings if she moved on with her life. I appreciated everything she'd done to help me and the time we'd spent together over the last six months. I wouldn't forget her, but it was fine if she needed to forget me.

"Let's just see what happens," she reassured me. "I'm here for you." I got the impression she already had in her head a maximum sentence she would wait through. If it was longer, she was out. Shorter, she'd hang around.

"Of course, she's going to run for the hills!" I thought.

"It's for the best. One less person to watch moving forward while I rot in prison." *One less person to worry about. One less person to long for.*

Sunday night I got in the car with Harry, and we drove to the Anne Arundel County police department. A while later I was in a patrol car on my way to jail. The officer didn't cuff me, and he let me sit in the passenger seat next to him. We chatted like old buddies catching up, and I wondered if he'd driven drunk and knew he could easily be me at that moment. He walked me into the Jennifer Road Detention Center.

"Just sit over there," he said, pointing to a concrete bench.

The jail intake officers took their time, and I sat in the waiting area for several hours. The bench was uncomfortably cold and hard, and it made my butt hurt, but I was scared to be locked up and grateful for the delay. Around 11 pm, they took me back to my cell.

As the door creaked open, my cellmate woke up. He was older than me, maybe late forties or early fifties, with a scraggly beard and sunken eyes. He glanced at me bemusedly, and I was sure he was thinking, *"first timer."*

He was on the bottom bunk, so I climbed to the top bunk as he rolled over and fell back asleep. I was exhausted from the emotional upheaval of the last three days, and, despite my fear of the place, I fell asleep quickly too.

While sleeping in a jail cell was different from anything I'd ever experienced before, what was not different was my snoring. Laura used to complain about how hard it was to fall asleep next to me, and Maria tells me it's like sleeping next to a freight train. Of course, when we slept in the dungeon, Maria and I actually were right next to a freight train. So the snoring must be even *worse* than a freight train!

Now I start to fall asleep again. I start snoring again, and I get kicked again. "Cut that shit out," my cellmate seethes. I start to fall asleep again, snore, get kicked. Sleep, snore, get kicked. It continues like that until I force myself to stay awake for long enough for my cellmate to reach a depth of sleep from which I doubt my storing will awaken him. But after forcing myself awake for so long, I can't fall asleep again, and I spend the rest of the night awake thinking about my life and the events of the last eight months. There are so many things that I've always taken for granted about myself. But I'm starting to understand the truth. I'm a bad guy who makes bad decisions and does bad things. I'm not upset about getting kicked for my snoring. *It's the least of what I deserve.*

❖

At what I assume must be 6 or 7 o'clock in the morning, the bright tube lights of Unit A-1 flicker on, and I look around the cell for the first time through squinting eyes. Besides the utilitarian bunk bed we sleep on, my cellmate and I share a small metal table hung from the wall, a stool, and a stainless steel sink and matching stainless steel toilet. The toilet, three feet from the bed and offering no privacy, is clogged with shit and toilet paper, and I hop down to pee on top of the mess.

"You're lucky they put you here," my cellmate offers helpfully, "You snore like that with some of these other guys, they'll cut your throat." Things can always get worse, I suppose.

Unit A-1 consists of a large triangular common area full of round tables and plastic stacking chairs, surrounded on two sides by two stories of two-person cells. The walls and doors are painted in neutral shades of tan and cream, and two tan metal staircases lead to the ends of a catwalk that offers access to the second-floor cells.

A correctional officer in a blue uniform pushes a tray through a slot in the cell door, and my cellmate hops down to grab it. I follow his lead and grab the second tray that follows immediately after the first. Breakfast consists of a piece of white bread, not toasted, what appears to be a single scrambled egg, and overcooked carrots. I push it around with the plastic spork but don't have much of an appetite.

"I'll take that if you're not going to eat," my cellmate offers.

"When do we get to go out there?" I ask, gesturing toward the common area and handing him my uneaten tray of food.

"After breakfast, we'll get an hour. If you need to shower, that's the time."

A-1 is a maximum-security intake unit. Since none of us have been assessed for risk by the correctional staff, we're all treated like we pose a high risk of violence or escape. We get one hour in the common area and twenty-three hours a day in our cells.

"I'll probably just sit at one of the tables," I say, scared of what might happen in the showers.

"You better not start smelling," he glares up at me sitting

in the top bunk, and I think it's a stupid thing to worry about. The place already reeks of desperate men.

After breakfast, our cell doors open, and we walk onto the common area for our hour of relative freedom. Some of the men pace around the room for physical activity, while others head for the showers, and still others sit at the tables, sharing gossip and intelligence about the jail and their cases. I sit in a corner by myself and try not to be noticed.

"Everyone back in your cells," one of the correctional officers yells at the end of the hour. After everybody returns to their cells, another officer with a clipboard walks around the common area opening individual cells and letting certain men back out.

"O'Brien, you've got arraignment," he says, opening my cell door. I know from my criminal law classes and Harry that this is just the first step in the criminal justice process after getting arrested.

Back in the common area, most of the men line up at a table where the public defender has set up a makeshift workstation. They take turns completing a form to secure the services of the public defender's office and sharing a few details about their case. The rest of us sit in rows of plastic chairs surrounding the door to a conference room on the side of the triangular common area where there aren't any cells. A court employee calls us in alphabetical order and spends a few minutes talking with each of us.

"O'Brien!" she shouts over the din of male voices echoing through the cavernous room.

I sit down at the table with her, and she taps her pen on the form in front of her.

"How many times have you been arrested?" she asks.

"One."

"Job?"

"I work in a restaurant."

"Education?"

"I have a law degree."

She looks up from the form and glances at me out of the side of her eye.

"This is serious. I don't have time to mess around."

"It's the truth," I protest.

"Fine. You can tell the judge about your 'law degree,'" she replies mockingly. "Follow me."

She gets up from her seat, and I follow her to the conference room at the end of the common area. Inside, there is a TV screen and camera. On the TV, I see Harry, the judge, and a man I assume is the state's attorney.

"I have Mark O'Brien," the court woman says to the camera.

"We are on the record in State of Maryland versus Mark O'Brien," the judge intones.

"Yes, your honor," the state's attorney begins. "Mr. O'Brien is charged with homicide by vehicle or vessel and eight other lesser charges resulting from a drunk driving collision in which one person was killed."

The judge looks up at the camera, and the court woman takes her cue.

"Mr. O'Brien lives in Baltimore, Maryland, and he has two sisters, his parents, and a girlfriend living in the area. He works at," she looks down at her clipboard, "the Rusty Scupper, a restaurant in Baltimore, and states that his employer will permit him to continue working if he is released pending trial. Mr. O'Brien also claims to have a law degree."

"Correction," Harry interrupts. "My client *does* have a law degree. He graduated from Georgetown last spring." I glance at the court woman who rolls her eyes at me. I don't hold the mistake against her. Most of the time, if you have my background, you don't wind up here—not because you haven't done anything wrong but because the deck is stacked in your favor to get away with it. This thing, though, this crime I've done, is so bad that it's not the kind of thing you just get away with.

"The state does not oppose Mr. O'Brien's release pending trial," the state's attorney continues. "But given the seriousness of the charges and Mr. O'Brien's access to resources that could enable his flight, the state requests that this court set bail at one million dollars."

"Mr. O'Brien has lived in Maryland for half his life. He could have fled at any time over the last eight months if he intended to avoid confronting the charges against him," Harry implores. "He has a family and a life here, and he intends to apply for bar membership and begin his legal career in Maryland as soon as he is able, acknowledging that, given the charges against him, that could be some time." Harry asks the court to release me on my own recognizance—that is, with no bail payment.

The judge sets bail at fifty thousand dollars, and Courtney and her partner offer their house as collateral, rescuing me again. If I don't show up to court, they'll lose their home.

"No drinking. No drugs. And you need to report to pretrial supervision twice a week. Dismissed."

I go back to my cell, expecting to leave the jail immediately. I'm wrong. They don't let you out right after you post bail.

"They gotta do a bunch of shit, like paperwork and shit," my cellmate explains. "They wanna make it official that you're not their problem anymore and make sure they're letting out the right guy."

Later that evening, I'm wondering if they've forgotten about me, if I'll have to spend another night here, when an officer opens the door to my cell.

"O'Brien. You're out of here."

❖

In Maryland, defendants are supervised on pretrial release in the county where their crime occurred. That means twice a week I need to be in Annapolis, about an hour from the row home I'm renting in Baltimore. My roommate and I had already signed the lease when Harry called to tell me about the charges, so even though I might go to prison in just a few months, I'm still planning to move out of the dungeon. I have no car and no way of getting to pretrial supervision. But if I don't show up, I'll be arrested and spend the next three months in jail awaiting trial. Maria says she'll drive me back and forth to Annapolis for all my appointments.

"It's no problem," she says, though it's an unmistakably loving sacrifice that will have her driving four or five hours a week and waiting for however long these appointments are going to take. It's going to be inconvenient, and it's going to get in the way of work and other things she could be doing with her time.

"Thank you. I really appreciate it," I tell her. I'm overwhelmed with gratitude, and I hope she hears it in my voice.

The next day, we get into Maria's Honda Civic. It's white, so not the purple that brings happy thoughts of Laura or the silver that reminds me of the crash. We get on the highway, and Maria presses down on the gas. She drives fast. Too fast. Faster than I ever would now. And it frightens me. I grab the handle on the armrest of the door as she speeds down the highway, and I put my other hand defensively on the dashboard.

"What's the problem?" she asks.

"We're going pretty fast, don't you think?" It's not the first time we've had this conversation.

"If I'm going to be driving you back and forth, you're going to have to deal with it."

Kara would call this "exposure therapy." That's when therapists help people overcome irrational fears by progressively exposing them to more and more of what they're uncomfortable with. It's supposed to be done by a professional, and I don't think Maria is qualified. But she's also right. She's doing me a favor, and driving fast is going to mean she spends less time in the car, so I fight the urge to grab the door every time she changes lanes and hits the gas.

Heading south on I-97 outside of Annapolis, the highway curves gently to the left just before it passes under Hawkins Road. The right side of the road dips down into a wooded area, and the guardrail is a couple of feet down the hill from the shoulder of the road. This is where it happened. I've only been here once since the crash. For the next three months, I'll have to pass it twice a week. Anticipation and apprehension fall on me as we approach. I sit up straight, looking ahead for the overpass that will signal we're nearing the spot. My heart races as we get nearer. I stare at the guardrail and make a silent prayer, apologizing to Laura, asking God for forgiveness, and wishing once again that I could trade places with her.

# CHAPTER 15

At the pretrial supervision office, I sit and wait for my supervisor to come out. That's what they call the person in charge of my life now, my supervisor. Maria isn't allowed in the building and waits in the car. I sit for an hour before being called back to my supervisor's office. My time is his time. And because for some reason she still cares about me, Maria's time is his time too.

My supervisor is a Black guy in his late thirties, with a kind smile and gentle eyes. His hand is disfigured, and he seems self-conscious about it, turning it away so it's not visible, sort of like I try to hide my pain from family and friends, probably with a similar lack of success.

He explains the rules and what happens if I fail to follow them. He's firm but not unfriendly. "You need to be here every Tuesday and Friday. Don't be late. I have a full docket. You'll take a drug test today and every time you come in. I don't care if the first one's dirty, but there should be less drugs in your system next time, and it should keep going down until you're clean."

I nod in acknowledgment. There will be some weed in the test from before my arrest. It stays in your system for about a month.

"If you get arrested for anything or break any of the terms of your release, you have to tell me right away. I'll have to send you back to the judge, and you'll probably get locked up until your trial. Do you have any questions or anything you need to report?"

"No."

We go to the bathroom so he can watch me pee for the drug test.

"Have you been drinking?"

"No." Right after Laura died, I was drinking all the time. But as I spent more time with Maria and started watching Lucky, I drank less and less. Now that I'm facing prison, I've decided that even though I hope my life is short so I can see Laura again sooner, I don't want to spend it locked up, even if being locked up is exactly what I deserve. Abstinence from drugs and alcohol is a condition of my release on bail, and I'm not going to mess up any second chance I might get by drinking or smoking weed.

❖

Being charged with Laura's death has plunged me back into a deep hole. If Judge Hackner, the judge in my case, decides that justice requires me to spend my life not only without Laura but also behind bars, I don't think I could disagree. The possibility that Maria and I could have a life together, that someday I might not hurt so much, seems like a silly fantasy now.

After my release on bail, Harry told me that I should start alcohol treatment while on pretrial supervision. "If you get sentenced to probation instead of jail, Judge Hackner's going to order you to do it anyway, so you might as well get started. It will look good if we get to sentencing, and you're already in rehab."

My insurance covers a place called Crossroads on Charles Street in North Baltimore. The Motor Vehicle Administration hasn't taken away my license because the state troopers filled out some paperwork incorrectly, so I'm still legally allowed to drive, but I don't have a car or money to buy one. Crossroads isn't far from my house, so while Maria or my roommate can drive me some of the time, I'll also be able to walk when I need to.

Crossroads is a private addiction treatment center in a not-bad part of town, so I assume it will be nice. When Maria drops me off out front for the first time, I think it's a dump. There can't be any other kind of healthcare that gets delivered in the kind of dilapidated settings where they expect people to recover from addiction.

I sign in, and a counselor calls me into his office. He goes through a long list of questions about my drinking and drug history. I've been drinking since I was fifteen. My first drink was the night I found out my parents were divorcing. I walked up the street to hang out with a friend; he wasn't home, but his mom was, and she gave me a few screwdrivers to make me feel better. It worked. I started smoking weed a year later and smoked a lot of weed during college. That also made me feel better.

"Have you ever been arrested or gone to jail for something related to your substance use?"

"Yes."

"How many times?"

"Just once." I tell him about the accident and the charges I'm facing. I spent one night in jail waiting for the arraignment last month.

"How often do you drink and how much?"

*Before the accident or now that I want to be dead again?*

"It was three or four times a week." And it was usually a lot whenever I did. "But I haven't had anything to drink in a few weeks, since the arrest."

"How about family problems? Have you had family problems or other relationship problems related to your substance use?"

*I killed my girlfriend and stole her parents' daughter from them. Does that count?*

"Yes."

They ask about family history, work history, education, and all kinds of things. In the end, they put me in an outpatient treatment program that meets once a week for two hours. It's the lowest level of treatment they have. The first hour will be an AA meeting, and the second hour will be group therapy. I don't think I have an alcohol problem, but if it'll keep me out of prison, I'll do whatever I need to do, say whatever they want to hear, and follow whatever rules they say I have to follow.

❖

But once I get started, it turns out that outpatient treatment and AA meetings are a massive waste of my time and money. There's a $10 copay for every session, and while it seems small, it's eating into the little bit of money I have. I'm waiting tables at the restaurant again, but I don't make a lot of money there, and almost all of it goes to rent, utilities, and food.

The people in the AA meetings fall into two camps. There are the ones who aren't required to be there as part of the treatment program, who come because they actually want to be in an AA meeting. They've been in recovery for a year, five years, twenty years, and this is how they stay sober. Their stories don't resonate with me at all. When they're talking, I'm sitting there thinking, *"I'm not like you."* They're mostly older, and while their drinking might not have led to a death, what they describe are heart-wrenching difficulties with not being able to stop. My drinking did lead to someone's death, but I've never not been able to stop when I wanted to.

"Hi, I'm Jim, and I'm an alcoholic. I haven't had a drink in ten years. After my seventh DWI and third stint in jail, my wife left me, and my kids wouldn't talk to me anymore. I lost my job, but I had thirteen dollars left in my wallet. I spent it on a fifth of Jack. After I drank that, I really had nothing left. That's when I found the rooms."

"The rooms" is what people in AA call the places where AA meetings take place. With the exception of a prison cell, I'd rather be in any other room on the planet.

"And now I take it one day at a time. The program works if you work it." People in AA have all kinds of sayings like this. "Thanks for letting me share." They always say "thanks for letting me share" at the end.

"Keep coming back." That's what you say after someone says, "Thanks for letting me share."

Many of their stories really are heartbreaking. And being in the rooms really does seem to have changed their lives for the better. But the meetings do nothing to help me get better. I can't relate to the problems they describe. I drink when I want to, and I don't drink when I don't want to. I'm not going to call myself an alcoholic, because I'm not an alcoholic.

The other camp is full of people like me, here because the treatment program requires it. And we're in the treatment program because court or work requires it, or our lawyers say it looks good. We don't actually buy into any of it. We go through the motions. In this camp, only one or two of us seems to have any kind of genuine substance use problem. The charade seems like a giant waste of resources. Maybe treatment should be only for people who need it, and with the money we save, we could clean these treatment centers up a bit.

❖

A few weeks later, Harry receives the discovery packet of evidence from the state. It has all the police reports, crime scene recreations, and everything else the state has to make their case against me. I review them, not to see what they have on me but to better understand what happened.

Corporal Weaver from the Anne Arundel County Police Department was first on the scene the night of the crash. He was patrolling on I-97 when he saw a group of cars stopped by the right shoulder with their flashers on. He saw my Honda Civic overturned and smashed on top of a guardrail on the edge of the road. My headlights were facing the wrong direction toward oncoming traffic.

He turned on his siren and stopped near my car. As he approached on foot, he passed a group of onlookers and asked if any of them were involved in the crash or saw it happen. Nobody was involved, and nobody saw it happen.

"I'm a nurse. He's in the car!" said a woman already on the scene. "His name is Mark, and he's still in the car."

It's so strange to read about the crash and all the details I don't remember. I still can't recall anything between being at Chris's and hearing the paramedic—who I'm now learning was actually not a paramedic but a cop on patrol— when I thought he was saying "he's gone" about me dying, but really was saying "she's gone" about Laura already being dead.

I don't remember people being around the car before first responders arrived, but I must have been talking to them since the nurse knew my name. I don't remember her, but I suspect having her with me must have been comforting. I wish I could find her, thank her, and ask her more about what happened that night, but her name's not in the police report.

❖

Corporal Weaver got down to look inside the car and saw a leg with the bones exposed hanging out the door. He could see me in the car, buckled into the driver's side and my head hanging down toward the ceiling of the car, which was now the floor of the car. It took him a moment to realize the leg wasn't mine and that there was another person in the car. He examined Laura and saw she wasn't breathing. There was no way to get to her to provide medical attention.

I'd assumed for the last ten months that the first responders on the scene didn't know Laura was in the car because I'd said I was alone. I thought maybe the guardrail was blocking their view and mine. But when he'd asked me if there was anyone else in the car, Corporal Weaver already knew Laura was dead. He wanted to know if there was a third or fourth person who might have been thrown from the car and if anyone else might have been injured.

"No one. It's just me," I'd said. I never even mentioned Laura, and he hadn't told me, "There's a dead girl hanging right next to you."

*How could I just forget her?*

"I shoulda died. I'm better off dead, aren't I?" the report says I asked him at one point. I remember thinking I was going to die but not *wanting to die*. I didn't know Laura was dead, and when I thought I was dying, I worried about her having to live without me, about how she'd suffer. The way I remember it, I wanted to live. I don't remember saying that I would be better off dead. Had I alternated between wanting to live, believing I was by myself dying in the car, and then knowing that Laura was already dead in the car with me and therefore wanting to die too? Had I wished I died because I already knew I was responsible for her death? Did I see her in the car with me? Did my mind erase the memory, or had it never been there?

*What is wrong with me? How could I not know she was there? I killed her, and then I abandoned her.*

Maybe my concussion made me forget that we were at a party together. But reading the report and the description of Laura's leg hanging by me in the car makes me think that her death and the injuries she suffered were just too unbearable for me to acknowledge, that my brain immediately put up walls to avoid confronting the horror of it all.

*How could I forget? Thank God I don't remember.*

❖

Trooper Bedell from the Maryland State Police was the lead investigator. Reading his description of the accident and wreckage, I know how lucky I am to be alive, and how unbelievable it is that I walked away with almost no injuries. Reading his notes, I accidentally feel thankful for having survived.

*I shouldn't be thankful. I should be dead. Laura should be alive, and I should be dead. Never be thankful to be alive. Never, ever be thankful to be alive, ever again.*

While I was driving down the highway, the car "for unknown reasons began to rotate clockwise." *Unknown reasons?* Not because I was drunk? Not because my tire blew out? Not because a deer ran in front of me and made me swerve or another car cut me off and left the scene? There were no witnesses to the crash; the reason was just "unknown."

As the car began to spin, it crossed from the left lane into the right, skidding for 184 feet, and then across the shoulder for another seventy-four feet, until it collided with the guardrail. The car flipped over and was traveling backwards and upside down atop a guardrail for another hundred feet, the guardrail cutting into the car and killing Laura when it struck her head.

Our seatbelts were buckled, and the airbags didn't deploy because it wasn't a front-end collision. We both would have been fine if the guardrail hadn't come through the top of the car. That's the thing about a deadly accident; there are a million little factors that have to align for it to happen. Any one of them could have changed, and Laura would still be alive. Any one of them could have changed, and I would be dead too.

My blood alcohol level was 0.19, three times the legal limit, and the blood sample was taken hours after the accident, so it must have been even higher when I was driving. We were traveling at seventy-four miles per hour in a sixty-five-mile-per-hour zone. Not too too fast, but they're charging me with exceeding the speed limit anyway. That's what they do. Pile on the charges to make it seem worse than it is, which almost makes me laugh, because how could anything be worse than killing her?

Trooper Bojnowaki from the Maryland State Police interviewed me in the hospital the morning of the crash. In her report, she writes that when she arrived at the hospital, I was lying on my back with my neck immobilized. She told me she needed a written statement on what happened in the accident, and I said I understood but couldn't write a statement because I couldn't move. I don't remember being immobilized. The way

I remember it, I was sitting up and talking to both troopers, but there's also no mention in the report of the second trooper who looked like Laura.

*Did Trooper Bojnowaki come alone? Did Laura visit me in the hospital?*

The trooper wrote down my statement so I could sign it. I told her that Laura and I left my house at 9:30 to go to Chris's. We stayed there a half hour then went to Bartenders, the bar with the pepperoni pizza around the corner from Chris's house.

The statement says we drove from Chris's to Bartenders, but we didn't drive. Chris's house and the bar were only a block apart. It's a reminder of how much information can get confused or wrong in these investigations. She was thinking about the car accident, so she assumed there was driving at that point. I probably assumed she would write it how I told it, so I just signed the statement without reading it closely.

*How much of this actually happened?*

I told her we left Bartenders when it closed so we could go home together. I didn't remember going back to Chris's when I talked to her in the hospital, or she got this part wrong too, but I remember it vaguely now, ten months later. I told her Laura was our designated driver, that she hadn't been drinking, and that I had no idea why I would be driving.

*Well, at least that part's true.*

# CHAPTER 16

It's the day before my court date, the day before I'll be sentenced for killing Laura. I've decided to plead guilty.

The police reports and crime scene photos prove I was driving the car when it crashed. Harry thinks the evidence that the car began rotating for "unknown reasons" and the fact that I'd been having problems keeping the tire inflated raised "reasonable doubt" about whether my drunk driving was the cause of the accident. Maybe the accident would have occurred even if I'd been sober. The state might not be able to prove a direct line of causation between my drunk driving and Laura's death.

"You could consider pleading not guilty to the manslaughter charges," he'd explained. "But you're going to be convicted of DWI anyway, and with Laura's family standing behind you, you're probably going to look like a jerk trying to avoid responsibility and piss off Judge Hackner. He could give you a longer sentence for the DWI if you plead not guilty to the manslaughter charge than he would for manslaughter if you accept responsibility for the whole thing."

"It doesn't matter. I want to plead guilty. Laura deserves that much," I'd told him. "She deserves justice." I wouldn't walk into a courtroom and deny what I did. I wouldn't put her family through that or dishonor her memory like that.

Harry talked to the state's attorney about what the terms of a plea agreement could be. The state wasn't out for blood, and they'd offered to recommend a sentence of no more than eighteen months if I pleaded guilty to the felony homicide charge. They'd throw out all the other charges: a lesser homicide charge, DWI, reckless driving, speeding.

"I'm hopeful that with Laura's family by your side, Judge Hackner may go below the eighteen months. There might even be no jail time," Harry said. "You're a good guy, Mark. He could give you a break." A middle-class, educated, white guy, I might get a break.

"But I *am not* a good guy," I'd thought.

I didn't want to go to jail. I was scared to death of going to jail. I wanted to move on with as short a sentence as possible. I knew the judge could give me ten years, and if I could limit that to a maximum of eighteen months, that sounded like a good thing to do. At the same time, eighteen months didn't seem long enough for what I did. I felt the man responsible for Laura's death should suffer more than that.

My best friend growing up had been another army brat, and we'd lived on two different bases together. He'd been killed by a drunk driver when we were kids. When I was a teenager, and the driver came up for parole, I wrote a letter asking the parole board to deny his release. He'd taken a life and destroyed a family. He should stay behind bars. But this time, I would be that man. Had the man who killed my friend also been just some "good guy" who made a mistake, or had he been the monster I'd imagined him to be, a killer? And if he was, doesn't that mean I'm a monster too?

"I'll take the deal," I'd decided.

So with a day left before my sentencing, I borrow Maria's

car to go to confession at St. Joseph's, the church Laura and I went to with her family on holidays, where we had her funeral, and where Courtney and I now attend weekly mass. I don't know if I'll be in jail for years, months, or no time at all— the judge can ignore the plea deal and give me any sentence he likes—but I feel suddenly compelled to ask for God's forgiveness while I still have time. *Why did it take me so long?* Maybe if Laura's family can forgive me, and God can forgive me too, I might be able to forgive myself someday. And maybe if God isn't mad at me, my sentence won't be as severe. That kind of magical thinking has continued to invade my thinking since the crash.

After a half hour drive, I arrive at St. Joseph's. I park the car and walk to the door. I reach to open it, but it's locked. The hours posted by the door tell me the church is closed, and I remember there is another church nearby. When Laura and I lived together, we drove by St. John's all the time. I get back in the car and drive straight there.

St. John's is open, and I decide to sit in the pews and pray. I'm alone in the church, and I sit there for an hour, praying for forgiveness, for some idea of what I should do with my life, and for a criminal sentence that doesn't include years in prison. I pray to God and talk to Laura. I pray that she's okay and that I will see her again one day. I ask God to take control of everything and say I'll trust him to be in charge, like that Carrie Underwood song *Jesus Take the Wheel*. Of course, if he'd taken the wheel a year ago, I wouldn't be hurting so much and so afraid of the future now. Or maybe he *did* take the wheel that night, he's a bad driver, and that's why Laura's gone.

A man comes in to sweep the floors. He walks by and smiles warmly. I do my best to smile back, wipe the tears from my cheeks and stand up to figure out where I can say my confession.

The office of the church is next door. I knock on the door, and a woman quickly answers. Tears are streaming down my face again, and I ask if I can talk to a priest.

"Confession is on Saturday only," she tells me and closes the door in my face.

*So much for a loving God.*

I walk back to the car, distraught and dejected, and decide to give up. This isn't going to work. Everything in my life is going wrong. Why should I expect *this* to be any different? I drive back to the interstate and turn north toward Baltimore.

It's been a few months since I moved out of the dungeon; my new place is on the north side of the city, nowhere near Courtney's house in south Baltimore. But I have to get off the interstate near Courtney's house to drive through downtown on Key Highway and get home. After getting off the interstate, I'm distracted, and, as if on autopilot, I turn onto Lawrence Street and then onto Fort Avenue like I'm returning to the dungeon.

*No big deal. I'll just take the next right and get back on Key Highway. Oops, missed the turn. I'll take the next one.*

I'm so distracted by my distress, and I really can't concentrate.

*Oops. There goes another turn I should have made.*

I can't even drive home correctly.

I finally make a right turn. I'm not familiar with this side of the neighborhood, but I know I'm heading back toward Key Highway, and Key Highway will take me around the harbor toward home. I stop paying attention again. The next thing I know, I'm turning left for no apparent reason.

*C'mon, Mark. Get it together.*

This part of the neighborhood is full of one-way roads and narrow alleyways. Wherever I try to turn, I can't. And when I can turn, I get distracted and forget to.

I pull over to get a grip on myself. When I look up, I'm right in front of a church. It's less than a mile from the dungeon, but I never knew it was here.

It's locked, but there's information about another church owned by the parish just a few blocks away. I walk over to Holy Cross and knock on the door of the offices. A priest answers the door.

"I was hoping I could make a confession."

Father Patrick opens the door and takes me to his office. He is younger than most of the priests I've known; but his eyes reflect a wisdom and worldliness beyond his years. It feels like a miracle, like I was guided here. Like I prayed to find a place to receive forgiveness, and God literally took the wheel to get me here.

*Kind of creepy, actually.*

"Forgive me father for I have sinned. It's been, I don't know, about ten years since my last confession."

"Go ahead," says Father Patrick.

"I killed someone." It's true, but I also say it for shock effect, like I'm play acting a confessional scene from a movie. I'm not sure why.

His eyes widen. He wasn't expecting that, but he's also accustomed to hearing people's darkest secrets. Now I walk it back a little.

"I caused a car accident about a year ago. My girlfriend died. I'm getting sentenced tomorrow."

"Is there anything else?"

"I stopped going to church. For a long time, I didn't have any relationship with God. I'm trying to fix that."

"Do you remember how to say the Act of Contrition?"

I nod and say the prayer I've known since I memorized it in second grade.

❖

The next day, I'm on my way to the courthouse to plead guilty and receive my sentence. Barack Obama is being inaugurated today, and all the radio stations are talking about the historic ascendance of America's first Black president. When Laura died, everyone assumed Hillary Clinton would win the democratic nomination. It's a reminder of how quickly the world moves on, how much things change, how much Laura will miss with her life cut decades short.

I walk into the courthouse with my family, pass through security, and see Laura's family and Harry waiting for me. Maria isn't here because I still haven't told Laura's family about her. David plans to ask Judge Hackner not to send me to prison, but if the judge doesn't show mercy, I could go straight from the courthouse to prison, and today could be my last one as a free man.

We wait outside the courtroom until the bailiff opens the door. It's a small room with four rows of benches on each side of a center aisle. Harry and I sit at the table in the front right of the courtroom. The prosecutor is at the table on the front left. In a show of solidarity, Laura's family and friends sit behind me instead of behind the prosecutor where victims' families usually sit.

Judge Hackner enters, and we all stand up. He reads from the sheet in front of him and announces the case of State of Maryland versus Mark O'Brien.

The state's attorney and Judge Hackner discuss the charges against me and the facts the state intends to present if I change my mind and plead not guilty. They talk about the agreement to recommend a sentence of no more than eighteen months. Then they turn to me, and Harry and Judge Hackner explain the long list of rights I'll be forfeiting by pleading guilty. At the end, Judge Hackner asks if, knowing all the rights I'll be giving up, I still wish to plead guilty.

"Yes. I plead guilty."

Once I decided to plead guilty, Harry told me to collect letters of support for Judge Hackner to consider while deciding on my sentence. With Laura's family by my side, and others attesting to my good qualities, he thought it was possible Judge Hackner might not give me any jail time at all.

Chris and one of my high school friends took the lead collecting letters from my friends. My mom collected letters from my family. And David collected letters from Laura's family. Forty of my friends and family wrote to the judge. Eighteen of Laura's family members also did.

I'd read some of the letters, but it felt like they weren't about the person I'd become. Some of them described me as a role model, as someone who was compassionate, someone who went to law school to make a difference. Others talked about how much I loved Laura. "I have never seen a couple that was more perfectly matched . . . Mark and Laura would have had a fairytale life together if the accident never happened . . . Laura was truly Mark's world." Laura's mom wrote one of the nicest letters about how much we loved each other.

*As if loving Laura is supposed to excuse the fact that I killed her.*

The only one who really seemed to get it was Laura's cousin, who was ten years old. "Mark would always play with me. He was a lot of fun. But after the accident, he is not the same. He always looks sad."

She's right. I'm not the same as the person in these letters. I'm a killer, unworthy and undeserving of their forgiveness. I'm not the good person they're writing about. I probably never was. I was always this bad person. I just didn't know it yet. They just didn't know it yet. I have no idea who I am anymore.

Harry hired a psychologist as an expert witness, and I met with him a few weeks ago to talk about my grief and therapy sessions with Kara. Out of respect for my privacy, the judge asks everyone to leave the courtroom while the psychologist testifies about my mental state. The prosecutor, who seems to be making only a half-hearted effort to condemn me, doesn't object.

Therapy "is clearly benefiting him, and he is getting better," the psychologist says. "It would be much more difficult for him to heal from this incident and to put his life back on a positive track" without continuing counseling. Harry is trying to convince the judge not to send me to jail so I can keep going to therapy, but I think they're making me sound like a crazy person. But I'm not a crazy person.

*I'm a monster.*

# CHAPTER 17

Once the psychologist finishes his testimony and everyone has returned to the courtroom, my mom walks to the front of the courtroom to make a statement. She says that if you asked her a year ago what would be happening in my life, she'd have told you I might be in a courtroom, but not as a defendant, as a lawyer. I might have been with Laura's family in a church, but for our wedding not her funeral.

It aches to see my mom in so much pain. I've long been able to tell when she's upset, even though she's usually so restrained. The muscles around her mouth tighten almost imperceptibly, hiding her anguish from all but the closest observer. Now she tries to exert control, but the tears are coming anyway, and there's no doubt she is completely heartbroken.

She says she was looking forward to Laura's joining our family. "Laura could light up every place she walked into. . . We've already lost a daughter," she says. "The grieving is unbearable."

She begs the judge not to take me away too. "Sending Mark to prison will only magnify everyone's grief," she implores before returning to her seat, sobbing.

My dad speaks next. He's been out of the army for five years after a twenty-year career, but he still carries himself like an officer. He participated in a number of courts martial during his time in the service, and he makes his statement as if giving an official report about a defendant's character and the appropriate punishment for their violation of the Military Code of Justice. He talks about our family's history of service and our beliefs in living up to a duty to others. He tells Judge Hackner he understands that justice requires some punishment, but he asks him to have mercy and tells him that he knows I'm the kind of person who will feel an obligation to do good for others because of my mistake. I think the message is as much an instruction to me as a statement to the court. "If you get a second chance, you better do something good with it."

Laura's aunt was one of the first members of Laura's large family that I really bonded with. The first time I met her, she didn't know Laura and I had moved from friendship to romance, and she tried to set Laura up with another guy while I was standing awkwardly next to her. We had a good laugh about it later.

She walks to the front of the courtroom, gestures to her family seated behind her, and looks up to the judge.

"We are a large, close, and loving Italian-Irish Catholic family. Everyone who meets my family wants to be a part of our family and is welcomed in with open arms. Laura is and always will be a huge part of our family. She is our bright and shining light."

She tells the judge that she liked me from the moment Laura introduced me to her—skipping over the part where she tried to get Laura, a different boyfriend. I was a part of their family, and she knew we would be married one day. "They are good and honest and wonderful young people." We still talk about Laura in present tense, avoiding the finality of speaking about her as part of the past.

On the night of the crash, she says, "Laura was the designated driver . . . We will never know the details of that night and what went wrong with their plan, but the events of that night have changed our lives forever." From the letters to the court and Laura's aunt's statement, I wonder if their forgiveness stems at least in part from a feeling that Laura bears some of the responsibility for what happened.

"Our family is devastated, Mark is devastated, and Mark's family, who loves Laura too, is devastated. I know that if Mark could take Laura's place, he would."

Tears are streaming down my face. I caused this family so much pain.

"On behalf of my family, including Laura, I would like to ask," she continues. "Please show leniency to Mark so that we can be together to love and support each other. Thank you."

"Why are you doing this? Why are you defending me?" I wonder.

David stands up to speak next, and after a quick glance in his direction, I can't even look up from the table. There is so much sadness in his eyes. They used to look so young and alive. Now they're heavy, weary. He's aged so much in the last year.

"I met Mark for the first time four or five years ago. This was before Laura and Mark were, as Laura would say, officially together," he begins. "I could tell then, Mark was in love with Laura."

*He knew before I even did!*

"I even told her so," he says. "After the accident, Mark

was afraid we wouldn't talk to him or allow him to attend the services. I told Mark then, we liked him because he was a good man, but we loved him because of the way he loved Laura. Their love was something special."

David tells the judge how we've continued to stay connected since the crash. "Mark even spent several days with us last May in Florida to celebrate my other daughter's birthday. Consider the character of the man that would do that. He was with us constantly, never knowing how we could respond and answering all the questions he could. There were a couple of nights, Mark and I stayed up talking about Laura and our feelings."

He tells the judge that if he were mad at me, he would have to be mad at Laura, "and that is not going to happen. Laura and I talked often, but on February 8th, we talked off and on for three hours. We discussed their plans for the evening, and they had a plan. For some reason, they didn't stick to it. Neither one of them should've been in the car that night."

He finishes his statement by saying that the only thing that has gotten all of us through the last year is having each other, and he asks the judge not to take me away too. "Whatever you decide will eventually end. What Mark has to endure every day will not."

"Why are you doing this? How can you forgive me?" I want to ask.

I think this is harder than if they just hated me. I've done this to them, and they are so nice, so forgiving and merciful. They don't deserve this pain, and I  damn sure don't deserve their absolution.

I wish they'd all stop talking about my good character. That's not me. I've known that wasn't me since I read the police reports and really knew what I'd done to her.

"Mark is a good man," David says. But that's not true anymore. I'm the kind of person who makes horrible decisions, puts lives in danger, takes lives, and destroys families and futures. I still *want* mercy, but there's no way I *deserve* it.

❖

David looks at me as he returns to his seat. He presses his lips together, and the right side of his mouth curls up in half a smile. He nods at me as if to say, "I meant what I said."

Harry asks me if I want to make a statement, and I stand at the defendant's table. My legs feel heavy with worry. They shake, and I hold onto the table's edge to steady myself. I spent hours working on my statement to make sure it would be exactly right. I'll never get to say my wedding vows to Laura, so this is the most public declaration of love I'll ever make to her. I take my hands off the table—they're shaking now, too—and pick up the piece of paper in front of me.

"I'm sorry for taking your beautiful and kind and talented daughter, Laura Marie, who I know you loved so much, away from you so early in her life," I say, turning to face Laura's parents with my knees wobbling uncontrollably. To her sisters, I apologize for the loss of their big sister.

Matching itself to my knees, my voice is unsteady; I'm so

nervous I can hardly speak. I apologize to my family and Laura's friends. "Theresa, I know you two were supposed to get houses next door to each other and travel across the country, and I know how painful it is for you not having Laura."

I squeeze my eyes shut, sending tears rolling down my cheeks, and squint so I can see the page better. "I cannot express in words the grief every one of you must feel for the loss of your daughter, sister, granddaughter, niece, cousin, aunt and friend. I know I can't put it into words because I can't express my own grief at the loss of the woman I loved."

I turn to David and his family and tell them I don't understand how they've forgiven me and can't explain how grateful I am to each of them for their support and kindness. "It's beyond my comprehension because I can't forgive myself for what I've done."

I turn back to the judge, hoping I can make him understand that this isn't just your run-of-the-mill lost love. My love with Laura was epic. Something was always missing until I found her. I hoped to spend the rest of my life making her laugh her beautiful laugh every day.

I had a long silly nickname for her. We never used it in public; it was too ridiculous. But I say it now. "Latte the Turtle, Princess of LaLa Land and Outlying Territories, queen of my heart, love of my life, and girl of my dreams." I leave out the "goddess of the bedroom" part, though, deciding decorum requires keeping it PG in the courtroom.

I tell the court about our little punch-buggy-jinxing-in-unison routine. It's the little traditions that make each love special. "Memories like that and others at the beach in Florida visiting Laura's parents and sisters for birthdays, spending time with both our families and spending holidays making the rounds to see all our relatives, or moving into our house in Magothy Manor and starting our lives together." Those are the memories that keep me going, "but mostly I'm just sad and lonely without her, and I still just wish I could be with Laura."

"I would give anything to go back to that night and change what happened."

*I love you, Laura, and I'm so scared of what comes next.*

❖

Yesterday I asked for God's forgiveness, and now I'm waiting for a different kind of judgment. A million thoughts rush through my head as Judge Hackner clears his throat and begins to speak.

"The court is unfortunately in a position where I hear tragic stories quite frequently, and this is certainly among the most tragic I've heard," he says. "Unfortunately, particularly in the context of this type of offense, it is not a rare occasion when I get folks who are eminently reasonable and decent people who just made one mistake that unfortunately has a devastating consequence, and that's what happened in this case.

I don't want to go to prison for a decade. *Just let me have my life back. No! I don't deserve that. I deserve whatever he's about to give me. Probably more. Probably a lot more.*

"Whereas on any other night given a different set of stars

aligning, he would've driven home without any incident," the judge continues. "He would've found himself tucked in bed, and nobody would've been the wiser for the fact that he had been driving drunk."

*He's being really nice. Maybe I won't even go to jail. Please, God. Don't send me to jail.* I'm terrified of going to jail.

Judge Hackner says he doesn't think the sentence for doing something should depend on how angry the victim's family is. He asks if someone should be treated differently because their victim's parents are vengeful. "Do I treat that individual differently than somebody whose family loves him as they do and say wonderful things about him? I think ultimately the question is, what is the message that goes out."

*You're right. I deserve whatever another person would get for this. Their forgiveness doesn't change the justice Laura deserves.*

Another purpose of punishment in the criminal justice system is to keep people from repeating their behavior. Judge Hackner says he doesn't think that's necessary in my case since the loss of Laura has already made the consequences severe for me. "I don't know whether putting somebody in jail is going to be more traumatic or more of an adverse memory than knowing that you killed somebody that you loved."

*Who cares? Just send me away already. I can't look at these people anymore.* The pain in their eyes is too much. *Send me away.*

"I certainly don't see too many cases where I've had quite as much expression and solidarity on both sides of the aisle," he goes on.

*This is not the kind of aisle I ever would have imagined for us.*

"It certainly gives me hope that he's well on the way to rehabilitation, but I do feel that an appropriate sanction has to take into consideration not only the punishment, which I believe he has experienced. The rehabilitation, which I believe that he's also experiencing, but some measure of deterrence. I think that the bottom of the sentencing is eminently appropriate, and therefore, the court is going to sentence the defendant to the period of five years."

*Five years! Five years? I can't do five years.* It might as well be a lifetime. *Why didn't I just die? Why am I still alive? Laura, you should be dealing with this, not me. This is your fault. This is your fault. This is your fault! I'm sorry. I didn't mean that. I shouldn't have even thought that. This is all my fault. I love you. I'm sorry.*

"I'm going to suspend all but 90 days of that," I hear him continue. "You're going to be on probation for a period of five years."

*Ninety days? I can do ninety days. Maria will wait ninety days. I think. Five years of probation. No problem. Thank you, God. Thank you.*

"But I think that to say to you that because everybody loves you and because everybody is supportive of you, you don't go to jail, and the other guy who comes in tomorrow whose family members aren't here and his victims are screaming for blood, they somehow get treated differently. Unfortunately, I think that would be a miscarriage of justice, and that's why I'm imposing a sentence."

This sentence is a miscarriage of justice. Laura deserves more than this. *I should rot in hell for killing her. I'm so sorry, Laura. I wish I were with you.*

"Thank you, Your Honor," I stammer. *Thank you for not throwing my life away.*

❖

Judge Hackner agrees to let me leave the jail once a week to continue grief counseling, and he grants a two-day reprieve before I start my sentence so I can get my affairs in order, even though I'm ready to be locked up today. I'd kissed Maria goodbye this morning, hoping that my sentence would be short enough that she might stick around. She and my roommate said they would care for Rocko while I serve whatever sentence I receive. I'd given my roommate post-dated checks to pay for three months of rent. If I was sentenced to longer than that, he'd said that would give him time to find a new roommate. Everything was in order, so the two days are just extra time with Maria and Rocko before the months apart.

My family and Laura's gather with Harry in the hallway outside the courtroom. There are hugs and tears. David apologizes for not being able to do more. I think his forgiveness is a superpower; he's who I want to be when I grow up.

Everyone wishes I could have avoided jail but agrees the sentence is not as bad as it could have been; all things considered, I'm relatively lucky, though it's still hard for me to use that word to describe anything related to the crash that took Laura from us.

"We'll visit as soon as we can."

"I'll write to you all the time."

"We can finally start healing."

"Laura loved you so much. She'll be looking out for you."

"You're going to be okay."

An hour later, I walk through the front door of my row home and fall on the couch, exhausted. I don't have any tears left to cry, and I don't really know what I'm feeling anyway. I'm totally numb, and I just want somebody to hold me and let me rest.

# CHAPTER 18

I call Maria and tell her about the sentence. I can hear the relief in her voice when she tells me three months is "not that bad."

"Harry said with the different credits they'll give me for working and good behavior, it will probably be more like two months."

I'm allowed to have visitors twice a week. We plan to have her visit on Sundays with my family. David, who has moved back to Maryland to be closer to his family, will come on Tuesdays. I still don't want them to cross paths, and she knows it.

"Can I be the one to drive you to counseling?"

"I was hoping you would."

"I'm coming over."

I spend that night and the entire next day with Maria. We go to my favorite sushi restaurant in Baltimore and get all the best rolls: the crunchy spicy tuna, the crab and cream cheese with spicy tuna and eel sauce, and the salmon, mango, and avocado roll. I haven't had a drink since I got arrested, and I'm worried that something, anything, could go wrong if I have one tonight, so I order a coke even though I'd really like a beer.

Maria looks beautiful with her smokey eye shadow and strapless shirt, something to think about while I'm locked up. I tell her I'm scared about jail. I've seen what it's like on TV, and during the one previous night I spent there four months ago, my bed got kicked all night because of my snoring.

"My cellmate told me other guys would kill me for it. I used to think nothing bad would happen to me. Now I assume everything bad will happen to me. If anyone's getting raped in jail, it's going to be me."

"You do snore pretty loud, she mocks me. "My friends said to tell you not to drop the soap."

I laugh. The gallows humor is a relief.

"You're going to be fine," Maria says. "It will all be over soon. I'll call you every day to check on you." She doesn't know that I'll actually be the one to call *her* every day. You can't call people when they're in jail. They have to call you. It has to be collect, and the fees are exorbitant. Locking people up is a lucrative business.

I was just learning to live in the world without Laura when I found out I was being charged with killing her. The official stamp of approval the charges placed on my culpability had renewed and strengthened my feelings of guilt, and I'd been terrified by the possibility that I might spend years in prison. I'd spent the four months since that first night in jail preparing for the worst and convinced I deserved it.

But now there's something else mixed in with the raw pain in these reopened wounds: a sense of relief, and maybe, even, *hope*. I'm grateful that I won't spend years in prison. After I complete what I know is a very short sentence— even if it doesn't *feel* like any time locked up could be short—I'll be able to start over. I've been in a holding pattern for nearly a year, grieving and wondering what would happen because of the crash, because of my crime. Now there's an end in sight.

CRASHING I LOVE YOU. FORGIVE ME.

And even if my sentence feels lenient, it also feels like a judgment has been rendered on the appropriate amount of punishment I should receive, which feels like permission to stop punishing myself.

*Maybe it's okay to have a future.*

Maria promises to bring Rocko to see me when she picks me up for counseling.

"You look hot in that shirt," I smile.

"Good thing you have one more night."

*She's going to stick around.*

❖

The next morning, I get in the car with Maria so she can drive me to jail. As we pass under Hawkins Road on the section of I-97 where Laura died, I close my eyes and inhale deeply, pressing the pain and panic down into my guts. In contrast to the gray I'm feeling, the mid-winter sun warms my face as it streams through the driver's side window, and I wonder if there will be any place in the jail where I'll be able to feel its glow.

"This is the last part," Maria says, reassuring herself as much as me. "It'll be over before we know it."

My first night in jail had felt like an eternity, and, while my sentence is objectively short, I'm worried that a lot of bad things can happen in three months.

"Yeah," I say, forcing a smile. "Almost there."

I'm going to miss seeing Maria. She's been an anchor for

me over the last year, and I've grown to care deeply for her. I've become accustomed to missing Laura, but now I'll be missing them both. In my head, I picture Maria driving right past the jail and off to start a life with me somewhere nobody knows any of this ever happened. Could we outrun the past and build a future as other people? I know she wouldn't want it, and I'm not sure I do either. But it's a nice escape for the moment.

We pull into the parking lot at the Jennifer Road Detention Center, and as I step out of the car, Maria walks around to my side and throws her arms around my waist, her head nestled warmly against my chest. I lean down to kiss her, then look over her shoulder at the imposing brick facade of the jail. I gently pull back from Maria's embrace, a grim determination to do what I must tightening in my jaw.

"It's time," I tell her.

"I'll see you on Wednesday," she says resignedly. Maria will pick me up for therapy, so I'll see her in a few days. I pull her to me one more time, kissing her before turning to walk into the jail.

I walk into the jail without looking back, the heavy metal doors clattering shut behind me. I'm shaking with fear and anxiety, scared of the correctional officers, the residents, and the loneliness of this place. Still, I force myself to march purposefully up to the front desk officer, a hard-looking man in a blue uniform and close-cropped hair. He's sitting behind a concrete-block counter painted the same neutral tan as the bars on the cells, the benches, and everything else in the room except the white and red AED that must be there in case someone's heart stops on their way in. He looks up from his newspaper as I approach.

"Can I help you?" he asks professionally.

"I'm turning myself in for a sentence," I say it more confidently than I feel, like I'm checking in for a hotel. *Is my room ready?*

"Name?"

"Mark O'Brien."

"Phone, keys, wallet," he demands after walking behind an imposing front desk.

"I left them at home."

"Smart, but I need identification." I hand him my driver's license, which I'd thought to remove from my wallet, and he checks it against information on his computer.

He escorts me to a sort of locker room around the corner from the desk and hands me a bag.

"Take off your clothes and shoes and put them in there." I fight my discomfort with the loss of bodily autonomy and force myself to comply without hesitation, then stand naked and embarrassed, holding the bag in front of me until he reaches for it and removes the last vestige of my privacy.

"Squat and cough." I remember the routine from my previous one-night jail stay, and I lower myself into a baseball catcher's crouch and cough as directed.

"Okay, get up," he instructs me. He hands me a pair of green pants and a green vest along with a mesh bag holding what appears to be another change of jail garb. "Go ahead and get dressed."

After I'm dressed, the correctional officer tells me to follow him down the hall. We stop a short distance from the desk, and he tells me to stand with my back against the wall. A camera is mounted in the hallway, and he pulls it down to take my photo.

"Go sit over there," he says after taking the mug shot, indicating a bench near the entrance. "I'll make your badge, and then we'll go down to the unit."

An hour later, I'm completely processed into the jail. Another officer walks me down to unit A-1, the maximum-security unit where I spent the night here four months ago. The whole place smells of sweat, fear, urine, antiseptic, and institutional food. I've been stripped of my dignity and identity. I'm a man in green in a sea of men in green, identified by a number, JID1304026.

❖

My cellmate, a small Black man with alert but comfortable eyes, has the top bunk, and I sit down on the bottom, deflated.

"I'm Leon," he offers. "Who are you?"

"Mark," I reply absently.

"What're you in for?" he asks, making small talk.

I tell Leon about the crash and my sentence.

"Damn!" he exclaims, drawing out the *a* sound in the word. "They let you off easy. Most people get 18 months for drunk driving deaths on a first offense. You musta had a good lawyer."

"What about you?"

"I'm on pretrial. Couldn't make bail and still pay rent, so now I'm not paying either. But I didn't do it," he tells me without mentioning the charges.

I know from my last time here that everyone who gets locked up starts out on the maximum security unit while the correctional officers determine their risk classification.

"After a few days, you'll get moved down to whatever level they decide is right," he explains with the wisdom of past experience. "White boy like you'll be down on minimum security within a coupla weeks if you mind your business."

I barely missed lunch when I arrived at the jail, and by dinner time, I'm starving. A correctional officer slides a tray of food through the slot in the cell door, and, grabbing mine first, I retreat into the corner of my bunk and prop the tray up on my crossed legs. Dinner consists of a small carton of milk, soggy steamed green beans with the stems still attached, two slices of stale white bread, three slices of slimy bologna, and a mustard packet. It's disgusting and inadequate, but I eat it hungrily.

After the same correctional officer collects our trays a half hour later, Leon rolls over in the top bunk and pulls the blanket over his head.

"I'd go sleep if I was you," his voice muffled through the fabric of the blanket. "Nothing else to do in here but drive yourself crazy."

Copying him, I roll over in the bunk and close my eyes, thinking about the last few days. My mind finally settles on replaying the sentencing hearing in the courtroom. Even after the last year, I'm astonished by the depth of kindness and for-giveness I've received from Laura's family. Can I ever deserve their forgiveness and the mercy the judge showed me? *I'm not even sure I deserve to be alive.* But with my short sentence, I now know I have a life ahead of me, and I have to make peace with what I've done, or I'll waste it, dishonoring Laura's memory and the goodness of her family. I owe it to them to try for happiness when this is over. I'm not sure what that could look like now, but I'll have plenty of time to think about it while I'm locked in this eight-by-ten-foot cell for twenty-three hours a day and then some other cellblock where I'll have more freedom but little to do.

For what must be the next fourteen hours, I drift in and out of sleep. At some point, the lights on the unit are turned off, and when they turn back on the following morning, I'm pleas-antly surprised that Leon hasn't slit my throat for snoring. After breakfast, a correctional officer stops by our cell door.

"Pack your things," he says to Leon.

"Guess they're moving me down," he says, referring to the lower security level of the unit he's likely being moved to. "Better watch that snoring with whoever comes next."

He hadn't mentioned it all morning, but I guess he knows it could cause me problems.

"Good luck," I tell him, then roll back over to sleep more.

Later that afternoon, I get a new cellmate, and he climbs up to lay in the top bunk. He pulls out a pocket-sized Bible and begins to read. I'm jealous that he has reading material to pass the time. During the hour I was allowed out of my cell earlier, I confronted my worst fears about the jail by washing myself in the communal showers on the unit, surprised I was able to enjoy the warmth of the water despite my trepidation. I walked around the perimeter of the common area to stretch my legs and burn some energy. But the hour had passed quickly, and, other than that, there's been no diversion. Nothing to do. Nothing to read. I'm so bored, and I doubt I can force myself back to sleep again.

"Where'd you get that?" I ask. "They wouldn't let me bring in anything to read."

"The chaplain gave it to me at intake," he says, and I curse him for his good luck. "He has a bunch of 'em. If you ask, I'm sure he'll give you one too."

I don't even know how to go about seeing the chaplain, but later that night the new cellmate gets released on bail.

"You can keep it," he says, tossing me the Bible.

"Thanks." I start to read, so grateful for the distraction of having *anything* to read. I would have taken an instruction manual for a home appliance at this point just to have something to do. But I'm also pleased to have the Bible because the stories are familiar and consoling.

# CHAPTER 19

"It still hurts, you know?" I tug on Rocko's leash as he gets distracted by a squirrel and tries to pull me across the street.

"What does?" Laura asks, reaching for my free hand as we stroll casually down our tree-lined street in Magothy Manor.

"My parents. It still hurts that they aren't together. My dad always told me Catholics don't get divorced. It really blindsided me."

"I bet. What made you think of that?" She pulls me closer so our hips are touching as we walk and looks up at me with what looks like gratitude.

"I just don't talk about it much. And I wanted you to know." I shrug.

"I'm glad you did, and I'm sorry it hurts." She stops and turns me toward her. "It's okay to tell me when things are bothering you. I love you." She puts her hand behind my ear and kisses me.

"I love you too."

We continue on past our house and down to the neighborhood beach on the river. I let Rocko off his leash so he can play in the water, and I take off my shoes so I can join him. The water is cool and feels refreshing as it splashes against my legs. The sandy bottom is soft and smooth, and the sun sparkles magically over the rippling currents.

It feels good to tell Laura about my parent's divorce. I'd never told anyone it bothered me before. The pain is somehow lighter now that I'm sharing it with someone. Deciding to share more, I walk back onto the beach and sit beside her on the bench that faces *the water.*

*"I didn't like having to move every couple years as a kid," I tell her. "It was cool to get to see so many places. But I missed my friends. I still get jealous of people who have friends from when they were little. I wish that were me."*

*Laura puts her hand on my leg and smiles. "What else you got, mister?" She laughs.*

*"My high school girlfriend. I didn't love her, but I hated that she didn't love me. She broke it off, or I kind of did, but I wanted her to want me back, and the rejection was really painful. It doesn't even matter. I have you. But the rejection still eats at me. And none of the big law firms I've applied to are offering me jobs. I'm worried I'm not good enough. And I'm fat. Ever since I was little, I've had this gut no matter what I do."*

*"I love your gut." She puts her hand on my belly and leans into my neck. "It's going to be okay," she whispers.*

❖

I wake in the medium security cell that has become my new temporary home. I was in the maximum-security unit for only a few of days before a correctional officer opened the door to my cell and instructed me to follow him. "You're going to medium," he'd said.

Most of the men on this unit are awaiting trial either for more serious crimes like armed robbery or gun crimes or because they can't afford bail, even though they objectively should be allowed to go home until their trial. Some of them will spend more time in jail awaiting trial than they would if they'd already been sentenced for the crimes they're accused of.

The two cells on the unit appear to be segregated by race. I'm in a cell with ten other white guys. The cell next door is all Black guys. I don't know if it's on purpose or not. I wonder if all the units are like this and think it's weird as hell. Seven of the men in my cell have been together for some time. It's clear they're a tight group. Only a couple of us are short-timers making our way through the jail's risk classification system and waiting to be moved down to minimum security.

So far, the first days in jail have gone slowly. I find myself in deep contemplation when I'm not reading from the Bible I got from my short-term maximum-security cellmate. The absence of conversation, affection, and a sense of security have me thinking about, *longing for,* my friends and family.

I lay in my bunk now reflecting on the wretched truth that I've spent my entire life hiding myself from the people around me. I unconsciously believed that the only way to be loved was to keep anything that might be upsetting from the people around me. They had enough on their plates without me adding to their problems. As an army brat, I had to make all new friends every few years, and it was easier as a cheerful, funny guy than it would have been as a regular whiny guy. So if I was happy, you'd get happy Mark. And if I was upset, you'd still get happy Mark. I thought this was strong, and I was embarrassed to show any weakness.

My friends often came to me for advice, poured their hearts out to me really. I was popular with the guys in high school, but at lunch, I always sat at the girls' table to hear about their insensitive boyfriends and annoying parents. I was good at listening, but I rarely shared my true self. Maybe I was a good listener *because* I didn't want to talk about myself. All the focus was always on the other person.

I never let people into my inner world. *I didn't even go there myself.* The psychologist who testified at my sentencing said that before Laura died, I was "not an introspective person or someone who found it easy to express his emotions." I spent so much of my life ignoring or controlling my emotions that I often had no idea what I felt.

"Breakfast," the correctional officer in the unit's small common area announces, and I step down from my bunk. Unlike in the maximum-security unit, we don't have to eat in our cell here. The common area is much smaller, with just enough space for a few round tables and a desk for the correctional officer, but we have more time out of our cells. Racial segregation continues even when we're not in our cells. The Black guys have access to the common area some of the time, and the white guys have access at other times. The residents from the Black-guy cell just finished breakfast, and now it's our turn.

Rubbing the sleep out of my eyes as I walk to the cell door, I bump into Jason, a long-haired, devil-worshiping, admitted armed robber with a tattoo of a demon having sex with an angel.

"Sorry," I mutter.

"All good," he replies, smiling. "It's early."

Breakfast is a slice of stale bread, canned peaches, a small carton of orange juice, and two pieces of slimy bologna—sweaty meat, as the more experienced residents of the jail refer to it. What I wouldn't give right now to have Laura make me a BEC the way her dad made it. Thinking of Laura reminds me that not only have I been hiding my whole life, but I've also been taking the people I love for granted. I took *her* for granted.

If you'd asked me before the accident, and I'd been honest about my feelings, I would have told you I loved Laura, and I wanted her, but I didn't *need* her. Our love felt to me like the kind of epic Hollywood fairytale people dream about when they talk about finding "the one." We were so in love, our own little insular world of two, giddy and smug, knowing with certainty that what we had was better than what anyone else had. It was an amazing, earth-shattering, unprecedented and wonderful love. I knew that to my bones, but still, on the rare occasions when we fought, or she got on my nerves, or I got on hers, I always had in the back of my head that if it ended, I'd be fine. Love was nice to have, but I didn't *need* anybody.

And because I feared that if I ever let anyone see all of me, they might not like me, I never let Laura know all of me either. I hid from her like I hid from everyone else. And that meant I never got to know all of her, the tenderness she could have shown if she'd known I needed it. Our most honest conversations have happened since she died, since I started bearing my soul to her ghost on a nightly basis.

I finish my breakfast and place my tray on the cart that will take it back to the kitchen, then return to my cell to collect my toiletries and take a shower. Everything in the medium-security unit is painted the same antiseptic tan as everything else I've seen in the jail. But the bathroom has a stall with a toilet and another with a shower. While there are no doors on the stalls, they offer more privacy than the open toilets and showers on the maximum-security unit.

The shame of knowing how indifferent I've been to the people I love feels like filth on my skin, and I turn the water as hot as it will go, hoping to burn away my self-disgust. I grab the jail-issued bar of soap from the mesh toiletry bag and rub it on my head to wash my hair. I scrub my body forcefully, but there's no removing this stain.

It's embarrassing and ridiculous to have thought I didn't need Laura. The hardest part of the last year has been going through the pain without her. She should have been there in the middle of the night when I was curled up in the fetal position or sitting with my arms around my knees, rocking back and forth because I just didn't think I could take one more minute of the hurt. The only time I ever cried in front of her when she was alive was before we started dating when my childhood dog Sam died. But I think I could have shown her the worst moments since the crash, and she would have known what to do.

Without Laura here, I've had to rely on the other people in my life for love, consolation, and all the practical support I've needed to survive. It's been weird to be in pain so publicly, to have people so actively concerned about my wellbeing. It's also been beautiful and profound. And I know now that I've been missing out on this my whole life because I never opened up like this before. I'd never before hurt so much that I couldn't hide it.

I turn the water off and read for my towel, drying off and wrapping it around my waist. I walk to the sink and pull out my jail-issued toothbrush, run water over it, and begin to brush with the jail-issued toothpaste. I run the jail-issued comb through my hair and rub the powdery jail-issued deodorant under my arms.

By holding people at arm's length for so long. I know I missed out on the closeness I could have experienced in my life. But now I begin to wonder if they also bore a cost. There is a benefit not only in being loved fully but also in being able to love someone else fully. My friends and family stayed by my side over the last year not because they had to but because, in my suffering, I'd finally given them a chance to live out the love they'd always felt for me. Being able to care for me was part of what made *their lives* meaningful. I would never have let them care for me like this before. The walls I put up my whole life made my life less meaningful, and they also deprived the people around me of the meaning and happiness that comes from expressing love through action.

Laura's death has made unavoidable the reality of how fragile life is. I know now that we can't take the time we have with people for granted. A meaningful life is one spent as a member of a community of people we depend on and who depend on us, and as I pull my drab green jail-issued shirt over my head, I promise myself that I'll do better. I'll show the people in my life how much they mean, and more than that, I'll let them get to know the real me. I won't take life for granted ever again.

I look up to the ceiling of the cell and whisper to Laura,

"I promise."

❖

"Wanna play?" Terry asks me, sweeping the tiles off the Scrabble board as I walk back into the common area of our unit. Terry is a muscular blonde 30-something man who looks like he'd be just as at-home in a surf competition as he is in jail. He's awaiting trial on fraud charges, the details of which he keeps murky.

We play a lot of Scrabble. I mean *a lot.* I've only been on the unit for two days, and I've already played six times. The other guys are unbelievably good. The first time one of them asked me to play, I figured that with a law degree, I probably had the most education of anyone here and would win easily. *Hubris.* I got my ass kicked, and I've gotten my ass kicked every time since. They all know more words than I do, and they have better techniques. "The key," one of my other cellmates explained, "is to know all the two-letter words and never leave an opening for the other guy to score." Their games drag on for hours, but when I play, I'm beaten in no time.

"Sure. Why not," I reply, sitting.

We divide up the tiles, and I place my first word—H-O-M-E— before he places his—M-E-T-H, and pretty soon, the board is covered, and there's barely any space to add a tile. When the correctional officer tells us to return to our cell, the game isn't over, but Terry has twice as many points as I do, so we declare him the winner. Everyone laughs at my poor performance.

"You'll figure it out," one of the guys says helpfully.

"I hope so," I reply sheepishly.

To my surprise, it's a pretty good group of guys. At night in our cell, we sit on our beds and talk about our families, our charges, and what we plan to do when we get home. It's a support group for troubled men, sitting up in our beds like adolescents at summer camp. I came to this place scared of them, but the men I'm with are just regular guys who made mistakes, like everyone does, like me. Even the guy who stuck up a store with a shotgun—I can't remember his name—seems pretty nice.

It makes me question how I've thought about right and wrong, good and bad throughout my life and especially since the crash. Everything I thought I knew about myself and so much of what I thought I knew about the world is proving to be misguided.

Before the crash, I thought I was a good person, and good people didn't commit crimes. They certainly didn't commit homicide. After the crash, something had to give. Either I was not a good person, or good people could commit homicide. Now I wonder if it's fair to focus on one giant mistake and discount everything else I've ever done on every other day of my life when I didn't hurt anyone.

Later that night, as my cellmates drift off to sleep, I sit on my bunk and tick off the particulars of my personal good-character balance sheet. I start with the good. I've always been able to make people laugh. Moving around so much taught me to make friends quickly and make others feel at ease in a group of strangers. I'm a good friend and a good listener. I'm intelligent and excelled in school. I care about helping people. I worked in special education before law school and volunteered as a swim coach for the Special Olympics. I went to law school because I wanted to fight for the little guy and make a positive difference in the world.

Then I move on to the bad. I'm proud and self-important. I like giving advice because I think I know better than everyone else. I believe I'm special and that the rules don't apply to me, which is why I make reckless decisions like driving drunk and getting in fights. I judge others for their bad decisions. I was on the admissions committee in law school, and I recommended rejecting applicants with criminal records because I thought their mistakes made them less deserving. So, add hypocrite to the bad side of the ledger. I started law school with the best of intentions, but by the time of the crash, I wanted to get a job at a top law firm so I could win law school, show I was better than the other guys, and drive a sweet car that would let everyone else know I was a winner.

For so long before the accident, I thought of only my good qualities and considered myself better than others. That was the proud and self-important me deciding to focus on only a sliver of my personality. Since the crash, I've thought of only the worst parts. And I've felt like I died in the crash too, like the good person I was died with Laura, because I haven't been able to think of myself as good since she died. But now, I'm discovering a third option. I am not horrible, and I am not perfect. I am just human.

I look up to the ceiling and silently send my thoughts to

Laura. "I'm good and bad, babe."

❖

After four days on medium security, I'm getting transferred to another medium-security unit but at another jail. The other three white guys on my unit who were already sentenced are coming too. We're leaving behind the seven guys awaiting trial. Two correctional officers escort us out of jail and chain us together by our wrists and ankles. We pile into a van, and two other correctional officers take the driver and passenger seats. We head out from the jail toward the highway where Laura died, *where I killed her.*

Like too many of us, I lived before the crash as if I were relatively invulnerable to harm. I knew bad things happened in the world. People died in car accidents, because they got cancer, in terrorist attacks or natural disasters. I just didn't expect any of those things to ever happen to me. I never woke up and thought, "today might be the day I die."

I still have my parents and all four of my grandparents. Before Laura, I'd been to funerals but not for anyone whose death deeply affected my life. When my childhood friend was hit by a drunk driver, we'd already moved away from each other, and I didn't fully grasp the sadness of his death as a child. The finality and pain of death were so foreign to me.

But now I know viscerally that death stalks all of us, all of the time. Our lives can end at any moment. The lives of the people I cherish the most can end at any moment.

If I'd known she would die on this highway, if I'd understood I might die at any moment too, what would I have done differently? Would I really have cared about making the most money, driving the best car, or owning the nicest house? What would have been important to me?

The transport van speeds up, and I can tell we're going too fast. There aren't seat belts for the inmates, and a lump of fear grows in my throat. I know from the police reports and from seeing the car that it's a miracle I survived the crash. I doubt I have two miraculous crash survivals in me, and I stretch my neck to look at the speedometer. A hundred and seven miles per hour. The speed frightens me, but I can't help thinking there's something poetic and romantic about dying on the same stretch of highway where Laura died.

The fear and whimsy wrestle for my attention, but in the moment, the fear wins out. My heart is pounding, and I start to shake. I close my eyes and take a deep breath. *I don't want to die. Please, God, keep us safe.*

The wannabe Dale Earnhardt up in the driver's seat speeds up even more and flies across two lanes, cutting off one car and flying up behind another. At the last second, he swerves back into the center lane and flies around another truck. I'm holding the legs of my jail pants so tightly my knuckles are turning white. They're the only thing I can reach to grab onto. The guy next to me appears alarmed too, but he looks at me like maybe I'm overreacting. The driver pulls back into the right lane and slams on the brakes behind a little sedan. We must be getting off at the next exit. I breathe a sigh of relief as the van slows down.

We pull into the secure lot at the new jail, and the gate closes behind us. Sweat is dripping down my face, but the cuffs prevent me from reaching up to dry my brow. My breathing is slowly getting back to normal when the driver comes around and opens the door.

"Everybody out," he instructs us. "Welcome to Ordnance Road Detention Center, your new home."

The four of us chained together pile out of the van as the correctional officers lead us inside. My new understanding of the world is reinforced yet again: Everything is out of my control.

# CHAPTER 20

The guys on the Ordnance Road medium-security unit aren't as close-knit as the guys on the Jennifer Road medium-security unit were. Most of those guys had been together for a few weeks or even months. People move in and out of this unit more quickly. The men here mostly keep to themselves. They leave me alone, except at night when I start snoring. Someone inevitably walks over to my bed and kicks it to wake me up, sometimes every couple minutes, as I quickly doze back off and start the freight train up again. So now I'm lying in bed trying to stay awake until everyone else falls asleep, thinking about the therapy session I just returned from.

The jail administrators wouldn't let me leave for my therapy appointments while I was moving quickly through the jail's classification system, but now that I'm settled on a unit where I'll stay for at least a week, Maria is allowed to drive me to the appointments. They'd given us three hours to make the one-hour round trip and attend the one-hour appointment, so we'd have a half-hour buffer on either side of the appointment.

This evening was my first leaving the jail for counseling. I walked to the desk in my unit where the correctional officer was sitting and explained that I needed to leave.

"You and everybody else here, brother," he said cheerfully while looking at me like I was out of my mind.

"I have permission from the judge and the warden," I replied.

"Fine. Have it your way," he said skeptically, picking up the phone and calling down to the administration to prove to me that he was right.

"I have JID1304026 here," he said into the receiver. "He says he's supposed to leave for an appointment." He'd said it more like a question than a statement.

"I've never heard of something like this," he'd said a moment later, putting down the phone. "But they say you can leave. You'll have to squat and cough before you leave the unit and then head straight to intake."

I walked down the hall, eager to see Maria, to touch and smell her. I've been talking to her every day, and she's already visited a few times. But talking over the phone or through a thick pane of glass hasn't been the same as holding her.

When I reached the intake unit, they gave me my clothes to change back into. I removed the dark green jail-issued pants and shirt and slid into my jeans and hoodie, which felt extra comfortable after just a few weeks of the stiff, abrasive jail garb.

"When you get back, you'll be searched and take a breathalyzer. It detects cigarette smoke too, so no smoking," the correctional officer at the front desk told me. I'd known the cigarette line was bullshit, but I don't smoke anyway, and I didn't say anything. I've been strip-searched a lot already, and I wasn't planning to drink, so even though getting naked in front of strangers over and over wasn't ideal, the rules didn't trouble me.

I left through the metal gate and saw Maria waiting in the parking lot. My feelings for her have grown so strong, but I still haven't been able to bring myself to say it out loud. I've seen in her eyes that she feels the same way and wishes I would tell her how much I care about her. But I just haven't been able to acknowledge how much she means to me now.

Maria had borrowed her sister's minivan and put the seats down in the back so Rocko could come with her. I hopped in the passenger's seat, and we fell into each other's arms. I kissed her deeply until Rocko stuck his head between us, and I scratched him behind his floppy ears. He's part boxer and part shar-pei, brown, big, and muscular with a wrinkly face, boxy snout, and perpetually serious expression, but his wagging tail betrayed his joy at seeing me as I hugged him tight around the neck.

Maria had brought Five Guys, my first *real food* in two weeks, a nice break from the stale bread and sweaty meat in jail. I devoured the burger and fries on the way to therapy, aware that the food and the freedom were luxuries none of the men I was locked up with would get during their sentences— another example of the kid gloves I've been getting. I felt a little guilty about it, but mostly I was relieved to have the time away from the dreary monotony of jail.

We'd arrived at the appointment ahead of time and hopped in the back of the van. I pressed my mouth to hers, and for fifteen minutes, we'd been any young couple hooking up in the back of a car.

Then I went inside to check in for my appointment, and it wasn't long before Kara called me back into her office.

"I've been thinking about you a lot. Your mom has been keeping me updated about everything going on," Kara said as

I sat down. Her office felt like a sanctuary of sorts, a bright, cheerful, and friendly place that could not be more different from the jail.

"How are you doing?" she asked.

"I'm actually okay."

"I know it can't be easy, but I've been thinking that finally knowing your sentence means maybe you can start considering what's next. It probably seems like a long time, but these three months will be over soon."

"I've been thinking about that too."

"There's a lot we could talk about," she said. "But why don't we start with how you're holding up in there."

"On the plus side, I was so scared of what jail would be like. You know how it is on TV, all rapes and fighting. But it isn't like that at all, at least not so far. The guys in there are fine. On the minus side, the place smells awful, the food is disgusting, and I'm so bored," I'd told her.

The jail reeks of institution and pee, which is strange, because I haven't noticed anyone peeing anywhere besides a toilet, and the sounds of creaking metal, footsteps, and conspiratorial whispering echo throughout the units and hallways.

"It's kind of like a high school cafeteria if someone peed in the corner, " I told her. "and two groups of students were whispering about a fight that was going to happen after school. Like there's a hushed anticipation of what could happen next."

"I'm glad to hear you're feeling safe, but I'm sorry the place is so bleak," Kara sat up straighter, imagining the place.

"If the idea is that you're not supposed to want to come

back, they're doing it right."

"I suppose, but it doesn't sound like a place where people are actually being rehabilitated."

"Yeah," I shrugged in agreement. "It's also like networking for people to exchange ideas that will just get them in more trouble when they go home," I laughed.

"Your birthday is coming up. Anniversaries can be tough. How are you feeling about it?"

My birthday is in two days. The anniversary of Laura's death is two days after that.

"She's been on my mind a lot lately," I admitted. Since the crash, I've thought about Laura every day. Some days, every hour. Some hours, every minute. The crash ended her life, but it hasn't ended my love for her. "I talk to her as much now as I ever did. Not out loud. I just talk to her like she can hear my thoughts."

"Does she ever talk back to you?" she asked, and I wondered if she was checking to see if I was psychotic.

"Ha, no, she doesn't talk back to me. Don't worry."

"I didn't mean it like that," Kara said. "What do you think she would say if she could talk back to you?"

"I don't know. She was always the better person out of the two of us. I guess I like to think she'd say, 'I miss you too, and I forgive you. Please be my happy Mark again. I want you to live. I love you, and I'll be here waiting for you when your time comes.'"

"Why do you think she was the better person?"

"She was perfect. Everything about her was just,

*exactly right.*"

"Nobody's perfect, Mark. Laura sounds like she was wonderful, and it has always sounded like the two of you loved each other very much. But she was also human. It can be easy to forget that when we miss someone."

It's this last part that stuck with me when I left the appointment and that I've been thinking about since I laid down in my bunk after returning to the jail.

Since she died, I've turned Laura into an angel of sorts. A guardian angel, an omnipresent companion in my heart and in my head. It's hard to remember any flaws she had now. I suppose that's what happens when people we love die. We turn them into perfect saints even though they were just humans like us. The love Laura and I shared was special. Our bond was strong. You might wonder if it was really that good. And the answer is yes, it was.

We were recklessly in love, gambling our friendship on a chance at life-changing romance. We were all in from the start because if the romance didn't work out, it was hard to see ever going back to being pals. We weren't going to be Joey and Dawson or Ross and Rachel going back and forth between romance and friendship, breaking up and hanging out while moving on with someone new. If it fell apart, it would have cost each of us the most important person in our lives.

But for three years, the bet paid off, and we had a magical run of exuberant, audacious, carefree love. She was my first love, and the rush of all those endorphins and all that dopamine and oxytocin had me transfixed. There was no stress; we both worked part-time, studied, and chilled out like any two twenty-somethings with few responsibilities. Our biggest domestic concern was whose turn it was to clean the bathroom. Our love was like that Jason Mraz song *I'm Yours* that everyone likes now: peppy, fun, innocent, and sweet.

But, in reality, neither of us was perfect, and our relationship wasn't perfect either. No person is, and no relationship ever could be. And I think now that it isn't fair to erase her by turning her into something she wasn't. It's like I'm killing her again. It's the inverse of how I dismissed all my good qualities after she died. I've dismissed all her flaws. But now, if I'm being honest with myself, I have to acknowledge that she really wasn't perfect. She was a person, just like me.

She could be dismissive of other peoples' feelings if she felt wronged or slighted.

"Try to see it from their perspective," I'd implore her.

"What's their perspective? They're an asshole."

She could hold a serious grudge if you crossed her. She'd been fighting on and off with one of her sisters the entire time I'd known her. They never got a chance to reconcile after the last fight.

For the first year we dated, she refused to meet my family even though I loved spending time with hers. I was so proud of our relationship and wanted my family to know my awesome girlfriend, but getting involved with her ex's family had made their breakup harder, and she wasn't ready to repeat that level of entanglement. A year into dating, I was ready to call it quits if she didn't let me introduce her to my mom. I never told her that, but the time she finally said yes to dinner with my family was going to be the last time I asked her if she'd said no.

Laura was a smoker, and I constantly asked her to quit. *What a nag I was!* I told her that since we planned to have kids one day, I didn't want my children to lose their mother to cancer. But really, I just hated how it made her breath smell and her kisses taste. She thought I was a hypocrite because I had no problem with us smoking weed together. *She was right. I was a hypocrite. Still am. Listen to me declaring my undying love for her every night while waiting to call my new girlfriend.*

The biggest problem we had, though, was that I was insecure and jealous. She'd had two long-term serious boyfriends before me. She lived with one of them before I met her. She'd been with each of them longer than we were together, and I always wondered if I was her favorite. I didn't ask her that, but I was annoying and pouty whenever they came up in conversation. She'd hooked up with some of the guys I knew, some of the guys who were my closest friends. I always wondered if I was the best one. She saw the problems coming when I asked her out. She asked if I would be weird about it. "I don't care about that," I lied. "Your past is what made you who you are, the girl I want to be with." I never told her how I really felt because it wasn't in my nature to be honest about difficult emotions, but whenever I felt insecure, I'd get snappy with her without telling her why. She didn't deserve that.

I was the jealous one, but now I wonder how she'd feel about Maria. I imagine her angel voice in my head telling me it's alright to move on, that she wants me to be happy, that it's fine if Maria makes me feel better. But I wonder, is that really what she'd think? Or would Maria make her feel insecure and jealous the way I'd felt about her other relationships? If the tables were turned, would enlightened heaven Mark want Laura to be happy, or would jealous insecure Mark want her pining after me for all eternity?

And for that matter, does she care at all? There's no way for me to know. Sometimes it feels like I can still feel her presence, like she wants me to know she is somewhere, that her spirit didn't die with her body. But that could just be my mind desperately hoping. She could be nothing more than the ashes we scattered in the river, nothing more than a memory in the people who loved her.

My eyes are getting heavy now. I say a prayer and tell Laura goodnight. As I start to slip into the quiet of sleep, I start to snore, and I'm jolted awake by a kick to my bed.

"Shut up, O'Brien!" one of my cellmates glowers from beside my bed. "I'm trying to sleep."

"Sorry." I better stay up just a little longer.

❖

Two days later, it's my birthday, a day that used to be a cause for celebration. But now it's just the beginning of the anniversary of Laura's death. And I'm spending it in jail, punished for killing her.

At the same time as I'm thinking about Laura and feeling morose over the gloomy anniversary, I'm also looking forward to seeing Maria and my mom this afternoon. Laura may have needed a year to warm up to meet my family, but Maria did not. She got to know Courtney right away when I was living in the dungeon, and now she's best pals with my mom, the two planning their visits together every weekend. Visits mean squatting and coughing to leave the unit and then talking on a phone through a sheet of plexiglass, but it's better than nothing.

I'm starting to see a future with Maria. I realize I've been keeping her at a safe distance since we met, not only because I've felt guilty about something-like-cheating on Laura but also because I didn't know if incarceration would mean losing Maria too. Now I know I'll be home in two or three months, not two or three or ten years. We've already exchanged a few letters, and I call her daily. The jail charges exorbitant collect call fees, and she's running up quite a tab. It will be nice to see her later today, and I'm looking forward to holding her when she picks me up for my next therapy appointment.

I'm sitting in the common area of the unit, distractedly watching TV, when a large group of correctional officers walks in.

"Shakedown!" One of the men in my unit shouts, and I wonder what it means.

"Everybody, out of your cells, *now*," one of the correctional officers bellows, cupping his hands around his mouth to project the instruction.

"Line up in two lines right here," he continues, pointing to the ground on his left and on his right.

Two other correctional officers stand at the front of the

two lines, facing the men lining up before them.

"They're going to search the cells," I hear one of the men whisper.

"Okay, listen up, everyone," the correctional officer at the head of the line on the right announces. "You're going to squat, cough, and then walk over to the unit door. We'll line you up outside. Let's make it quick."

While each of us removes clothes, squats, and coughs—so they can make sure we aren't hiding any contraband in our butts—and then proceeds to the hallway, three correctional officers ransack the cells, flipping over mattresses, searching the metal rafters, opening the lockers, and dumping out trash cans.

Two guys in my cell have non-jail-issued pens—in their beds, not their butts—so the guards punish our whole unit by placing us on lockdown for two days. None of us can leave our cell except for meals, and nobody can receive any visitors. Maria and my mom won't be able to see me when they come today, and the guys tell me they won't even be told why they can't see me. The next time I leave my cell will be the anniversary of Laura's death which feels like salt in the wound at a time that would have been tough regardless.

In the last letter I received from her, Maria was upset because she thought I was hiding my feelings about Laura from her. She didn't want me to do that. I could tell she wanted more from me and from our relationship. She wanted to know where we stood. It had been nine months since we met. She'd stuck with me through so much already. Most people would have made their exit long ago, maybe the first night. She was right to want more than I'd given her, but I couldn't find the words to acknowledge any of it.

"I know we haven't talked as much about Laura recently," I write now in response. "I worry I'm hurting you when I express the love I feel for her or talk about my continued sadness over her death."

I tell Maria I'll always love Laura, that there still hasn't been a day since the accident when I haven't thought of her. I still sometimes pray that my life will be short so I can be with Laura soon. When I feel happy with Maria, I also feel like I don't deserve to be. I took Laura's life, and sometimes feel I have no right to enjoy mine. I fear that moving on means losing what little I have left of Laura.

"It can't be easy to be with me when you know there is always another girl with us. I find myself unable to express my feelings for you out of fear that telling you how I feel will minimize or trivialize my feelings for Laura."

I tell Maria about Stu, a burly gray-haired man on my unit with massive hands who knew about my accident and sat down with me at dinner last night to see how I was doing. Stu was in jail for killing his wife in a drunk driving accident. She was a doctor, and he was high up in the construction business. A little over three years ago, they were out drinking and celebrating her birthday, and he wrecked the motorcycle they were on. His wife was killed instantly by hitting her head on a guardrail. The similarities to my crash were striking, but unlike Laura's family, Stu's wife's family refused to forgive him and pushed for a heavy sentence. He was sentenced to fifteen years;

all but one year was suspended. So I got three months, and he got one year for the same thing. In Virginia, the minimum would have been five years. If someone else had taken Laura's life, I would have said five years wasn't enough. There is often no rhyme or reason for how people get sentenced.

Tears streamed down my face as I told Stu about Laura and Maria.

"After my wife died, I fell in love with her best friend. We bonded over the grief," he'd told me. "I think you can probably relate." His case took longer to resolve, and it had already been three years since his wife died. "We're getting married when I get out of here."

"I just don't know if it's okay to be happy," I'd said.

"Laura wants you to be happy. When you're happy, she's happy. When you're sad, she's sad."

I tell Maria his words relieved some of the guilt I'd felt about dating her so soon after the accident. Stu told me I owed it to Laura to live the happiest and most fulfilling life I could. I don't write it in my letter now, but I'm starting to think there could be a life for me with Maria.

# CHAPTER 21

Sunday is my favorite day of the jail week. We get the two best jail meals: coffee cake for breakfast and real chicken for dinner. That alone would make it the best since every other day of the week has horrible food. But Sunday is also commissary day, making it extra special.

The commissary is a way to order extra snacks, coffee, socks, and toiletries. My family adds $20 a week, the maximum, to my account, so I can order from the menu of items. We place our orders on Thursday, and they arrive on Sunday. I've always gotten the same things: instant coffee, Ramen, envelopes with postage for sending letters, a few bags of chips, and a cheese danish to substitute for Thursday breakfast. Thursday breakfast is shit on a shingle (creamed chipped beef on biscuits), and it's as disgusting as it sounds. But some of the other guys love shit on a shingle. So I trade mine on Thursdays and get extra chicken thighs on Sundays.

Sunday is also hook-up day—not that kind of hook-up. The hook-up is a sort of casserole made with thrown-together ingredients from the commissary and dinner. It's similar to what residents in other facilities call a prison spread. Cook up some Ramen noodles, mix in some commissary tuna or leftover chicken from dinner, add cheese whiz or crushed-up chips for extra flavor, and top it with diced pickles. I eat the chicken that comes on my dinner tray, and then I add the extra chicken I traded for to the hook-up. It's as close to delicious as anything

I've had since I got here.

I spend a lot of time writing letters, but it gets expensive to keep up. I get letters from Maria, my mom, my sisters, David, other members of my family, other members of Laura's family, and even some of my mom's friends. I write back to all of them. Sometimes I write four or five letters a day.

The commissary envelopes come with postage, but they're expensive, and so is the paper. I've developed a letter-writing system to save money. I order three envelopes a week: one for letters I will send to David for him and his family, one for letters for my family that I will send to my mom, and one for letters to Maria. I ask everyone to write letters on one side of the paper so I can use the back sides to reply.

The costliest and most highly prized item on the commissary list is a Walkman radio. Being able to listen to music is a great distraction, and a lot of the guys save up to get one. Since it costs $20 and that's the maximum amount you can spend on a commissary order, getting one means not getting any new snacks, paper, envelopes, or coffee for the week.

I've wanted to be able to listen to music, but I'm attached to my instant coffee and Thursday morning cheese danish— the rituals are important— so I've stocked up over the last couple of weeks by rationing the items from a single commissary order to last two weeks. That means my Walkman is in this week's commissary order.

"O'Brien!" the correctional officer bellows, holding up my commissary package.

Knowing I'll be able to listen to music is the best and

most exciting thing that has happened to me since I got here. It's strange because I tried to avoid music as much as I could over the last year— I didn't want to hear a song that would remind me of Laura and send me into a tailspin of anguish— but now I'm ecstatic about the potential to tune out the ambient jail sounds of clanging metal and chairs on concrete and the din of dozens of men living in close quarters.

I bound purposefully across the common area to the correctional officers' table and claim my order.

I open the package and solemnly insert the included batteries. I put on the headphones, switch on the radio, and turn the dial. At first, I can't get a station to come in and hear nothing but white noise. After several minutes of twisting the dial back and forth and pacing around the unit, hoping to find a place where the signal will come through clearly, I hear the staticky crackle of a radio station trying to break through. I gently adjust the tuning knob, hoping not to lose the signal, and the clear sound of music erupts in my ears. The cacophony all around me disappears as I turn up the volume on the radio.

The song is unfamiliar, and I listen closely, trying to determine the genre. It has a sort of mid-nineties grunge beat to it, but it's nothing I've ever heard. Then I hear the lyrics, something about Jesus and the resurrection. Christian rock. *No thanks.* I keep searching for another station, adjusting the tuner for a few more minutes before giving up and returning to the Christian rock station.

The purpose of the music is to block out all the noise around me so I can enjoy the solitude of the place instead of suffering through the ironic loneliness of being locked up with dozens of other men amidst the jail sounds echoing around the place. It's not what I want, but this music will have to do.

❖

I'm in my cell, listening to the Christian radio station—it turns out the music isn't *that* bad, and some of the lyrics speak to my inner struggle—when the correctional officers announce another shakedown. I've moved into a minimum-security unit where everyone is either leaving in a few days because they have such a short sentence or because they're waiting for a spot to open on the work unit.

I've learned that my sentence is too short to get work release and go back to working at the restaurant, but once I get to the work unit, I'll be assigned a job within the jail. I'll have something to pass the time each day, and I'll get additional credit toward my sentence, which means fewer days in jail. Everyone on minimum security is on their best behavior, trying to show the staff that they deserve to move to the work unit quickly.

We line up without complaint, strip naked, squat and cough. They look around each cell, open all our lockers, and flip our mattresses. When they're done, they let us return to our cell, and we assume all is well. Nobody messes around and gets in trouble in this unit. A few minutes later, one of the correctional officers comes into our cell.

"Your sink is damaged," he says, gesturing to the bathroom. "Whoever did it is going back to medium security, and if nobody fesses up, you're all going back." Moving back to medium means moving one step further away from the work unit and spending more time in jail.

In each unit here, there are multiple cells, and each cell has twelve beds and a bathroom with a shower. In general, the facilities in this jail are well maintained, even if they're all the same ugly tan, so I immediately noticed when I got here that the sink in our bathroom was damaged. If anybody in the cell caused the damage, it was one of the guys who got here before I did. And I'm hoping one of them will take responsibility, but nobody does.

"You have until the end of the day to let us know who did it," the correctional officer concludes after nobody speaks up.

I lay down in my bunk, despondent at the realization that I'll be here for a week longer than I thought. I pull out the Bible—I'm reading the New Testament for the second time since I got locked up—and try to distract myself from what feels like a very big setback. A week is a long time when you're longing to be home. But a few hours later, Vinny walks into the cell and clears his throat, and everything changes.

I've changed units a few times since getting to Ordnance Road. After Jennifer Road, the cells haven't been segregated by race, which has made the place seem just a little more normal. I've met a bunch of guys in jail, and, with a few exceptions, they're not at all scary; most are good guys who made stupid mistakes or got hooked on drugs and needed help, help they still weren't getting in the jail's BS addiction treatment program.

Jail is an intense environment, and while some days I've seen people at their worst— depressed, angry, and anxious— other days I've seen them at their best— contrite, hopeful, and earnest. Some of the deepest and most emotional conversations I've had with other men have happened in the last few weeks. We talk about the challenges in our lives before we got in trouble, our fears for the future, our plans for improving ourselves when we get home, and our relationships, beliefs, and dreams. I feel fortunate to have gotten to know many of them.

Vinny has stuck out as a big exception to this unexpected harmony. He's been more in line with my most frightening expectations. I met him two weeks ago in my second Ordnance Road medium-security unit. He was muscular and intimidating, a neo-Nazi with a large swastika tattooed across his chest. Most of the guys steered clear of him. He tried to share some white supremacy literature he printed out in the library with me, but I politely declined. I had no interest in getting to know him better. His belief system was reprehensible to me, and the guy was downright scary. I was courteous and respectful to him because I had to live on the same unit with him, but I made it clear I was not interested in his ideas. That seemed to be the default way of interacting with him. Even the Black guys didn't try to mess with him; they just stayed away from him. And he seemed okay with that too.

When I found out I was moving to minimum security, I was happy not only because I'd be getting closer to the promised land of the work unit, but also because I'd be getting away from Vinny. "No way that guy is moving to minimum security," I'd thought.

But I was wrong. A couple days after I moved to minimum, I was lying comfortably in my bunk when Vinny walked in. He *had* progressed to minimum too. And he wasn't just on my unit again, he was moving *into my cell*. The cell that just got busted by the correctional officers for the broken sink.

Vinny tells everyone in the cell he's going to take responsibility for the sink so the rest of us won't have to share the penalty. I know for sure that he didn't do it. He moved to the cell after me, and the sink was already broken when I arrived.

"Somebody has to get in trouble. No reason for us all to go down for it," he says.

Vinny walks to the table at the center of the common area where the correctional officers sit and confesses to damaging the sink. I can't believe what I'm seeing. On the one hand, this guy is a monster, and his beliefs are absolutely disgusting. He is full of hate and ignorance. He represents so much of what is wrong with our society. On the other hand, I know he didn't break the sink, and he is sacrificing his wellbeing for the rest of us, including the Jewish, Black, and Latino men in our cell he professes to hate.

I lie in bed, torn between my conviction that society is better off the more time he spends in jail and my commitment to fairness and justice for all people. I went to law school to ensure everyone, even those I vehemently disagreed with, had the same rights. Vinny deserves to be condemned for his animosity and racism, but he doesn't deserve to be penalized for the sink. Maybe all I can do is try to live the values I believe in, without holding myself up as judge and jury; I'm responsible for somebody's death, and I'm starting to think maybe I don't have room to judge anyone, ever, anymore.

I've been thinking about the coincidences of the last few weeks, and I've wondered if they were more than coincidences. Before my court date, it felt like I was on autopilot when I wanted to go to confession and found the church I didn't know was there. Then when I was on the maximum security unit, the only book I was able to get my hands on was the Bible. And then the only radio station I found on the Walkman was Christian rock.

I wondered if God was trying to call to me or if I was just imagining it. The priests I knew growing up told me God would be there if I needed him, and I have needed him this last year. I've cherished the idea that God might be reaching into my life to help heal me. Maybe it's silly, but I've thought maybe Laura died because she was already complete and ready for heaven, and I survived because I'm still a work in progress.

I've always sort of believed in God, but my belief has been mixed with a healthy dose of skepticism. It still is. It's been comforting to think that God might be real because it might mean that something good can come from the crash if I become a better person. It also might mean there's an afterlife, and I'll get to see Laura again. So I like believing even though I also know I'll never be sure any of it is real. I know it could all be just a comforting fairy tale.

I have come to believe with certainty, though, that the values I learned growing up— forgiveness, grace, mercy, love, and sacrifice— represent the ingredients of a good and meaningful life. Even if God isn't real, if it's all just a fairy tale, a life lived in accordance with these values would be a life lived well. The root of those values is to love your neighbor as yourself. And the best way to live this out is to love even those you might otherwise consider your enemies. Helping Vinny is a chance to try this belief system out.

Later that evening, Vinny is packing his things to move back to medium security. He comes around the corner into the bathroom as I'm washing my hands at the sink next to the one he falsely confessed to damaging. I haven't told any of the guys about my law degree, and I've been hiding my education, thinking my law degree will make me seem even more out of place than I already feel, but now I feel compelled to tell him I can help.

"Hey Vinny," I blurt out. "I need to tell you something. I have a law degree, and the first thing I did when I got here was read the entire jail handbook. It says you're entitled to a disciplinary hearing, and you can name any other inmate to represent you. Tell them you want Mark O'Brien to speak on your behalf. I know you didn't do this, and I can get us all out of it. Please don't tell anyone I'm a lawyer."

Vinny raises his eyebrows at me as he processes this new information about me and tries to understand why anyone would want to help him out.

CRASHING   I LOVE YOU. FORGIVE ME.

❖

The next afternoon, a correctional officer comes to re-
trieve me for Vinny's hearing.

"He says he wants you to represent him, but you don't
have to."

"I'll do it. It's no problem."

"Are you sure? Why would you speak up for a guy
like that?"

"Because he didn't do it, but you and your buddies were
going to punish all of us for it, so he stepped up and took
the blame."

We walk to a little office on the other side of the jail where
the hearing will be held. Hearing makes it sound a lot more formal than it is. The correctional officer who will decide Vinny's
fate sits behind a small desk. The office is more like a closet,
barely suitable for one person, and there are three of us plus the
correctional officer waiting to bring me back to the unit when
I'm done. Vinny sits in a chair facing the desk.

"Stand right there," the correctional officer conducting
the hearing instructs me, gesturing to a square of tile next to
Vinny's seat. "Tell us what you know."

"Thanks. Well, I just graduated from law school at
Georgetown, and while I was there, I worked for a non-profit
law firm that focused on conditions of confinement for people
in institutions." That was during my second year, before I went
to the tax court, back when I still dreamed of being a do-gooder
to help people. "I learned to pay attention to the facilities in

places like this."

Growing up in a military family and moving to so many places, meeting brand new groups of people every two years, I've learned to be a chameleon, to fit in anywhere and with anyone. I never feel like an impostor, because I'm not acting. The different speech patterns, accents, and mannerisms I unconsciously adopt to suit any situation are all a part of me, a part of who I learned to be growing up with so many different people in so many different parts of the world. I'm multicultural. Vinny has only met jail Mark. Now he is seeing lawyer Mark, and after a moment of surprise, he grins at me. He's enjoying the show. The guard looks alarmed that this hearing isn't going according to plan; the inmates are taking over the asylum.

"I have to say, overall, this place is in great shape. Most of my lawyer friends would say you're mostly respecting everyone's civil rights," I continue, wanting to plant the seed in his mind that violating someone's rights could cause problems, bad problems that involve lawyers and lawsuits. "That's why I noticed right away when I got to the cell on our unit that the sink was ripped away from the wall. I arrived several days before Vinny, and the sink was already damaged. I honestly don't think anyone currently on the unit did it. But since you were going to punish all of us, Vinny stepped up to take the blame. I know for a fact he didn't do it, and I don't think he should spend more time in jail because of something that happened before he even got here."

"Anything else?"

"Nope. I think that's it."

The next day, Vinny is back on the minimum-security unit, and the correctional officers seem to have decided to drop the issue of the damaged sink. Vinny thanks me, and I ask him again not to tell anyone that I helped him. "I just want to mind my business." I don't want to draw any attention to myself. I just want to do my time and go home to build the rest of my life.

He promises to keep my secret, and I find myself in the uncomfortable position of having to trust the guy with the swastika tattoo.

# CHAPTER 22

The janitor crew is supposed to work for four hours a day, but we don't have nearly enough work to fill four hours a day. I've been on the job for about a week, since a couple days after Vinny's hearing, when a case manager stopped by and told me to come to his office.

"This is it," I'd thought. "I'm getting a job. I hope it's an every-day job."

Getting a job in jail was a big deal. Once I started working, I'd get a day off my sentence for each day I worked, so if I worked every day, the rest of my sentence would be cut in half. Instead of serving two more months, I'd serve one more.

I know my sentence is short, but it seems to go on forever. Every day seems so long. Every week feels like an eternity. So much happens in such a short amount of time.

Most moments are filled with a combination of anxiety, fear, and boredom. Everyone is constantly on high alert. The drama of being locked up together, of spending every waking and every sleeping moment together, is nonstop. Just imagine being locked in a room with twelve of your friends and family members for a month. Now imagine them as strangers. There's a ton of gossip about how this guy wants to fight this other guy, or that guy is getting out soon because he's a snitch, or that other guy may or may not actually be a sex offender instead of a burglar—being a sex offender is considered the worst, lowest thing you can be in jail. There are cliques, and they're constantly shifting since people are constantly moving in and out of the units.

I countdown the days, the hours, and the minutes, and it makes the time pass so slowly. I can't imagine what it's like for someone who's locked up for years or decades, or their entire life. If those guys spend as much time thinking about time as I do, the sentence must grind on forever. It must drive them crazy.

When I'd walked down to the case manager's office and he'd told me I was going to be a janitor, I was ecstatic. Not only are janitor jobs seven days a week, they also provide freedom to walk around most of the jail while you work. Janitor was a coveted job. It was probably *the best* jail job.

I started the next day, and right away I enjoyed the early mornings required by the position. Everyone gets up at 5:30 for breakfast, and everyone except me goes back to sleep after they eat. The janitor job starts at 7:30, and I've developed a habit of making myself a big cup of instant coffee and watching the news by myself between breakfast and work every morning. It's been the only time I've had control of the community TV, and I've appreciated sitting in the common area while it's been so quiet. The solitude has been nice for breathing and thinking.

The correctional officer who's usually on the unit in the morning is a nice guy who treats us like actual people, not caged animals. He's respectful and self-deprecating in his humor. He's a good one, not like the sadistic weirdo who processes me back into the jail after my counseling appointments and seems to enjoy the strip search a little too much. The weird correctional officer makes me strip down and then stares for too long. Job benefits for him include health insurance, paid time off, and gawking at involuntarily naked men. He's also generally an asshole. But he's young, so maybe it's just the over-exuberance of being inexperienced and wanting to get it right, doing his job by the book. And he's been trained that his job is to assert his dominance and maintain control over the inmates.

But the morning correctional officer is older and knows how to do a strip search.

"Make it quick," he jokes gruffly when the other janitors come out at 7:30. "Nobody wants to see that shit." He doesn't enjoy it and has us quickly pull our pants down, squat, cough, stand up, and pull our pants back up. One fluid motion, maybe two seconds, and then we head off to work.

I always start my work day by cleaning the health suite. I sweep and mop, then clean the bathrooms. To kill time in the bathrooms, I clean a little section, then lean against a wall and count to 200. That way, it takes me almost an hour.

Toilet seat.

*1, 2, 3 . . . 200*

Back of toilet.

*1, 2, 3 . . . 200*

Mirror.

*1, 2, 3 . . . 200*

After finishing the health suite each morning, I get assigned another part of the jail to sweep and mop, vacuum, or dust. Sometimes they have us move furniture or scrape paint, but other than telling us what to do each morning, nobody really supervises us. The freedom is nice.

There's an office suite with a janitor's closet where they keep all the cleaning supplies. In the closet behind a set of shelves, there's a strange dark corridor barely wider than my shoulders and maybe sixteen feet long. It leads nowhere, and there doesn't seem to be any reason for it to be there. During my first week on the job, I noticed that someone had flipped a milk crate upside down and turned it into a seat at the end of the hallway. They'd left a pile of old newspapers too.

Visiting the corridor became a part of my morning routine. After cleaning the health suite each morning, and before moving on to other tasks, I'd steal a newspaper from the big stack in the office that leads to the closet and head back to the mysterious corridor to read and enjoy some relaxation.

I was sitting there one morning when the door started to open. It could have been one of the other janitors, but I wasn't sure, so I jumped up, grabbed a sponge, and started scrubbing the shelves that block the way to the corridor. I was standing suspiciously on the backside of the shelves where nobody would ever go unless they were hanging out in the weird dead-end corridor, and there was no good reason to be hanging out in the weird dead-end corridor. The young creepy-sadistic-lingering-strip-search correctional officer stepped in and looked right in my direction, but he never acknowledged that I was there. He didn't do anything. He didn't say anything. He just turned around and left.

"Did he even see me?" I wondered. He had to have seen

me. We were no more than two feet apart. But it had been dark back there—though not too dark; I could read— and I wasn't sure. "That guy's a jerk. No way he would let me slide on this," I thought. "But how could he not have seen me?"

If he'd busted me, I'd have lost my job and been in jail longer just for taking a few minutes off. That and taking the newspapers would have gotten me sent back to medium security.

The next day, the milk crate and newspapers were gone from the hallway. My reading nook was no longer safe, and my reading material was no longer available. But nothing else happened. Creepy sadist had done me a solid, it seemed.

I hadn't expected that. The small kindness made me dislike him a little bit less and think more about how all people are really a mix of good and bad. There isn't much difference between the guys who wind up locked in this place and the correctional officers entrusted to supervise us. We're all just human.

But this morning, as I clean the health suite bathroom, I have something else on my mind, or rather, two *someone* elses: Laura and Maria. Nothing new there. I can't shake my guilt over being with Maria when Laura has only been dead for one year, one week, and six days, and I feel bad that I haven't been able to give as much of myself to Maria as I know she wishes I would.

Maria and Laura are so different. Laura was laid back and relaxed. Maria likes to be on the move. Laura liked to party. Maria never had a drink until she was twenty-one. Laura was quiet, a bit of an introvert, at least until she felt comfortable around you. Maria makes new friends standing in line at the grocery store. Laura liked lying on the beach. Maria likes hiking in the mountains. Laura had straight, dark brown hair. She was short and soft. Maria has curly, lighter hair. She's taller and more athletic. When Courtney met Maria, she told me that I'd found Laura's opposite. If Maria had reminded me of Laura, I don't think I would have wanted to be around her. Maria touches different parts of my heart, engages different parts of my mind, and shares different parts of my interests.

Maria's companionship has been fulfilling in ways that are entirely different from Laura's. She is wonderful, and I know that Maria is falling in love. I can see it in her eyes when she comes to visit, and her actions—taking care of Rocko, driving me to pretrial supervision, bringing me my favorite foods when she picks me up for counseling— are unmistakably loving. But I've worried that I might be incapable of ever falling in love again, even if she is deserving of it. It's not fair to her that I'm unable to let go and let her all the way in.

I stand up from leaning on the wall and clean the bathroom sink.

*1, 2, 3 . . . 200*

Maria has become such an indispensable part of my life; she's a safe, calm harbor in the storm that has been my life since the crash. I need her in so many ways, ways I never thought I would need another person.

She's the companion who spent so many days and nights with me while I suffered through the devastation of the crash, the grief of losing Laura, and the trauma of surviving. She's the one who always makes sure I get where I need to be, sacrificing her time to focus on my needs while I've had so little to give in return. We have our favorite restaurants downtown, like the sushi spot we went to before I turned myself in for jail—we mostly like the same sushi, although I'm still working on getting her to eat eel—and the bar in South Baltimore with its own beer and those great little gourmet pizzas. She knows me better than anyone else ever has. I've grown so much since I met her and shared parts of myself I'd kept hidden my whole life. She knows exactly how to act when I cry. She doesn't get uncomfortable or try to make my feelings disappear. She pulls me into her arms, and I know she understands.

I wipe the paper towel dispenser next.

*1, 2, 3 . . . 200*

She loves romantic comedies, and now I love romantic comedies, too. She watches the same ones over and over to go to sleep. She started doing that when her dad was dying. I watch them because the themes are light and breezy, and I need light and breezy. We complete each other's movie quotes all the time. The night we met, she started the line from *Clueless* when the girls are out on the tennis court with the gym teacher, and one of them refuses to play.

"My plastic surgeon doesn't want me doing any activity where balls fly at my nose," she'd said.

"There goes your social life," I'd replied. She told me later it was the moment she knew I was special.

We're both swimmers. I was the captain of my high school team. She was a division 1 swimmer in college.

We both know about loss. We have our own little short-hand, like riding the waves, to tell each other when we're having an especially hard time. She doesn't mind that Laura is a part of our relationship. Seeing how understanding she is about Laura, how she doesn't think of our relationship as a competition with my relationship with Laura, I finally see how stupid I was to worry about Laura's ex-boyfriends. Every love is different. Every relationship that is good is good because it's the one you need at the time you're in it.

Where Laura reinforced my instinct for being a home-body, Maria brings me out of my shell. She signed us up to play kickball together in a league in Baltimore and takes me to meet all her friends and family members.

She's wonderful, amazing, and sexy as hell. Our physical chemistry is off the charts, and I ache to see her again.

I start to stand up from leaning on the wall so I can clean the toilet when it hits me. I slouch back against the wall and sigh.

*Holy crap. I'm in love.*

How did I not notice?

I read an article once about the three phases of romantic love. It starts with lust, a crush, that little voice in the back of your head that says, "I want to mate with this person."

If things go well, it progresses to the attraction phase. That's when our brains get a huge jolt of dopamine, norepi-nephrine, and serotonin. This is the phase we think of as the falling part of being in love, when we lose our appetite, can't sleep, agonize over every detail of our conversations with our love interest, want to talk about them all the time, and make fools of ourselves because our heads aren't on straight.

If it doesn't fall apart in the attraction phase, we finally settle into the attachment phase. Oxytocin and vasopressin cement the bond for the long haul. We aren't head over heels like the first months or year of the relationship. Our brains could never keep that up, and I'm not sure our species would survive if they did. But we are committed and bonded in the most tender way. This is the kind of love that can last.

Maria and I are in the attachment phase. With everything that's happened since the crash, falling in love while coping with grief, trauma, and the fear of prison was just so different from any relationship I've had in the past. The love snuck up on me. But it's unmistakable now that I'm willing to see it for what it is.

*I love her. I love her so much.*

And I'm terrified by it.

# CHAPTER 23

The next day, Maria takes me to my counseling appointment. I've been locked up for about six weeks, and it's such a relief being with her, being out of jail for just a few hours, with the woman I love. *One of the two women I love.*

Jail really isn't horrible. It's mostly just boredom and bad food, but it's still occasionally punctuated by fear and violence. There was the time in the second week of my sentence when I'd taken too long on the phone, and the big white dude with fat rolls on the back of his massive neck shoved me off my seat so he could make a call. I didn't do anything in response, and the other guys told me if I let someone push me like that again, I'd get messed with the rest of the time I was locked up. It wasn't like me to let someone push me around, but something about the fact that he was in jail made him scarier, even though I was in jail too. I decided I wouldn't let it happen again.

One time, I watched the correctional officers kick the shit out of a guy in the hallway while I was working my janitor job. *That* had been disturbing; the correctional officers seemed to think it was good sport. Another time, I'd almost gotten into a fight with Pookie, a teenager with a high metabolism who I caught stealing food from my locker. Some of the other guys broke it up, and his buddies made him give the food back. I regretted afterward that I wasn't more compassionate. He was young and hungry. The food they gave us never seemed like enough, and he didn't have money to get some extra snacks from the commissary. When I found out why he was stealing, I gave him my weekly danish and told him to let me know if he needed anything else.

But *the closest* I came to getting into a real fight was with a cellmate who was covered in muscles and tattoos. I farted out loud, which is a little crass but not at all out of the ordinary in jail; manners in jail are about the same as in a men's locker room. He told me I had to say "excuse me" to him. I remembered how embarrassed I was when I let the other big guy push me off my seat by the phone, and I knew this was a similar challenge. I jumped down from my bunk to step toward him.

"I don't have to excuse myself to anyone, bitch," I'd said.

He'd pressed his chest to mine, invading my space, and I decided that the only way he was going to win the fight was to kill me. I stared into his eyes with no fear, anger, or excitement. I was completely impassive, and I think he was alarmed by my calm. In the moment, my superpower was that I didn't really care if I died. In general, I didn't wish I was dead anymore, but being with Laura would be nice, so I was ambivalent about living or dying. It was really quite liberating.

We stood chest to chest for several seconds. The tension in the cell was palpable. Nobody was moving; nobody was trying to instigate us the way the young guys sometimes do for excitement. Everyone was just holding their breath.

"Fuck you," he finally said and walked away.

I tell Kara about it now, and she asks how I felt when it happened.

"I guess I was a little scared, but I also kind of wanted to just beat his ass, to take everything from the last year out on him. I thought he would have to kill me to win, but, actually, I think I might have killed him if he'd hit me."

"There's something else too. It's not related," I say, quickly changing the subject.

"Okay. But I want you to think about being more careful. It's easy for people to lose their temper in situations like yours. I don't think the guy who thinks he would kill someone is who you are."

*I did kill someone.*

"What else is on your mind?" Kara asks.

"I think I'm in love. Well, I'm in love. I know I am."

I tell her that it's frightening to acknowledge it. I'm worried now that I might lose Maria too. I'm worried something will happen to her now that I love her. Every girl I've ever loved has died, even if that represents a small sample of one. Why should this one be any different?

"Mark, are you listening to yourself? Your crash was a tragic accident. Anything can happen at any moment, but that kind of tragedy is very, very rare, and you can't let that fear control the rest of your life."

"But what if I do something, and she dies? I can't be the guy with two dead girlfriends. I can't be the guy who kills two girlfriends."

"I've known you for a year now, and you're a smart guy. What would you say to yourself if you were me right now?"

"I guess I'd tell me that I'm being crazy. That this is a good thing."

"I wouldn't call you crazy. We don't say that to your faces," she smiles, and I smile too. It's a good shrink joke. "But you're right that this is a good thing. You're never going to have a relationship with no risks. That's not the world we live in. But you are strong, Mark. I think you're ready for this. What are you going to do?"

"I think I should tell her."

"I think so too."

❖

I walk out of my appointment and across the parking lot to the minivan where Maria and Rocko are waiting for me. I open the door and scratch Rocko on the head before nudging him into the backseat.

"How was it?" Maria asks. I breathe in the familiar scent of the Sui Dreams perfume she wears and smile as I sit down in the passenger seat.

"Not bad. Pretty good, I guess." I don't usually tell her much about the counseling appointments. I tell her most of the things I tell Kara because I tell her most of the things that I'm feeling. I just don't tell her that I tell Kara those things too, and she never pries about the conversations I have in therapy.

I want to tell her I love her, but I'm nervous. It's a different kind of nervousness than when I first told Laura I loved her. Unlike with Laura, I'm sure Maria loves me back. I'm not concerned she won't say it back. I'm worried about what happens after she does.

Maria backs out of the parking spot and turns onto Kenilworth Drive to take us back to the highway. I glance over and look at her a little longer than usual.

"What is it?"

"Nothing," I tell her. "You look pretty tonight. I'm taking it in while I can." She glances at me flirtatiously with big blue smokey eyes, and I can hear and feel the hot blood in my ears and cheeks. It's getting warm, and my palms are sweaty. I wipe them on my pants and change the subject.

"What are your plans for the weekend?"

"I'm coming to visit you, of course."

"Besides that."

"I'm going to Michelle's tonight, and she's having a party on Saturday," she says. "The kickball crew will all be there."

"Nice. That sounds like fun. Tell them I said 'what's up?'"

Michelle is her friend from college, the one whose house, near my old dungeon, Maria took me to for the after-party the night we met. I wish I could go there with Maria. Being in the car feels so normal, and even though my sentence is nearly over, I don't want to go back to my new dungeon. It's so lonely. When I'm in the visiting room, I try to imagine what it's like for the guys seeing their children through the glass, unable to hold and squeeze them. Everyone is so happy when they're walking to a visit and so miserable when their family leaves. Maybe Maria and I could just keep driving and never go back.

The light in front of us changes to green, and Maria turns the car onto the highway.

"I'll miss you," I tell her.

229

"I'll miss you, too," she replies somberly. "But I'll see you Sunday, and then it's just three more weeks until you're home."

"As long as nothing goes wrong," I say.

"Nothing is going to go wrong."

She's probably right. I'm obsessed with doing everything I have to do to get as many days off my sentence as I can. If I work every day and stay out of trouble, I'll be out in a little over three weeks. Still, the last year has taught me to anticipate the worst. I guess that's why I'm nervous even though I know Maria loves me back. Once I tell her, once it's out there, that's when things will go wrong. Maybe she'll die. Maybe I'll die. Maybe we'll die together. Maybe the jail will cave in on me, and I'll never get to leave.

I take a deep breath and try to calm myself down. Nothing is going to happen to her. I'm going to come home in three weeks. Nothing is going to go wrong. But I can't shake the feeling. Maybe tonight isn't the night to tell her. Maybe I should wait until I'm home with her. But at the same time, I can barely contain myself. I love her, and I want her to know it. I want her to say it to me too.

We get back to the jail, and I get out of the car. Maria comes around the front to hug and kiss me before I return to lock up. I'm willing myself to say the words, but nothing will come out.

*"I love you." Just say it.*

The words are screaming in my ear. I love you. I love you. I love you. The blood is rushing to my cheeks again, and I can't make my mouth say the words, so I lean down and kiss her again to keep my lips busy. Her lips are so soft and taste like the strawberry lip balm she's wearing. The kiss ends, and she looks into my eyes.

"I love you," I finally say. I want it to be the last thing I say before we're apart again.

I smile down at her, and she looks up at me with contentment because of what I've finally said and resignation because she knows I have to leave.

"I love you, too." I kiss her again, then turn and walk into jail, the gate clinking closed behind me and between us.

# CHAPTER 24

The next day, I'm beaming about Maria and looking for a place to eat my breakfast. I can't wait to see her again. I keep to myself during meals, so I'm looking for an empty table. One of the other guys on the unit asks me to sit down. Sam is massive. Probably six feet, five inches and easily 350 pounds. He's known as a high-level leader in the Dead Men Incorporated, a white prison gang that started in Maryland. Their main business is murder for hire. All of the inmates and most of the guards are afraid of Sam. I don't even think of refusing.

"Vinny told me what you did for him. I have an issue I want your help with," he says.

"Fucking Vinny." I try to be chameleon jail Mark and act hard. "I told him not to *fucking* tell anyone."

"The warden isn't counting my days right. I'm not getting all the good-time credit I'm supposed to," Sam explains. Good-time credit means getting time off your sentence for good behavior. It's less time than you get off for having a job, but it still adds up and matters to anyone who wants to be home as soon as possible, which is everyone. "I told the warden about it, but he won't listen."

We spend the next half hour going over the details of his problem, his letters to the jail administration, and what he thought was wrong with the calculation. As far as I can tell, he's right. They're messing up the count and planning to keep him in jail longer than they should. I draft a letter for him to

CRASHING  I LOVE YOU. FORGIVE ME.

submit to the warden, explaining the error, citing the relevant sections of the jail's handbook, and asking that it be corrected immediately. It's fun to use my legal training, even just a little. I tell him to send it to the warden and let me know if I can help with anything else.

I call Maria later that evening and tell her about my introduction to Sam.

"That's crazy," she says. "I had something crazy happen too."

She tells me that after she dropped me off after therapy the night before—after we exchanged our professions of love—she drove to her friend's house to hang out. While she was there, someone broke into her car.

"The strange thing is, they didn't take any of my stuff," she tells me. "But they took all of yours." My phone, my wallet, and my shoes were gone when she got back to the car, and the passenger door was wide open.

We whisper apprehensively about our suspicion that Sam's gang might be responsible. Maybe my ability to leave every week—the arrangement is unheard of—combined with my short homicide sentence and understanding of the law raised concerns that I might be an undercover cop or snitch. There isn't a lot of trust in jail.

"Maybe their gang members waited outside the jail and followed you to Michelle's after you dropped me off," I whisper. "Maybe they think I'm under cover or something, but they also wanted my help getting Sam out sooner." So they had someone break into Maria's car to see if they could find any evidence to confirm their suspicions. But they didn't find anything because I was just a random guy who got a better deal because I was middle-class, white, and had Laura's family supporting me.

The possibility that I was being vetted is reinforced a couple days later when Sam asks me to sit with him again and tells me the warden fixed his good-time credits. He thanks me and tells me that DMI is always looking for smart people to help with their businesses. "If you're interested . . ." He shrugs as if to say, "ball's in your court."

It's intriguing to be offered this glimpse into an underworld I never would have seen otherwise, but I'm ready to get past my brief life of crime. "Thanks, man. I appreciate the offer. But I'm putting all this behind me when I get out."

"It's not easy finding work with a record," he tells me, and he's not the first of the guys I've met to warn about the challenges of life with a criminal record, "so keep it in mind. But I hear what you're sayin'." He tells me they know where I live and that I'm under protection as long as I live in the townhouse I rented before getting locked up. He doesn't say it like a threat, and I don't take it as one. I assume they know my address from whatever IDs were left in my wallet, but I don't ask.

After that, I sit with Sam for every meal. We become friends. He tells me about his family, and I tell him about mine.

❖

"I'm going to go play basketball," I tell Mike, gesturing toward the group of Black guys on the other side of the gym and tossing the ball back to him. "Wanna come?"

Mike is a young, aspiring DMI member from my unit. He's a nice kid, if a little misguided. He's short, blonde, and loves to work out.

"You wanna play with the Black guys?" he asks with dismay, using a racial slur that white people should never lose." I cringe, but he doesn't say it in a way that's meant to be derogatory. He doesn't consider them to be beneath him. To Mike, it's a normal label to differentiate *his people* from *those people*. He's mystified that I would cross the line meant to divide us.

"Yeah, why not?" I say, strolling across the wooden floor toward the basketball court. He doesn't follow me.

Mike's casual divisiveness is minor compared to what really concerns me. My military upbringing instilled a deep patriotism and a strong belief in liberty and justice. I grew up believing our system was unique in the world and worth defending because it was the most free and fair civilization in history. I wrote my college thesis on the ways the Constitution and amendments secured our freedoms. I knew we weren't perfect and that injustices occurred. I'd volunteered with the Innocence Project to try to exonerate people who were wrongly convicted. But on the whole, I believed our system of justice was righteous.

Now I can't square those beliefs with what I'm witnessing in jail. I knew racism was still a problem, but how can half the people in jail be Black in a county that's overwhelmingly white? Why are we so divided from each other? And how can a country that prides itself on liberty and freedom imprison so many people who did nothing more than put a substance in their bodies? So many of the men I'm locked up with are here for drug possession. At worst, they were harming themselves, but most of them are going to be locked up for longer than I am, and incarceration is causing more harm than the drugs ever were.

*How is this a free society?*

"You guys mind if I play?" I ask as I approach the court. The Black guys look a little surprised that I'd want to join them.

"You any good?" asks Dante, a young, friendly Bloods gang member who I've gotten to know on the unit.

"I'm okay," I shrug.

I grew up playing basketball. There was a youth center with a basketball court on every army base, and every army-brat boy I knew played basketball almost daily. I had basketball hoops in the backyards of all the homes I lived in between the fifth and twelfth grades. All told, I probably played street basketball ten hours a week for fifteen years. I know I'm more than okay, but I don't want to overpromise.

"We need one more to make the teams even," another of the guys says. "You're with us."

A minute later, one of my teammates gets a rebound and passes the ball to me as I run toward the other end of the court. Only Dante stands between me and the basket. As he lunges for the ball, I dribble around my back, and he falls on the ground. I cross under the hoop and score easily on a reverse layup. My teammates are jumping up and down, laughing and whooping. They can't believe the white guy just schooled their buddy.

"Oh shit," one of them yells. "Alright, white boy, I see you."

After the game, I sit in the common room off the catwalk on our unit. It's a small room with a table and chairs used for programs offered by volunteers and religious services. Over the last couple of weeks, I've started using it to offer legal advice to the other guys. After they heard about the help I gave to Vinny and Sam, a lot of them started asking for my help. At first, it was pretty informal, a bit of advice to Mike while he was doing push-ups with his feet up on the bunk—I was on lookout for correctional officers since it's against the rules to use the furniture to workout—or a brainstorm about his case with Dante while sitting at breakfast.

But now it's become a little more formal. After returning from my janitor job or the gym, I sit in the common room and respond to letters from friends and family I received the day before. The guys leave me alone while I'm writing letters, and when I'm finished, they take turns sitting down so we can go over their cases and the paperwork they've received from their public defenders who are overworked and unable to pay much attention to their cases. We strategize on their defense and write the arguments down to make it easier for their lawyers. Someone's always doing pull-ups from the TV mount, and someone's always on lookout since it's also against the rules to do pull-ups from the TV mount.

Helping them is a good distraction from all the "what ifs" I've been grappling with. Not remembering the crash feels like a barrier to making meaning out of it. Ideas about what I could have done differently to prevent Laura's death or why I survived and Laura died intrude on my thoughts about what a future that honors her might look like.

What if I had gotten my tires replaced? Did someone cut me off and make me lose control of the car? Did a deer run in front of me? What if we left the party half an hour earlier? Half an hour later? A minute later? Would we have made it home? What if Laura drove? What if I didn't have a birthday party? *Would she still be alive?*

Once I start playing this game, it's easy for me to go way back, fast.

What if I went to Penn State instead of Towson? What if Laura and her ex-boyfriend never broke up, and then she didn't move in with Theresa? If I never met her, would Laura still be alive? What if I never told her I loved her? What if she never loved me back? *Would she still be alive?*

I'd rather she were alive, even if that meant I never would have known her. She would be fine. Her family would be fine. We both would have met someone else. Life would be fine.

*She would still be alive.*

"Are you that white guy that helps people with their cases?" asks the young Black man I've never seen before, but instead of "guy," he uses the same racial slur that Mike used earlier to describe the group of Black basketball players. I'm not offended when he says it. If anything, it feels like I'm being included in a community I wasn't a part of before.

"Yeah," I tell him. "Did you just get on the unit?"

"This morning, but I already heard what you did to Dante, baller."

"Do you need some help with your case?" I ask, grinning proudly.

Over the next half hour, I help the young man respond to detainers sent to the jail by other states where he has some outstanding warrants. I write responses telling about his sentence and the programs he's participating in to rehabilitate himself. The goal is to convince the out-of-state prosecutors to drop the cases against him. They're minor, and he's already doing time.

It feels good to help the men on my unit with their legal problems. This is why I initially went to law school, to fight for people who needed help to fight for themselves. To show love to people in a world that would throw them away. To seek fair outcomes and make their lives a little better. Now it's a small way to give back and make up for what I did.

"I appreciate you," he tells me when we're done.

"No problem," I reply. I appreciate him too, and I'm thankful for the time away from my thoughts.

When I'm analyzing every decision either of us ever made to see how it led to Laura's death, I sometimes forget that life is too complicated for the exercise. The causal chains are too long to fully understand. Every decision we make in life keeps us from experiencing other realities that may have been better or may have been worse. Each action opens a different set of options for our next decision. And that decision opens still more possibilities and more options for us to choose from. So over time, the difference of one decision as it leads to another and then to another becomes huge.

There are millions of ways my life or Laura's could have gone. But the sum of millions of our small choices led us to the reality in which Laura died in the crash. It led us away from all the other lives we could have lived. Any number of those decisions, if changed, could have made our lives completely different. But nobody thinks about that when they're making all the small day-to-day decisions that are part of life. When you pick a college, you think about its cost, the quality of the education and the opportunities it will provide, how far away from home it is or how much you like the campus; you don't think about how choosing one college might lead to someone's death or someone's birth, or dozens of other possible consequences, because there's no way to know how the choice will affect those outcomes. We do our best with the information we have and hope things work out. We don't know what long-term consequences will result from our daily choices, and we can't control the outcome one month down the road, let alone several years.

Life is so random. I wonder about the paths that led Sam, Vinny, Mike, Dante, and all the other guys to this place. A lot of them started out in pretty bad spots. And a lot of them also made some pretty bad choices. But some choices they made were probably only bad in retrospect. My decision to drive drunk was a bad choice, and the consequence of that choice was the worst possible outcome. But it makes no sense to second guess my choice of college because it ultimately led to meeting Laura. And I have to accept that even on the night of the accident, a million things came together to result in the moment of her death. My actions and decisions were a big part of that, but so were Laura's, and so were innumerable factors we had no control over. I can't go back and change any of it, but maybe I can choose how it changes me. I can choose not to let it destroy me, but maybe I'm supposed to let it direct me.

I wonder how things will work out for the guys I've helped. I'm not going to be here long enough to find out, and I have no intention of staying in touch. Like every other place I've left before, I'll cut ties and move on. Put it behind me. Put them behind me. In this one sense, I should have been well prepared for losing Laura. I've lost almost everyone I've ever met. I'm so used to moving on. Losing her has hurt so much because she was the first person outside my family I ever thought would be around for good.

# CHAPTER 25

I'm sweeping the hallway outside of the health suite. A group of young people carrying notebooks walks by with the warden. They must be college students on a tour, getting a close-up look of the animals in the zoo. Maybe they're studying criminal justice, social work, psychology, or something like that.

As they approach, I pull the mop bucket back and apologize for being in the way. Two of them—a bouncy girl-next-door brunette who's attractive in the same ways Laura was attractive and a young guy who seems interested in her—look up from their notebooks and make eye contact with me.

"Hey, how's it going?" I say, smiling comfortably.

They both look startled and visibly recoil from me. They're disgusted, and it shows on their faces. They back away urgently, and it's like a hot poker shoved into my chest. I've never experienced people being so disgusted by me before. But from their perspective, I'm just one of the dangerous animals in the zoo they've come to explore. The bars are missing, and I got too close.

It's still so uncomfortable and foreign to me to be treated as something less than human. Before the crash, I was someone other people admired. The moms of girls in my high school wanted them to date me. Life has come easily to me. I went to a top law school. I had a beautiful girlfriend and lots of friends. I felt entitled to it all.

But now I'm the guy who destroyed his life and killed his girlfriend, and everything that's happened since Laura died has been mortifying too: living in the dungeon, Maria paying for all our dates, crying in public, peeing in cups with someone peering over my shoulder, recounting the worst moments of my life to a group of strangers at drug treatment, standing in court to be sentenced, changing into my jail uniform, stripping down and squatting and coughing over and over, cleaning toilets, mopping floors, and now repelling students on their jail field trip.

Grief, trauma, and fear were at the core of my pain in the year after Laura died. Being in jail has given me space and time to explore the pain I've felt since Laura died and the way I want to change things for the future. I've accepted that I'm neither a good nor a bad guy. I'm just a guy doing his best. I'm more spiritually connected and know I can harness this pain for a new purpose. I love Maria, and—and this is new—I'm happy to be alive. But even with all that, it's humiliating to know that strangers find me disgusting and unworthy, and even my friends and family who used to admire me now just pity me.

But even with all I've been through over the past year, one of the hardest things to come to terms with has been this change I've felt in my status.

"Have I ever looked at someone like that?" I wonder, turning away from the tour group to hide the crimson shame and anger rising in my cheeks.

Later that morning, I'm in another part of the jail, sweeping another corridor, when my pre-trial supervisor approaches.

He's here for training taking place in one of the classrooms. He says hello, and I say hi back.

"How much time did you get?" he asks.

"Ninety days," I reply. "I'll be out in a couple days."

His colleague sneers at me. "How long 'til you come back?"

"He's not coming back. He's one of the good ones," my pretrial supervisor responds.

He's right that I'm never coming back, but I disagree that I'm the good-guy exception in the jail. Most of the people here are as good as people I've met outside the walls.

"We've got our hooks in him now. He'll be back," his colleague replies.

The guy is an asshole, and I want to tell him so. But, I have two more days on my sentence, and it's more important to me to get out of jail on schedule. I've had a horrible sore throat for a week and a half now. A lot of the guys in my cell are worried I'll get them sick too, and they've pressured me to go to the health suite and get antibiotics. But if I go to the health suite for any reason other than to clean it, the nurses might make me take a day off of work. A day off of work means another day in jail. So I haven't complained to the nurses. And now, if I tell this guy the truth about himself, I'll probably lose my jail job, and that means staying here an extra two days at least.

"Leave him alone," my pretrial supervisor says mercifully.

"Asshole," I whisper under my breath. As the two walk back into the classroom, I wonder why his words matter so much to me, and I realize it's because I still think I'm better than he is. It's an affront to the status I used to have to be insulted by someone I would have looked down on a year ago.

The remaining vestiges of my self-centered pride are the problem. I wouldn't care so much what others thought about me if I had more humility. It wouldn't be possible to be humiliated if I were less concerned with my status. While I've been locked up, I've taken a deep and hard look at myself, and in many ways, I've become more humble through the odyssey of the last year.

My knee-jerk anger and embarrassment at sudden indignities like the disgust of those students or the disregard of my pretrial supervisor's buddy are still colored by the vestiges of my self-importance, but when the emotion passes, I know in my bones that I'm no more important or deserving than any other person. I'm not that big of a deal. We aren't taught to think like that in our individualistic, army-of-one society, but it's true. My family and friends would be sad if I died, but the other seven billion people on earth would never even notice.

I finish sweeping the corridor and empty the dustpan in one of the empty classrooms lining the hallway. As I walk back to the janitor's closet to return my supplies, I chuckle ruefully to myself, thinking of the wild swings in my self-appraisal since Laura died. Sometimes I've felt none of it could be real because it couldn't happen to someone *like me*, meaning someone who was better than other people. Other times, I've thought it could *only happen* to someone like me, meaning a horrible screw-up destined for failure.

*What a mess I've been.*

"Ready to head back?" Justin asks as I drop the broom

and dustpan in the closet, where it looks like he's been waiting for me. Justin is one of two other janitors who lives with me on the unit. He's a short, chubby white guy with a black buzz cut, and he's here for stealing a backhoe and an excavator from a construction site.

"They left the keys, and I thought it would be fun to drive them around," he told me when we first met. I'd laughed, and I never thought his comically bad decision reflected on him as a human being. Our choices and circumstances don't change our value as people. I think I've always thought that was true about other people, but it's been harder to separate my own worth from my accomplishments and my shortcomings. Every single person has inherent dignity and value. That was true of me before the crash, and it wasn't because of how well I did in law school or how charming I could be to other people. My mistakes—even huge, devastating mistakes like the crash—haven't depleted my value either.

"Yeah, let's go," I reply to Justin, and he walks out of the closet behind me, closing the door with a soft kick. We walk onto the unit, pull down our pants, squat, cough, stand up, and pull our pants back up. It's really not a big deal.

❖

I finish my dinner—steamed vegetables and the few tablespoons of bland sloppy joes on a stale piece of white bread—and walk upstairs to my cell to organize the few possessions in my locker into "keep" and "leave" piles. It's my last night in jail, and I'm feeling contemplative, maybe even a little preemptively nostalgic, reflecting on the men I've met over the last two months: Leon, my first cellmate who taught me to sleep through the boredom, Terry and the other guys on medium security at Jennifer Road who kicked my ass in Scrabble, Stu, who lost his wife in a drunk-driving motorcycle accident, Pookie, the hungry kid who tried to steal my food, Sam, the gang leader, Justin, my fellow janitor, and Mike, Dante, and the other young guys in the unit I had the privilege to help with their cases (and, in Dante's case, to embarrass on the basketball court).

As I'm folding one of the white t-shirts I've been allowed to wear under my stiff, forest green jail uniform and dropping it on the leave pile, Mike walks into the cell and, without saying a word, plunges down to do a set of incline pushups holding the bar on my bed.

"You out tomorrow?" he asks, hopping back to his feet and admiring his biceps. He glances at my Walkman sitting on the keep pile. I'd thought I might keep it as a souvenir of sorts.

"Yeah. You want the radio?" I ask. He hasn't been able to afford one, and he needs it more than I do. For all his high energy and lightheartedness,  Mike has been through a lot. Violence, abuse, neglect, and danger colored his entire childhood. The trouble he'd gotten himself into—too many repeated thefts for the courts to ignore—was less surprising than his good humor about it all.

"Thanks," he says, looking down to the ground. "You're alright." For an instant, I think I see a flash of melancholy in his eyes before he looks up brightly, nods meaningfully, and bumps my fist.

"Good luck out there," he says over his shoulder, bounding out of the cell.

A thread of pain runs through the stories of the men I've met in here: trauma, grief, desperate times, desperate measures. The world is full of suffering people. Since the crash, I've noticed it so much more than I used to. I've become more aware of the little signs on people's faces, their eyes and mouths, of the ways they move, how they hold their shoulders, and their posture. I hear the pain in their voices, even if they try to hide it. I'm not the only one who has ever pretended that everything is okay when it's not. People do it all the time! I've noticed that too. I've always been good at reading people. It was how I learned to get comfortable in a new town every few years. But since the crash, it's become so easy to penetrate the facades people put up. I see my pain in them, and I feel theirs in me too. Nowhere has that been more true than in this place.

I pick up the two white t-shirts from the "leave" pile and walk down the stairs to the cell on the bottom left where Cliff has his bunk. Cliff has been in most of the units with me since the Scrabble unit, and he was in the van with me when I moved from Jennifer Road to Ordnance Road. Cliff is homeless, and he looks like he's in his mid-sixties—though maybe he's younger—with scraggly snow-white hair and a scraggly snow-white beard. He'd look like Santa Clause if he weren't so skeletal, and his eyes didn't droop so much. Last October, when the temperatures started dropping, he'd punched a cop at a playground so he could ride out the winter months in jail. He isn't in his cell, and I leave the shirts on his bunk.

I walk back up to my cell, the metal steps to the catwalk clattering under my feet, and wonder what will happen to Cliff after he's released next month. My heart aches knowing how hard his existence is. I don't pity him. I know his suffering. Empathy is sympathy but with humility. Instead of feeling bad for people, suffering has taught me to feel bad with them. There's a leveling power in deep pain. When you've felt it, you know what it feels like. You can't help but be aware of what it must feel like for others.

How broken is our world when a man's only option is to punch a police officer so he can be warm and well-fed, spending winter in a jail cell? Over the last year, as I've become more aware of the suffering around me, I've wished I could do more to stop all the suffering. For most of that time, I couldn't do much to help because I could barely care for myself. While I've been locked up, I've been able to help some of the guys locked up with me, and it's felt good. But it's also felt so small, like trying to empty an ocean of sorrow by sucking through a straw.

All that's left in the leave pile now are a stack of books and a few commissary snacks I won't need to eat before I leave in the morning. The books are highly coveted because they're hard to come by. There are older, worn options in the library, but the only way to get newer books is to have someone on the outside send them directly from a distributor like Amazon. Most of the guys don't have anyone able or willing to do that for them. My grandmother has been sending me three or four James Patterson novels a week, and I've been passing them on to a fellow Patterson fan as I've finished them. I walk over and hand the last one to him.

"What about that *Lord of the Rings?*" he asks. I've already read the three massive novels held in the single volume my mom sent, but I think I'll read them again someday.

"I'm keeping that one," I tell him.

"The Bible too?"

"Yeah," I say, a little guilty knowing how easy it will be for me to replace on the outside and how valuable it might be for the soul searchers who are common in this place.

"This is his newest, right?" he asks, raising the Patterson novel.

"I think so. My grandma said there's another one coming out soon. But I think this is the most recent one out now."

"The guys are gonna be mad I get to read it first," he says, grinning at the prospect of holding it over their heads. James Patterson is huge with the Ordnance Road work unit crowd. Then he reached out, slapped my hand, and patted me twice on the back in an acceptably masculine embrace. "Be good."

My last stop is at Pookie's bunk. It's still hard to believe he's old enough to be locked up with all these men. I've learned that he turned 18 just a few days before he got arrested for selling PCP. He's another young one with a lot of energy, and I've never stopped feeling bad for having almost fought him over some snacks.

"I don't need these, and I don't want them to go to waste," I say nonchalantly, handing Pookie a bunch of chip bags, a cheese danish, and the last of my instant coffee as if I don't know he's been starving for months in here. He looks up and takes them from me, a tough scowl on his face, then places them in his lap and returns silently to the book he's been reading.

There's a story I heard—I'm not sure where—about a man walking on a beach that's covered in starfish that have been left by the receding tide to die in the sun. He sees a woman up ahead picking them up, one at a time, and throwing them back into the ocean, barely making a dent in the countless echinoderms dying on the beach.

Approaching her, he asks, "Why are you doing that? There are too many of them to help. It makes no difference."

The woman picks up another starfish and throws it into the ocean. Turning to the man, she replies, "I made a difference for that one."

# CHAPTER 26

*I'm driving down I-64 in my silver Honda Civic, singing along to Tim McGraw's song "Just to See You Smile," and imagining having Laura in my arms again. I'm on my way to pick her up at the Staunton, Virginia train station. She's coming from Baltimore to visit me at law school. After a week apart, I'm so grateful that this long-distance relationship isn't really that long-distance. We're close enough that we can still spend every weekend together. I got a full scholarship to Notre Dame—it had been my dream since I was a child to go there, Irish Catholic boy that I am—but decided to stay closer to home so I could see Laura more often, even though it means I'll have $100,000 in student loan debt by the time I graduate.*

*It's a cool, moonlit night when I step out of the car. The pleasant musty smell of fall leaves and earth fills the air. As I step down onto the train platform, a gentle breeze makes my skin feel even more alive with anticipation. The train should be here any minute. It's the first time I'm picking Laura up from the station, and I turn in circles, imagining the route I took to get here, trying to orient myself enough to guess which direction her train will come from. I figure it out just in time to see the light of the train coming over the horizon and hear the blast of the train's horn signaling its arrival.*

*I'm giddy with excitement, practically ready to explode with joy that she's here. As the train slows to a stop and passengers begin to disembark, my gaze shifts from car to car, hoping to catch a first glimpse of her through the windows before she leaves the train.*

*Three cars down the train, I see her step off the train, looking up and down the platform for me. She turns, and our eyes meet, a ridiculous grin spreading across my face. I want to run to her, but I'm too embarrassed to make a scene and feel frozen to the spot where I'm standing. Everything on the platform except for her is a blur, and the light fading around her is somehow brighter than everywhere else, as if the light were coming from her rather than bouncing off her.*

*She walks toward me, drops her bags, and falls into my arms. I pick her up and twirl her around before dipping her back and kissing her deeply, her long brown hair flowing toward the dusty ground. I'm no longer self-conscious about anyone who may be watching this scene, and as she stands up, we linger in a tight embrace, repeating a cycle of kissing, talking, hugging, and laughing over and over. I grab her hand, walk her to the car, and open the passenger door for her before putting her bags in the trunk. My person is here.*

❖

I wake up in my cell for the last time, the glow of my slumberland reunion with Laura radiating through my consciousness and slowly dissolving into wakeful buoyancy over my impending freedom and real-life reunion with Maria. It's March 20th, four hundred and six days since Laura died. I've been in jail for less than two months, but it's felt longer, like a turning point has passed, and I'm on the verge of beginning a new life. It's not that the pain of loss or the shame of my guilt has shrunk. Rather, there is so much more in me—purpose, hope, meaning, love—that the hurt is a smaller proportion. I'm relieved to be going home. I'll be on probation for five years, but meeting with a probation officer once a week is no big deal. The worst is behind me. I can build a new life Laura would be proud of, a life I can be happy with.

After breakfast—a carton of milk, a fruit cup, and a small pancake; not a bad jail breakfast—I stay in the common area while the other guys go back to bed. When I'm supposed to leave for my janitor job, I approach the correctional officer on duty, the nice one who jokes and makes the strip searches fast, and ask him if I should go to work.

"If you're getting out today, just hang tight," he says. "They usually call you guys down for release around 10." It's clear from the context that he means 10 in the morning. That's just three hours away.

I sit back down for a few more minutes, then walk back up to my cell, then walk back down to the common area and watch more TV. I don't know what to do with myself. When 10 o'clock comes and goes, I begin to wonder if I'll ever get released, but before lunch, the correctional officer gets a call and beckons me over.

"Grab your stuff," he smiles. "You're out of here."

I grab the mesh bag with my underwear and a few other possessions and walk toward the exit from the unit.

"Squat and cough," the correctional officer says as we approach the door.

I pull down my pants, squat, cough, stand up, and pull them back up, one last time for old times' sake.

"Good luck," he says, opening the door and letting me walk through.

"Thanks," I say gratefully. "I'd say I'll see you around, but I don't plan on it."

"At least one of us gets to get outta here," he laughs.

The corridor is quiet and empty, but it's more peaceful than eerie. The echo of my footsteps off the institutional tan walls is a drum beat announcing my march out of the place. I quicken my pace as the anticipation of leaving rises, and when I turn the corner, I nearly run right into a correctional officer. She's stepping quickly too, but there's no lightness in her stride. She nods politely as we step past each other, but I can see she's upset.

I slow down, take a deep breath of the dank air, and pray silently for her. Over the last couple of weeks, I've learned that I'm stronger than before. The pain has tempered me. I still hurt, but I can bear it. I'm not afraid of it anymore. I don't think any amount of it could ever feel worse than what I've already survived. I'm less concerned about myself and more concerned about helping others who are suffering. Sometimes the only thing I can think to do is pray for them.

The corridor ends at the security station by the entrance--or now, maybe I should think of it as the exit— to the jail. I tell the correctional officer that I'm being released, and after confirming my identity and release information, he directs me to the locker room behind his desk and hands me the mesh bag with my clothes inside. He watches me change but without the skeptical interest I've become accustomed to in most of the correctional officers. I hand him the mesh bag with my jail garb, and he throws it in a laundry pile.

"You're free to go," he says indifferently, sitting down behind the desk. As I approach the door, it buzzes my release, and I push it open. The fresh air of early spring hits me in the face like a refreshing splash of water. It's sunny out, and despite the unseasonable coolness, the excited songs of birds getting a jumpstart on the season surround me. The 15-foot high chain link fence with barbed wire at the top begins to roll away, and I spot Maria's white Honda Civic across the parking lot. She's looking down and hasn't seen me yet. Who knows how long she's been waiting. I told her I could be released any time after 8:00.

I walk across an island in the parking lot, dodging the purple crocuses poking through the fresh mulch, tap gently on the windshield, and smile widely when Maria looks up. I get into the car and slide my hand around her waist. She reaches for the back of my neck and pulls me in for a kiss. "The last time I'll have to pick you up here."

We sit in silence for two long breaths, inhaling the reality of our togetherness and exhaling the separation we're leaving behind. The uncertainty that's lingered between us evaporates. I kiss her again and put my hand playfully on her inner thigh. She slaps it away, smirking mischievously.

"Calm down, sailor," she says. "Let's get you home."

As she pulls out of the parking lot, I turn on my cell

phone, and a voicemail notification pops up. I navigate to my voicemails and see his name: Harry, my lawyer. I flash back to the night of the kickball game when I got his call telling me I was going to jail.

"Mark, give me a call as soon as you can," Harry says in the message, and the uncertainty and anxiety settle right back down between Maria and me. *What now? I thought this nightmare was finally over.*

My heart is pounding, and I'm sure I'm about to find out something has gone wrong with my case and my release. Nothing good ever happens when you get a call from your defense attorney telling you to call *as soon as possible.* But what could it be? *They can't change my sentence now that I've served it, can they?*

I hit the button to call back and wait for Harry to pick up. "Hi, Mark. It's great to hear you from the outside!" he answers in his thick Irish brogue.

"Hey, Harry. What's g-goin' on?" I stammer.

"Now that you're out, I was wondering if you'd want to come work as a paralegal in my firm. I have a big death penalty case, and I could really use your help."

I catch my breath. "I'd love to. Thanks so much for thinking of me," I say, and then chuckling continue, "You just scared me half to death. I heard your voicemail, and I figured something went wrong with my release."

"Oh, man. I'm sorry. I just wanted to talk to you right away so you wouldn't be stressed about finding work. I know how hard it can be."

Harry is one of the best guys I've ever met. Being a lawyer isn't just a job to him. He cares about his clients and genuinely concerns himself with their wellbeing. I know he needs the extra help with his case, but more than that, I think he wants to make sure I land on my feet.

I hang up the phone and sigh with relief. Maria grabs my hand and intertwines her fingers with mine.

"It's okay. Everything is okay," she says soothingly.

And she's right. Everything is okay now. *My person is here.*

# CHAPTER 27

"I really needed this," I tell Maria, intertwining my fingers with hers resting on the gear shift as she drives over the Bay Bridge to the Eastern Shore of Maryland. She's driving a little fast, but I try not to let it ruin the serenity of the Chesapeake Bay views. "It's going to be so nice to just relax and be with you. Thank you."

I've been out of jail for ten days, and Maria is taking me for a weekend away at a bed and breakfast. She planned the trip while I was locked up and kept it a secret until she told me to pack a bag yesterday afternoon. She looks over to me and smiles, her long curls bouncing gently over her shoulders, then shrugs in mock modesty, proud of having surprised and pleased me.

"You're welcome," she says. "I could use a break too."

I thought that getting out of jail would make everything easier, but it's just been a different kind of hard. I've had appointments with Kara, appointments with my probation agent, and appointments for drug treatment that seem to take up all of my time. Maria has been driving me everywhere, so the appointments are taking up all of her time too.

"I know. I'm sorry it's been so much," I reply, guiltily squeezing her fingers. "Hopefully things will slow down soon. At least I don't need to go to Kara anymore after next week."

I've had two appointments with my therapist since leaving jail, and at the last one, she told me I was ready to stop meeting with her. With my sentence complete, it was time to rebuild my life on my own. We agreed to have one final appointment.

"True," Maria agrees. "But now you've got Crossroads three nights a week, so that doesn't help much."

As part of the requirements of my probation, I'd returned to Crossroads to restart drug and alcohol treatment the week I got out of jail. The place had been just as I'd left it: a run-down old row home on Charles Street, the sidewalk littered with cigarette butts. The inside was as poorly lit as ever, and the walls were scuffed like they hadn't been painted in decades. The decor at Crossroads, if you can call it that, consisted of faded flyers taped to the walls, the corners drooping in, and thrift store chairs with tears in the upholstery. I wondered how anyone was supposed to get better in a dump like that. And I couldn't imagine how depressing it must be for the staff to have to go to work there either.

I'd checked in with the receptionist and walked over to the cart that sat in the corner with the coffee urn and styrofoam cups. After pouring myself a cup, I sat on the stained sofa and waited.

As I reached the bottom of the cup of coffee, the same guy who did my intake assessment last time, a short, fat, balding white guy with a judgmental gaze and a grating tone, poked his head out of an office and waved me over, then returned to his desk without waiting for me.

"Welcome back," he said without looking up as I took the shabby chair across the desk from him.

"Thanks. The program has been really helpful," I lied.

"I'm hoping to continue from where I left off since it was going so well before my sentencing."

The staff at Crossroads had known I might go to jail, and I'd told them about my sentencing hearing at my last appointment. It had been three months since I last attended, but since I'd never missed an appointment and met all the requirements of the program before I was locked up, I'd hoped they'd let me start back up where I left off. If they did, I'd be done in just a few months.

"I'm afraid that won't be possible," he replied. "You've missed over two months of appointments, and procedure requires us to do a new assessment."

Before I could protest, he started peppering me with the same litany of questions he'd asked me last time, as if we'd never spoken before.

"How much do you drink?"

"I haven't in the last five months."

"Any family problems?" None. The crash has ironically drawn my family closer together.

"Have you ever tried to quit?" I did quit, and it was easy.

"How many times have you been to jail because of a crime related to substance use?"

"I guess technically twice since I was in for one night before I was arraigned and then for two months after I was sentenced, for the same offense." I assumed he wouldn't count that as two separate times since they were both part of the same case, but I also didn't want to call it one and be seen as dishonest.

"And how many times have you been in treatment?"

"Does this still count as the first time, or is this the second?" I figured I'd let him decide.

I went back out to the waiting area while the counselor reviewed the assessment. He called me back into his office a while later.

"Given everything that's changed over the last two months," he began, "we're going to take you out of the OP program and put you in relapse prevention."

He meant they were taking me out of the once-a-week program I'd been halfway finished with and making me start over in a six-month, three-times-a-week program. I was appalled. I'd followed all their rules. I hadn't had a drink since I got arrested, and it hadn't been hard to stop because *I never had a problem with alcohol or drugs.* I didn't need more of their crap treatment. What I needed was time to find a job and rebuild my life.

"This is bullshit," I'd thought. But I knew I had to be nice to the counselor who had so much control over my life, so I didn't say it out loud. The look on my face must have given me away, though.

"You didn't comply with your last round of treatment, Mark. You left partway through, and we haven't seen you in months," the counselor explained. "Failing at treatment boosts your score on the assessment."

"But you already knew I was probably going to jail when I started here in the fall. I didn't 'stop coming.' I came back as soon as I was allowed to."

"Well, that's the other thing. Now you've been to jail

twice for substance-related crimes. That also bumps up your score on the assessment." So if I'd just stayed in jail between getting arrested and getting sentenced, if I hadn't made bail, then I'd have only been to jail once, and my "addiction" would be better. It didn't sound any more scientific to me than it does to you.

"But it wasn't a new crime. It was the same one you already knew about."

"We're just following the guidelines. Now that you've failed in one treatment program and been to jail twice, the assessment says your addiction is more severe."

"But literally nothing has changed except I haven't used any drugs or alcohol in five months," I protested.

"Because you were locked up."

"So jail counts against me for staying clean, but doesn't count for me not coming to treatment?" I asked angrily.

"The assessment says the severity of your addiction has changed, and I'm starting to wonder if it isn't related to your anger," he said, raising his eyebrow and pressing his lips together judgmentally.

I gritted my teeth and breathed in heavily through my nose. There was no point in getting upset. My jail sentenced had been short, and I knew I deserved whatever other punishment probation threw at me.

"I'm sorry," I told him. "I didn't mean to get upset. When do I need to start?"

Before my sentencing, I'd chosen Crossroads because it wasn't far from the house I was renting. Walking to the treatment center would only take an hour each way. It wouldn't be fair to Maria to expect her to drive me to three appointments a week. None of it was fair to Maria. But I could get to Crossroads without relying on her.

"Don't worry about Crossroads," I tell her. "I'll walk. I'm so grateful that you're getting me back and forth to probation."

"We're here!" Maria exclaims as she turns into the driveway of an old gray colonial backing up to the Chesapeake. The sign out front says "The Old Gratitude House," and I feel grateful just taking in the view.

The pleasantly subtle scent of lavender greets us as we enter, and the innkeeper, a graying but lively woman, checks us in.

"How long have you been married?" she asks.

"We're not," Maria offers, and I wonder if it scandalizes the innkeeper to have an unmarried couple sleeping together in her home. Some people are old-fashioned that way.

"Maybe someday," Maria continues, glancing up at me.

"Just a beautiful couple in love then," the innkeeper beams, recovering.

She leads us to the stairs, and we follow her to the Oriental Room on the top floor. The room has a pitched roof with skylights across one side, a queen bed with a heavy maroon comforter, a large decorative Japanese fan on the wall, and an oriental rug. In the corner is a massive bathtub surrounded by candles, plush towels, and two robes.

"Enjoy!" the innkeeper says as she leaves, closing the door behind her.

I walk to the bedside table to pick up a book of matches

with the logo of a local bar printed on the outside and, shrugging, gesture to the bathtub.

"I'm one step ahead of you," Maria says, reaching to turn on the water. I light the candles surrounding the tub, and we slide into the luxuriously warm bath. Maria lays back against my chest, and I kiss her neck as she sighs contentedly.

❖

The next morning, we put on the plush bathrobes and walk out to the private deck overlooking the water. After a couple cups of coffee, we meander downstairs for a big breakfast with fresh-squeezed orange juice and the most perfectly crisp bacon you've ever tasted. Maria and I grin at each other across the table, thrilled to be doing a normal couple thing without a piece of plexiglass between us or the possibility of years in prison to separate us.

We hop on two of the bikes outside and pedal off to explore the town. Everything in Rock Hall revolves around the water. We pedal around all the piers and find a wildlife observation deck to watch the birds fly. It's so nice to slow down in nature and be in the sun together.

We ride through a marina and stop to pose for photos with all the dry-docked boats we like, dreaming of owning one someday and learning to sail, then walk along the beach and write our names in the sand, mine in print, hers in script. We spot a home designed to look like a lighthouse with a huge porch wrapping around most of the second floor. We stop and take pictures of that too.

"I've always wanted a house with a big wooden porch like that," Maria tells me meaningfully. "What kind of houses do you want to have?"

"Big porches are nice," I agree, uncomfortable discussing the future and eager to change the subject. "I need to get through all this probation nonsense before I start thinking about that though."

"Has your probation agent figured it out?" she asks, and I know she's referring to the community-service debacle.

The morning after I got out of jail, Maria drove me to meet the probation agent who would be in charge of my life. He had a friendly but firm voice and a warm African accent. He was tall and broad shouldered, and he wore a well-tailored suit with a gold tie and pocket square.

"This guy is put together," I thought.

"You'll report to me once a week for at least the first month," he explained. "If it's going well after a few months, we can switch to once a month."

I had no doubt it would go well. This was my second chance, and I thought it might be my last chance. There was no way I was going to mess things up again.

"You need to leave here and immediately report to the court's community service program," he explained. Even though I was on probation in Baltimore City, where I lived, the community service would be monitored in Anne Arundel County, the county where my crime occurred. "It's back at the Ordnance Road Detention Center."

I left the probation office, and Maria drove me to register for community service. Instead of entering the jail through the metal gate that led to the jail cells, I walked in through the front door.

"Can I help you?" The stern older woman behind the reception desk asked.

"I'm here to report for the community service program," I replied.

"Name?"

"Mark O'Brien."

"Hold on."

She picked up the phone and turned her back to me. A few minutes later, another stern-looking older woman stepped behind the desk.

"Mr. O'Brien?"

I nodded in confirmation.

"I understand you think you're here for the community service program. I looked up your record, and you can't participate in the program because your felony is a violent crime."

"But Judge Hackner required it in my sentence. I have to do it," I implored.

"That may be, but the law says we cannot have you in the program because you're a violent criminal," she said.

"Probation told me I had to report to you and enroll in the program, or they'd send me back to jail."

"You need to tell them you're not eligible," she said, clearly bored with the conversation.

"Can you tell them or give me a note or something? I

don't think they'll listen to me."

"No, you're not in my program, so giving you a note is not my job," she explained dismissively. "Judge Hecker needs to figure this out."

"So you're saying that even though the judge sentenced me to participate in this program, I can't? And I need to explain the requirements of the program to the judge who sentenced me to it?" I asked.

"No. I'm saying you can't be in this program, and it's not my job to clarify your sentence for you."

I got back in the car and told Maria what happened.

"That's crazy," she said. "That makes no sense."

On the ride home, I called my probation officer from Maria's car and told him that I couldn't be in the community service program because of my conviction.

"You're required to participate in it," he said. "It's a condition of your probation to participate in it."

"I understand. That's why I went to sign up for it right after our meeting like you said, so I could enroll and get started right away. I'm trying to do what I'm supposed to, but they won't let me because I'm a violent felon."

"But it's part of your sentence. If you don't do it, you'll be in violation of probation and go back to jail for the full five years of your sentence."

"I don't know what to do. What should I do?" I'd thought my legal education would help me navigate probation, and I was already struggling on the first day. I couldn't imagine how hard it would be for someone who didn't have a background like mine.

"I'll look into it," my probation agent said, hanging up the phone before I could thank him.

At our second meeting, I asked him what I should do about the community service program, but it seemed like he had forgotten to find out.

"I reminded him about it," I tell Maria. "But I'm not sure he's doing anything to fix it."

After returning to Old Gratitude House, putting the bikes away, and curling up warmly in the bed for an afternoon nap, Maria and I push two kayaks off the shore and into the Chesapeake Bay. A blue heron flies across the sky, and we gaze up at its majestic wingspan silhouetted against the soon-to-be-setting sun. The water laps gently against the sides of our kayaks as we paddle smoothly into a shallow cove. It's early spring, so the water is still chilly, and I shiver briefly when a nearby fish splashes me in its surprise at our approach.

The water always makes me think of Laura. The Magothy River, the Chesapeake Bay, and the ocean were so central to our love. Her family and I spread her ashes last year in a river that empties into the bay, and I believe that her essence is physically present in these waters too. We'd be planning a wedding now if she were still alive. Getting married, planning a life that is half yours and half someone else's, is an act of optimism. "Til death do us part" is an endurance athlete.

Maria slides her kayak alongside mine. Both our paddles rest across the two boats, and they begin to rotate together, like two dancers gliding across a gleaming glass floor. The golden-hour sunlight shimmers off the water and through her hair, making it glow like a yellow halo.

I still haven't told Laura's family about Maria. I visited them over the weekend, right after I got out of jail. David visited me every week while I was locked up, and Laura's sister and mom came a few times too. It was so nice to see them at their home instead of in the visitation room, and everyone was in a celebratory mood. I'd borrowed Maria's car to get there, which felt like an extra betrayal.

Even though I'm still scared to tell Laura's family about Maria, I'm no longer ashamed of loving her. My feelings for Maria don't diminish what I had with Laura. We can love with all our hearts, and still have space for more. Our capacity for love grows with the objects of our affection. And right now, my heart is enormous. I love them both, deeply and differently. And still, I can't help but wonder: Will I ever be optimistic enough again to want to make *my* future into *our* future?

# CHAPTER 28

"I don't understand," Maria says. "He'd rather die than have people know he has a learning disability?"

Harry's big case is a capital murder and conspiracy case involving drug trafficking in Baltimore City. There are multiple defendants with multiple attorneys, and the defendants are accused of multiple murders, including the murder of a witness. The state's case is strong, and it appears close to certain that the defendants will all be convicted.

Earlier today, I went to visit Harry's client, Danny, in a Baltimore supermax facility that holds about 500 inmates considered to be among the state's most dangerous, whether they're awaiting trial or already sentenced to death row. They probably wouldn't normally let a felon on probation inside, but since I was there on behalf of Danny's lawyer, they didn't even ask about my background. I walked through security and into the wing where he was being held. The sound of metal on metal as the heavy door clattered closed behind me reminded me of the sounds from my jail, and a shock of apprehension straightened my spine. One look around, and I knew the place was very different from the jail I had done my time in. It was older, darker, and more imposing. It wasn't a place for people to rehabilitate and reflect. It was a place for them to rot and die.

The correctional officer opened the door to a small cell, no more than four feet by five. Danny, a thoughtful looking middle-aged man in glasses, sat at a small desk, waiting for me. After greeting him, I handed him some paperwork for review. Handcuffed and chained to the table, he struggled to flip through the pages, and I turned around and banged on the door until the correctional officer returned.

"Can you uncuff him? We're trying to work." I hollered through the door.

"Not allowed."

I was secretly relieved. The truth was, this man scared me. The things he was accused of having done and that witnesses claimed to have seen him do made me believe he was capable of extreme violence for any reason or no reason at all. At the same time, I wanted him to know I was on his side and willing to fight for him. I wanted him to feel trusted and cared for. I wanted him to know that he still mattered.

"How are we supposed to work with you tied up like that? This is bullshit," I said to him after the correctional officer walked away, wondering if he could tell I was scared.

We talked for about an hour. My job was to find out as much as possible about his childhood, the traumas he was exposed to, and other challenging circumstances he may have confronted. If he gets convicted, which seems likely, we need to show that he deserves mercy so his life might be spared.

He was very sharp, and he had a lot of ideas for his case. He didn't want us to highlight the extreme trauma of his youth. He hated that to save his life, we might need the jury to know how broken he was and how the circumstances of his childhood contributed to the psychology that made him capable of the ruthless, violent behavior he was accused of. He was too proud to have the abuse and indifference to which he was subjected aired publicly. He said he'd rather take his chances with death row than have people laugh at him for his struggles with reading.

I can't tell Maria much about the case because it's privileged, but that last part really stuck with me.

"I mean, I kind of get it," I tell Maria, my head in her lap as she strokes my hair on the couch in her living room. "The whole criminal justice process is so degrading, and having all your problems trotted out in public is so humiliating, like being strip-searched in front of an audience."

"He's lucky to have someone who understands what that feels like working on his case, but I don't know how you do it," she says. "He must have done something pretty bad if they're going for the death penalty. What's his name?"

"I can't tell you, but if he did what they say he did, he's going to be punished enough," I reply.

"Okay, Mr. Fancy Lawyer," Maria laughs. Being on probation makes me ineligible to apply for bar membership for at least the next five years, so even though she means it playfully, the reminder of my lost career stings. The meaningful silence tells me she knows it was a slip.

"The state shouldn't be in the killing business though, and if he's dead, there's no shot at redemption," I say, breaking the awkward moment. "People can, and do, change."

"I guess. But it would creep me out anyway."

"The creepy thing was being in the facility," I say with a shiver. "Hearing the metal door close behind me made the hair on my arm stand up, like my skin cells rejected their prison cells, and even though it was way different from my jail, my blood knew it was in the same category."

Maria purses her lips ruefully, stands up, and pulls me up off the couch.

"Okay. It's time for ice cream," she says, sweeping me out the door.

❖

"O'Brien!" my probation agent yells into the waiting area where I've been sitting for the last hour waiting for our meeting. We're only meeting once a month now. After I showed up for my first eight appointments on time, and he knew I was working for Harry and regularly attending treatment at Crossroads, he decided I was the least of his worries and more of a pain in the ass than I was worth.

"Any word about the community service?" I ask him for what seems like the hundredth time.

"Still working on it," he replies, biting into a sandwich, and I assume he means that he hasn't done anything to find out how I can comply with the judge's order requiring me to participate in the community service program the law says I'm not allowed to be in.

"How's everything else going?" he asks after finishing chewing.

"Everything is good," I say, nervous about the next part. "But there is another thing I could use your help with."

"Mmm hmmm," he says with suspicion, glancing up from the file sitting next to his lunch. "What is it?"

"I don't think I can afford to keep going to Crossroads," I say, telling only half the truth.

I'd been back at Crossroads for a few months, and I hadn't missed a session yet. I'd consistently been the first one to arrive, pay my copay, and sit in the waiting area until the AA group started in the basement.

The AA part continued to be a complete waste of time. Half the people didn't want to be there, and the older AA veterans who relied on meetings seemed to be there out of a sense of charity to recruit new struggling alcoholics into their program. It was admirable, but it was also annoying. My rock bottom was the night Laura died, and while alcohol was involved, I wasn't an alcoholic, and the thrice-weekly assembly of sorrows would not be what saved me.

Speaking in the meetings was supposed to be voluntary, but they'd call on me to tell the story of losing Laura over and over. I guess it was because I didn't have all the "I'm Mark, and I'm an alcoholic" stories that they did. But the one story I did have was good for scaring all the new people who were there against their will. It still hurt, and it was none of their business. But I guess they figured, what's a little more trauma for one guy if we can help this whole room of people remember how dangerous drinking can be? At the end, they'd always say, "keep coming back," as if I had a choice.

My job with Harry was only part-time, and I was making $20 an hour with $100,000 in student loan debt hanging over my head. I'd started waiting tables at the seafood restaurant again to make ends meet. The money was fine, but the $10 copay three times a week was eating into my limited disposable income. Even though it was an emotional and financial burden, I knew I had to stick it out at Crossroads so I could meet the requirements of probation. At least, that's what I thought until the other night.

The grandfatherly counselor who usually leads our group therapy sessions after AA had the night off, and we had a different counselor for the session. He was younger and friendlier than the regular guy, and he didn't put me on the spot, which I appreciated. I just wanted to attend the garbage sessions for the minimum amount of time required, pass the drug tests they gave me every week, and move on with my life. No participation, no extra credit, just the basic package, please.

He introduced himself to me at the end of the session since he forgot to ask any of our names at the beginning. It's weird to think that someone could be in charge of helping a group of people change their lives without actually even knowing who they are. But hey, these are the experts.

"I'm Mark. It's nice to meet you."

He chuckled. "Oh, you're the guy with the insurance who never misses a copay. Putting you in the three-night program was genius. It's really helping us stay afloat."

He said it half jokingly, but it had the ring of truth to it. I had no money, and these guys were scamming me. I walked out fuming and kicked the door open so hard it slammed into the wall. "Keep coming back, my ass," I thought.

"Is there any other option?" I asked my probation agent, keeping the whole story to myself.

He stops munching on his sandwich long enough to tell me he can get me into a publicly-funded program that won't cost me anything, but I'll have to go back to meeting with him every week and start taking drug tests at the probation office in addition to the ones they'll make me take at treatment.

The more frequent meetings and additional drug tests are clearly meant to be punishment for asking for help and making him do his job. But being in jail and dealing with the probation system have taught me to be more patient. I spend so much time sitting in waiting rooms, hours upon hours some weeks. So, what's one more meeting per week? I'll sit out there in the waiting room, wasting time I could be using for something of value, something that would actually help me move forward. I'll pee in their cups. It's no different from peeing in the cups at Crossroads. Bring it on.

"That works for me," I say jovially. "I hope you have a great week, and I'll see you next Tuesday."

*Asshole.*

❖

The addiction treatment center my probation agent sent me to is disgusting. The moment I walked in for my assessment, I began to question my decision. Maria is more risk averse than I am, and she warned me that quitting Crossroads might not have been the best idea. "Was this another huge mistake?" I wondered when I arrived.

The dilapidated entryway to the center was crowded. The building, a mess of chipping lead paint and asbestos tiles exposed through holes in the worn carpet, looked like it should have been condemned years ago. Tiny offices surrounded what, in a nicer place, might have been called the lobby. Each office was crowded with multiple counselors conducting "confidential" assessments and counseling sessions. One group of clients was taking a break, and there was hardly any room to move among them.

Since I "failed" at Crossroads by going to jail and then "failed" again because I found out the program was a scam, and since I was sent to the new place as part of probation, the assessment said I needed an even higher level of care than I was getting at Crossroads—an intensive outpatient program—which meant I'd be attending meetings for three hours a day, four days a week. I hadn't had a drink or used any drugs for almost a year, but to these supposed healthcare providers, my addiction just kept getting worse. I was politely enraged when my new case manager told me, but he promised to move me to a once-a-week program if I passed all my drug tests and didn't miss an appointment for five weeks.

"You said you're only working part-time for that lawyer, and your restaurant hours are at night," he said. "Coming here four mornings a week might feel like a pain, but it won't be impossible. You can do this." I'd given up and agreed to the deal—five weeks and I'd be out of here.

The next morning, I was surprised by the number of people in the group therapy sessions—about a hundred people in a stuffy room with fifteen rows of five chairs each and additional seats shoved against the walls. The counselor leading the session looked at me like he hated me for taking up space in this free program for people with actual drug problems. I was too broke to keep paying for the Crossroads scam, but I didn't look as far down on my luck as the others in the group. And no matter how far I'd fallen, I'd started life with advantages most of them could only dream of. I kind of understood why he didn't like me.

"Trust me, buddy," I thought. "We both agree I don't belong here."

Since that first angry glare, the group leader hasn't called on me to confess my sins for the benefit of the group, which has been a nice change from Crossroads. In fact, he hasn't paid much attention to me at all, so I've gotten to coast anonymously, and as long as I continue to pass all my drug tests and attend every appointment for just two more weeks, my case manager will keep his promise and put me in a once-a-week program.

This morning, I'm sitting off to the side of the room, daydreaming and nodding along to the discussion in feigned attentiveness, when I notice the unusual silence in the room and  refocus on my surroundings. Everyone is staring at me, including the group leader.

"Welcome back, sir," the group leader says mockingly. "Remind me of your name."

"It's Mark."

"That's stupid. I'm going to call you Whitey."

I'm one of three white people in the group and often the only white guy at the Baltimore probation office on Preston Street, but I'm still not used to being singled out for my race. I know it happens to other people, but white guys in America just don't experience this, and I'm so uncomfortable with it when it happens.

After telling me my name is stupid, he makes me walk to the front of the room full of strangers and explain why I'm in the group. "How did a rich white boy like you wind up here?"

I bet he knows why I'm here but enjoys the prospect of dragging me back through the trauma. He'll probably start making me do it every week for his own entertainment, making me an example of what can happen to even "rich white boys" who screw up.

"A little over a year ago, my girlfriend planned a birthday party for me over in Canton." One sentence in, and I feel my body shrinking into itself, my soul sliding back into the dark hole I thought I'd dug myself out of.

❖

I walk into the brick row home Harry's law practice is in and ascend the aged wooden staircase to his top-floor office. I wave hello to Harry, who is talking animatedly about a case with what sounds like one of his friends from the defense bar on the other end.

"Top of the mornin'," he says to me, embellishing his Irish brogue, as he hangs up the phone.

"Hey, Harry," I reply with a grin. "Did you have a good weekend?"

I've been working with Harry in the afternoons for five months now. Having a part-time job has been good, especially since I've had to continue getting abused in the four-days-a-week intensive outpatient program. Instead of keeping his promise to move me to the once-a-week program, my case manager said the group leader told him I wasn't ready. That's the same group leader who's been calling me Whitey and trying to make me cry in front of the group. At least I've stopped giving him the satisfaction of reacting to how he hurts me.

"Whitey, please come up and tell everyone why you're here," he says during our group sessions. There's been a lot of turnover in the group, so each time there are a few new audience members.

"Hey guys, Whitey here. As a lot of you already know, I got in a car crash, and probation is making me do this bullshit, just like the rest of you. I don't believe in it either." That type of response has elicited a lot of nodding in agreement.

Harry and I got the verdict in Danny's case a month ago. The jury found him and all his co-defendants guilty. Then last week, the jury sentenced Danny to life in prison instead of giving him the death penalty. It was a small victory, but being a part of saving his life after being responsible for Laura's death felt meaningful and even noble. There was little doubt Danny had done some very bad things, but I believed his life still had value, and it was good that it would be spared because of the work we did.

"We had a pretty good weekend," Harry replies, referring to himself and his wife. "Listen, there's something I need to talk to you about. It's not urgent, but with Danny's case winding down, things are going to be a little slower around here. I don't think I'm going to have enough work to keep us both as busy as we've been. It might be time to start looking for something more permanent."

# CHAPTER 29

"Hello, this is Mark O'Brien," I answer the phone in my serious professional chameleon voice, the one I use now anytime I get a call from an unknown number. It's a sunny late-summer afternoon, and I'm walking to the bank on 37th Street to deposit some of the tips I've earned at the restaurant.

It hadn't come as a surprise when Harry told me it was time to look for other work. His wife was pregnant with twins, and with Danny's case winding down, I'd known my time was winding down too. I'd already been thinking about what I wanted to do next.

My experiences in jail and working with Harry made me want to help people in the criminal justice system. Probation meant that becoming a defense attorney was out of the question, but maybe I could help people get a second chance and rebuild in other ways. I was a little worried about losing my income, but I was also inspired by the opportunity to find a higher purpose. I took on more hours at the restaurant and figured that as long as I had *a job*, I could keep searching for *the job* that would make meaning out of the painful ordeal of the last year and a half.

But after a month of searching with no success—not even a call back—the urgency to get a steady paycheck began to outweigh my desire for a meaningful career. I began applying for every job I could find, even if it had no relationship to my skills and interests: retail manager, sales, administrative assistant. You name it. I desperately needed a way to pay the rent and something to do besides wait tables, but the economy had been in the tank for a year, and even people without felony convictions were having trouble finding. Nobody had called me in months.

"Hi, Mark. This is Jane. I'm calling about your job application for our Jericho program," the woman on the other end of the phone says.

I'd applied for the job at Jericho two months before after pulling myself out of a particularly gloomy mood. I'd been sitting in the basement of my house at the white Ikea table I converted into a desk, half-heartedly sending out cover letters and resumes, when a shadow descended over me.

I couldn't stop comparing myself to my friends who didn't have felony records and who started working when the economy was still growing. They were getting promotions, moving ahead in their careers, and buying their first houses, while I had nothing. Law school was supposed to put me on a fast track to success, but all it had fast tracked was an enormous debt and a degree I couldn't use. I didn't think I'd ever catch up, and I wondered how long Maria would stick with an unemployed and unemployable loser. I knew she loved me, but she also had expectations about her life, and I doubted she planned to support me forever. I didn't want her to have to. On top of my employment woes, addiction treatment was going horribly, and I still didn't know how to complete the community service requirements for probation.

The optimism I'd felt over the last several months vanished, and the stress forced me to recognize, yet again, that I didn't deserve the life or the career I wanted. I'd been fooling myself thinking I deserved anything but misery. Why should a door open for me? I was the kind of person who drank and drove and put lives in danger. I was the kind of guy who killed his girlfriend. I leaned back in my chair, closed my eyes, and ran my hand neurotically through my hair. And there it was again: the gun floating in the air.

*Click. Bang. Oblivion.*

"No," I'd said out loud with firm resolve. "I am not going back there."

Nothing that was happening would ever be as difficult as what I'd already been through. The challenges I was confronting stood in the way of the life I wanted, but they couldn't destroy my life. I could make ends meet working at the restaurant, and no matter how long it took, I could—no, I *would*—find a meaningful job where I could use my experience to give back. And so, that day, I applied for the Jericho job where, ironically (or maybe serendipitously), I'd be helping men returning from prison find work. It felt that maybe it was meant to be, and I wanted the job so badly. But then they never called.

"Hi, Jane. How are you?" I say with a smile.

"I'm good. I was just reviewing your resume. It looks like you may be a great fit for our organization. I'd love to schedule an interview if you're still interested."

I am *very* interested, and when she reminds me of the address, I realize I'm standing directly out front of her office.

"Crazy enough, I'm walking in front of the building now,

but I'm wearing shorts and a t-shirt. If you don't mind that, I can come in now."

❖

I love my new job, and I'm so glad I didn't let the addiction treatment program keep me from taking it. A few days after my first and second interviews with Jane and her team, she called and offered me the position.

"Thanks, Jane! This is so exciting," I'd told her. "When can I start?"

I was ecstatic, but working full-time would make it impossible to continue going to addiction treatment four mornings a week. In the four months I've been in it, I haven't missed a single appointment, and I've passed every drug test, but they still haven't let me move down to a less intense program. Whitey keeps taking up a treatment spot that should be for someone who needs it even as dozens of group members with serious substance use disorders have dropped down to lower levels of care and finished treatment.

My second probation agent was much less hands-on than the first one, but she still required me to report to probation and take a drug test every Friday. I'd gotten two jobs and done everything they'd asked of me, but they were still punishing me for switching treatment programs. Still, just as I'd never missed or been late for treatment, I'd never missed or been late for a probation appointment. The problem was, while I'd attended every weekly appointment I'd had with her, the new probation agent stopped returning my calls or showing up for our meetings months ago. Every Friday, after I'd signed in and taken my drug test, the receptionist told me that my agent wasn't there.

After my job interviews, I called her to ask her how to manage the conflict my potential new job would cause with addiction treatment. She didn't answer the call, so I left her a voicemail. When she didn't call back, I called the main line at the probation office, but nobody would tell me how to reach her or how to resolve the problem I might be facing.

"You can keep trying her at the number she gave you," the receptionist said. "I can't tell you to stop attending treatment. Only she can tell you that."

After accepting the job offer from Jericho, I called her another dozen times with no response. I had to decide whether to lose the job or stop going to treatment, and I decided the job was more important. If my probation agent refused to meet with me or answer my calls, how mad could she really get if I stopped going to treatment? I wasn't even sure she would ever know, and I didn't see any other good options. I couldn't pass up the job.

The work at Jericho matters. My new colleagues are wonderful, compassionate people. Everyone cares so much about each other and the men we serve. I'm proud to have a full-time job that makes a difference. I love being a part of the group of men we serve, men like me who need a second chance.

I feel as much like a client as an employee. I sit in the classroom with the guys as they go through the two-week training leading up to their job placement. The morning sessions are always inspirational— "you made a mistake, but you have your whole life ahead of you"—and the afternoons are more practical—"if they ask about your criminal record, be honest, but then tell them about your good qualities and the positive changes you're making in your life."

Every day of work feels special, but today feels extra special. I'll be meeting Marty this morning.

Marty was one of Harry's clients and had been convicted of stabbing another man to death during an armed robbery decades before. He was a teenager when he committed the crime, but he'd been sentenced to spend the rest of his life in prison. Over more than forty years in prison, he'd grown into a loving and contrite man, a model inmate who was respected by the men incarcerated with him and the correctional officers at the prison. Even though his sentence made him ineligible to ever receive parole, after receiving letters from the correctional officers about the positive changes he'd made in prison, the parole board decided to reopen his sentence.

When Marty's parole was approved, Harry called to ask if I could get him into the Jericho program. Jericho's work was supported by several different grants, and some of the funding excluded people with convictions for violent crimes—just like the exclusion that keeps me from completing the volunteer work that was a part of my probation. One of the grants allowed Jericho to help people with violent convictions if they lived in certain parts of the city. Marty had a grown daughter who lived in one of the eligible areas, and even though Marty had another place he was planning to live when he got out, we listed his daughter's address on his enrollment forms so he could get into the program.

Jericho's office manager calls to tell me when Marty arrives—everyone knows that I'm invested in his doing well in the program—and I walk to the front desk to greet him. I introduce myself and show Marty around the office.

"I got to help Harry with a couple things on your case," I tell him. "I'm really happy to get to meet you."

"Thanks," he says brusquely. His voice is deep, and his tone is terse. He has the eyes-wide look of a wild animal deciding whether it's fight or flight time. I can't imagine what he's feeling two days out of prison after forty years locked up.

We talk a little more about the program. I tell him what to expect.

"For the first two weeks, you'll be in the training program," I tell him. "It's really great. You'll get to meet the guys and learn some strategies for your job search.

"Hmmm," Marty grunts, nodding his head skeptically.

He seems so deep in thought like he's somewhere else. There's a sadness and bewilderment about him, like he was resigned to dying in prison and doesn't quite know what to do now that he has his life back. The last time he was free, he was sixteen, and now he's an old man.

❖

On Wednesday nights, we gather in the basement of a nearby church, and the Jericho staff serves dinner to the men and their families. Serving them brings me great satisfaction. The camaraderie and fellowship that comes with sharing a meal, with serving a meal to others, is healing and humbling. The irony of my divergent reactions to waiting tables in a fancy restaurant versus serving these men dinner is not lost on me. I felt ridiculous waiting tables after earning my law degree, but I serve these men food with grateful joy in my heart.

I borrowed Maria's car to attend the weekly dinner, and I'm driving Marty home to his house in north Baltimore, off Greenmount Avenue, where he's rebuilding his life a few blocks from where it veered so far off course forty years before.

My first impression of Marty had been that he was a kind, gentle man who was abrupt with me because he thought I was full of shit. Just another well-meaning do-gooder who had no clue what he was talking about and no idea what it was like to be him. But I was one of the only people he knew, and I'd been surprised over the last few weeks that he seemed to seek me out to talk, even though it was actually me who did most of the talking. He'd chime in with a grunt, an "uh huh," or a "yeah" every now and then so I knew he was listening, but he never made eye contact with me. He'd just stare off into the distance, chin set hard against some unseen foe.

After a while, Marty opened up a bit. He would never be talkative, but he told me about Baltimore in the '60s and '70s and the two daughters he had while in prison. I'd been curious to know how he had his children. *Did Maryland allow conjugal visits back then?* I meant official ones. Not like me and Maria in the minivan during my therapy breaks from jail. He said he had both daughters with the girlfriend he left behind after his conviction. They never married, but she visited him in prison. Early in his sentence, he'd been allowed to leave prison to visit his family as a reward for good behavior. I'd never heard of anyone besides me getting to leave jail or prison, but I didn't push for more details. When he told me, I wished Maria were with me. She would have gotten the whole story if she were with me. It was a talent of hers.

On the way to his house, Marty points out storefronts that changed while he was gone. "That used to be a hardware store . . . That one was a bar . . . I kissed my daughters' mom for the first time over behind that house."

Marty was locked up while rotary phones became cordless phones became cell phones became smartphones, and he's fascinated by them. "Did you know they can send messages with typed words?" I stifle the urge to laugh when he asks me. The world changed so much while he was away. Prison is a little like death in that way. The world moves on.

I tell Marty about Laura, about the accident.

"I'm sorry you missed so much while you were away. I think about that with Laura, how she's missing everything she would have seen in her life because of me."

"Don't be sorry about what I missed out on," he says. "The guy I killed is missing his whole life just like your girl."

Marty and I make an odd pair. He's a six-foot-seven, sixty-year-old skinny Black man, and I'm a five-eleven, twenty-six-year-old chubby white dude. He went to prison for four decades. He was supposed to die there, and now he's facing all the challenges of being an older Black man with no education and no work history in a city with no jobs. I went to jail for two months and got to turn my crime into a new career. The family of his victim hates him. Laura's family loves me.

You might think the different outcomes are fair because our crimes were different. And you're right that our crimes were different, but you're wrong if you think the difference in our crimes makes the difference in the consequences obviously fair. He made a terrible decision, and I made a terrible decision. He was a child, his brain and ability to control his behavior still developing, but I was an adult with a fully formed mind, totally responsible for my actions. He had nothing and was trying to get money to survive the only way he knew how. I had everything and was out for a good time. It's not as simple as saying he deserved so much worse of a punishment than I did. Both our decisions ended up with somebody dead, and we're both trying to do our best with the life that we have left. I guess that's what makes Marty and me friends: We're both looking for redemption.

CRASHING I LOVE YOU. FORGIVE ME.

# CHAPTER 30

"It's absolutely crazy," I say to my roommate over the glass coffee table that separates the grubby couch he's sitting on from the grubby couch I'm sitting on. "There are thousands—literally thousands—of state and federal laws that bar people from certain kinds of jobs if they have a criminal record. How is anyone supposed to move on after *doing their time* when they're set up to fail."

Some laws bar people from certain jobs only if they have certain types of convictions, but more often than not the crimes that are covered don't have any connection to the jobs they prohibit people from holding. Some apply to people for the entire rest of their lives. One law permanently bans anyone with a drug conviction from working in the healthcare industry. They can't even serve food in a hospital. Other federal laws ban people from working in transportation, finance, insurance, and other industries. And that's before you even get to the state laws. I've learned all this in my new job at Legal Action Center.

One of my co-workers at Jericho, Daryl, was a health coach, and he'd been helping me improve my nutrition and fitness during weekly sessions at his home in Canton, the neighborhood where my birthday party was the night Laura died. One Saturday morning, we were sitting at his kitchen table, and he asked me what I liked about our work at Jericho.

"I like that we're helping. We're making a difference for the guys. And I like the training program. I get so much out of sitting in on the classes and hearing how their lives are changing."

"I know it makes you happy, but Mark, it's not the right job for you," he'd said. I hadn't been expecting that. "You spent *three years* getting a law degree. You could make a much bigger difference for a lot more people if you were using it. Just think about it."

"I have thought about it," I'd thought to myself. "But who in the world would hire me?"

I continued to think about what Daryl said, but I also knew from my previous job search that Jericho might be the only place that would ever hire me. I loved my job at Jericho, and I wasn't sure I wanted to leave. It felt safe.

But I also had no idea how to do the job well. Helping men find work after prison was not what I'd been trained to do. I was doing my best, but I didn't really know how to get employers to hire the men we served, so many of whom had very little education and very little work experience to go along with their criminal records. I was barely able to find myself a job, and I was pretty sure I wouldn't be able to find myself *another job,* even if I wanted to.

I was determined to do better for the men in the program, so I started researching strategies for getting hired with a criminal record. I took a three-day course to become an Offender Employment Specialist trained by a National Institute of Justice program to help formerly-incarcerated people find jobs. One afternoon, I was searching for information about a tax credit for employers who hire people with criminal records so I could explain the hiring incentive to managers who might consider hiring the guys at Jericho.

I found a website for the National HIRE Network. HIRE stood for Helping Individuals Reenter Through Employment. The website had great information about the tax credit and other resources for people looking for jobs after jail or prison. I learned that HIRE was a project of Legal Action Center, a nonprofit law firm with an office in DC. The firm represented clients and lobbied to change laws and policies that made it harder for people with criminal records, addictions, or HIV.

I poked around their website and saw that they were looking for someone with a background in law or public policy to promote changes in federal law to better support people coming home from prison and get rid of legal barriers that keep us out of jobs, school, housing, and programs to meet our basic needs. I was well-qualified for the role, and the job posting said that people with criminal records were *encouraged to apply*. I showed it to my boss at Jericho the next day.

"This is an incredible opportunity, Mark. You'd be great." I'd only been at Jericho for five months, but my boss believed in what Jericho did, even if that meant helping me move on to another opportunity. Daryl was excited for me too. "That's what I was talking about, Mark. That's perfect."

I applied for the job, but I didn't get my hopes up. Getting your hopes up is what you do before your world collapses. *Never, ever, ever get your hopes up.* I didn't even tell Maria about it because I was sure it wouldn't work out. I wasn't at all surprised when I didn't hear anything back, and I assumed somebody else must have gotten the position. Probably somebody without a record, despite what their job description may have said. I was used to disappointment, so I just moved on. I enjoyed my job at Jericho, so it was no big deal. I needed to learn to be content.

"Be satisfied with what you have," I told myself. "Just be grateful to be alive."

Then, two months later, someone from Legal Action Center called to ask if I was still interested in the role. After two rounds of interviews, I got the job. Marty was out of the Jericho program by then, working full-time and catching up on life. He'd stopped by for a few dinners at the church after he'd gotten a job, but I hadn't seen him in a few weeks. I was proud of him and didn't begrudge his moving on, and everyone at Jericho seemed to feel the same way toward me.

"You're gonna do great things," Daryl said.

"Just don't forget us little guys," another of my colleagues quipped.

There were hugs and high fives all around, and I knew I'd never forget any of them.

"I'm happy for you, man," my roommate says without taking his eye off the flat screen showing the game of Fifa Soccer we're playing on his PlayStation. "It seems like you really love working there."

Working at Jericho didn't feel like a job, and neither does working at Legal Action Center. Using what happened—what I did—to make a difference for others is an act of love and a small step toward redemption. I'm not convinced that any amount of good I do will ever be enough to make up for Laura's death, but I want to try.

"It definitely feels lucky to get to do this job," I tell my roommate as Maria opens the door and walks into the house. I look up just long enough for my roommate to kick one past my goalie in the video game.

"Gotcha!" he shouts, throwing his hands in the air in celebration.

"Dammit!" I shout back. And then more calmly, "Taking the train in the morning is awesome. I love walking around DC. I love the work I'm doing. It really is great."

"What are you boys up to?" Maria asks, sitting down next to me and kissing me softly.

"Getting my ass kicked in Fifa," I tell her. "And talking about LAC."

Maria had been excited for me to find a job where I could use my law degree. As my growing understanding of the legal structures in place to keep people down after an arrest or criminal conviction reinforced my own observations and beliefs about the criminal justice system, the empathy I felt for the men and women entangled in it grew too. I knew what it was like for me, and how much worse it was for so many of them who didn't have the resources I had. I was horrified by society's willingness to cast human beings aside. The more I saw of the inequities in the system, the more disgusted I became, and the more blessed I felt to get to fight against it.

Jail was unpleasant, but, in some ways, it was easier than what came after. I realize I say that having served a very short sentence. I don't mean to imply that incarceration is preferable to parole or probation, just that parole and probation are supposed to ensure that when people return to the community, they have the support and structure to make healthier decisions and become contributing members of society. Instead, from what I've seen, they're perfectly designed to demoralize people and push them back into the negative habits and unhealthy behaviors that got them into trouble in the first place.

"How are Gab and Toni?" Maria asks.

Gab, my new boss who lead's LAC's work on federal policy, exudes serenity with an easy smile and drive to soothe everyone around her. The phrase she says the most is "no stress," and she really lives by it. Even when she's having a lousy day, she never lets it affect the way she treats others. Toni, her counterpart working on state-level criminal justice policy, is a no-nonsense fighter with a heart of gold. Over the last few months, Gab and Toni have been training me to do my job and challenging me to grow and learn. Everyone at Legal Action Center is so smart, and I've wanted to catch up as quickly as I can.

"They're good," I reply to Maria. "I was reading today that the American Bar Association catalogued all the laws against people with arrests and convictions, and they found over forty-five thousand. *Forty-five thousand.* I didn't even know there *were* that many laws." Sentencing is supposed to reflect the severity of the crime, but it seems like every crime in America carries a life sentence.

"Here we go again," Maria says sarcastically, elbowing me playfully in the ribs. She's heard a few of these speeches before.

"I still can't believe you were in Reid's office an hour after being at probation. That's badass, man," my roommate chuckles. "Your life is kind of like a movie."

The other day I went from the probation office to a meeting in the Senate Majority Leader's office. I always wear casual clothes to probation. You don't want to be the guy in a suit there. The train station is just a a half mile away, and if I have meetings at work, I change into a suit in the train station bathroom. Spending the morning at the Baltimore probation office and then the afternoon in the Capitol fills my days with the strangest contrasts. One minute I'm peeing in a cup with a person staring suspiciously over my shoulder, making sure it's actually my own pee going into the cup. The next, I'm in a congressman's office talking about how to reform the dysfunctional system that supervises me. In the morning, the system is trying to fix me. And in the afternoon, I'm trying to fix it.

"Life is strange," I laugh. "I don't think anyone in D.C. could picture me at probation, and I don't think anyone at probation could picture me in Congress."

Being on probation is like having another part-time job even though I haven't seen my probation agent in almost a year. I still show up for my appointment every Friday to sign in and take my drug test. Then I wait an hour for my probation agent before asking the receptionist whether she's available to meet with me. The receptionist won't answer me—she won't even acknowledge me anymore—if I haven't waited at least an hour after signing in, even though I know the answer will be the same each week: "She isn't in today." Gab and Toni never make me feel bad about the amount of time probation takes up. I'm acutely aware of how fortunate I am in this regard. Most bosses wouldn't be so understanding. Most businesses wouldn't be so accommodating.

"I'm going to take Rocko for a walk," Maria says, putting her hand on my knee to push herself up from the couch. "Don't beat him too badly," she says to my roommate.

Rocko's ears perk up at the sound of his name, and he lifts an eyebrow to look up at Maria from the dusty wood floor by my feet. He jumps up, tail wagging to follow her to the door.

"How are things going with her other than that?" my roommate asks after the door closes behind Maria and Rocko. "Has she brought up the lease again?"

Maria has been living downtown with her friends, and their lease is about to end. She's hinted a few times that she'd like for us to move in together, but I've told her I'm not ready for that. We've been seeing each other for over two years, but our relationship hasn't progressed much since I got home from jail. We spend almost every day together, but moving in together seems like a big step into the type of entanglement that would mean I'd be destroyed all over again if I lost Maria like I lost Laura.

Even without the crash, Maria and I would probably have different expectations about our relationship. Our social circles are very different. I went to a state university, and she went to a private Catholic college. Her circle of friends is both more affluent and more traditional than mine. Many of them are getting married and starting families at twenty-seven with their high school sweethearts or college boyfriends. Maria's photography business thrives on shooting weddings of girls she went to school with. None of my friends are even close to settling down. Laura and I would have been the first couple in our crew to get married. I'd be comfortable dating for several more years before thinking about marriage; Maria thinks about it for a living.

"She hasn't brought it up in a while. I think she gets it. I'm just not there."

"Do you think you will be?"

"I don't know," I shrug. "I love her. But I'm just starting to get my bearings, and I don't want to mess with that." I flick the controller, and the player on the screen kicks the soccer ball to the far corner of the goal, where another player is waiting to head it in for the score.

"Nice shot," my roommate says.

"Tie game."

"I get what you're saying," he says to me. "I wouldn't rush anything if I were you. You've got nothing but time."

I'm not sure that's true. The crash taught me that death is random. We might not have as much time as we think. But even if we don't have time, I know it's not the right time for any major changes now. I'm just getting comfortable.

# CHAPTER 31

"You're not pregnant," I told Maria on the phone last night. "You take birth control."

"But I'm never late, and I just have this feeling," she said.

"I guess take a pregnancy test?" I muttered.

"I'll wait until the morning if my period hasn't started by then."

"It's a false alarm," I'd thought as I ended the call.

Maria and I both want to have kids someday. I love children, and I love Maria. I know she would make a wonderful mom. I think I'd make a pretty good dad too. It would be nice to start a family. Just not yet.

"And that's not what's happening now. She's just late," I thought last night, pushing it out of my mind for the rest of the evening.

But as she creeps through the front door, the crumpled brown leaves of late fall trailing in behind her, and flops down on the couch next to me, I'm not so sure. She looks like she's been crying and puts her head on my shoulder. I look into her blue eyes and the red circles that surround them.

She takes a deep breath. I already know what she's here to tell me, but she can't find the words or doesn't want to say them out loud. This is not her plan. People in her social circle don't get pregnant before they get married. And they definitely don't get pregnant with a guy who isn't even ready to move in together, a felon on probation who's barely starting to put his life back together. She's upset because being pregnant before she's married is embarrassing for her.

"I'm pregnant."

Even though it wasn't the plan, I'm not at all fazed by the news. There's a big difference between an accident and a surprise. Accidents are unexpected, and the outcome can be painful and costly. Sometimes people die because of accidents. Surprises are unexpected too but in the most beautiful way. Sometimes people are born because of surprises. A child is good news. A reason to celebrate.

"Don't worry. I have great health insurance. This is going to be fine." I smile and put my arms around her shoulders to pull her closer, her arms hanging at her sides. I kiss her on the forehead and squeeze a little more.

She pulls back again so she can see me better and searches my face for *something*.

"You *want* to have a baby with me?" she asks, her gaze traveling from one of my eyes to the other and then back.

*That's* why she's upset. She's not worried about her reputation. She's worried I'm going to reject her and reject the family we could have together. It hasn't occurred to me until she asked that this is still optional. My religion says that there is no choice but to have the baby, but our culture says there is. And now I think of all the ways having a baby will change my life. The tension between wanting this baby and not wanting my life to change is palpable.

"I know this is your decision, and I respect that. I won't try to make up your mind for you," I tell her. "But I think we'd make good parents. There's no reason we couldn't do this."

It's a cop out. I'm glad to make the decision all hers. If she decides it's not the right time to have a child, the responsibility is on her. My life stays exactly how I like it, and I don't ever have to agonize over a hard decision. Her right to choose is my right to abstain from choosing. We sit in silence for a few minutes before she speaks.

"You're right. There's no reason we can't do this," she says. "We have good jobs. We love each other. Let's do this."

"We're going to be a great family."

"But I don't want you thinking we have to get married or something because of this," Maria clarifies. "If we get married someday, I want it to be because we both want to."

"Don't worry. I know I can still dump you," I joke. But my parents' divorce was so painful for me that I know I won't let our child grow up without me in their life every day, whatever that looks like. I'm here to stay.

And the more I think about it, the more excited I become. *We'll be a great family.* I'm overwhelmed, actually overjoyed, with thoughts of being a parent. I want to know everything Maria is feeling and will feel over the next ten months, everything that is happening to the child she's carrying, *our* child. I feel like a giant, an incredible elation vibrating through my body. The only other time my mind has ever been so focused was right after Laura died, but that focus was on agony. Now, there is only one thought: *I'm going to be a dad.*

I want to buy something for the baby, even though I have no idea what a newborn baby needs. While Maria rests on the couch, I walk up to the top of my street and turn onto the main road, looking up and down for any store that might have baby items. It turns out there's a fancy baby store right around the corner from my house. *Who knew?*

They sell cloth diapers and not much else that I can afford. I think the diaper is a baby bathing suit, and I'm too embarrassed to ask, so I buy a neon green bathing suit, aka, a cloth diaper, the first gift for the little clump of cells that is going to be my son or daughter, my new beautiful reason to still be alive.

❖

"Do you want to tell her, or should I?" I ask Maria, who is sitting next to me in the driver's seat of her little white Honda Civic. "Do we make small talk for a bit or just say it right away? It's your mom, so you decide. How do you want to play this?"

"We can just feel it out."

"That's not a plan."

Once Maria and I settled down from the initial excitement, we decided to wait until she was eight weeks pregnant before telling anyone about the baby—apparently, that's what people do. That would have meant keeping what felt like a huge secret for four weeks. The day after we found out was Thanksgiving, and after dinner, Maria sprawled across my mom's sofa and complained of feeling sick. "Maybe you're pregnant," my mom joked. Maria and I made eye contact and raised our eyebrows at each other but kept our mouths shut.

But a week later, Maria couldn't stand not telling her mom and sisters. They're a close-knit group. She's only five weeks along, but we've just driven the half hour to visit her mom and tell her the happy news.

We walk across the driveway and toward the garage. I can't believe we are going into this without a plan of some kind. We open the door inside the garage and walk into the kitchen. The house isn't close enough to just drop by, and Maria's mom is surprised to see us. She gives us each a big hug and asks what made us come over.

"We were just in the neighborhood and thought we'd say hi," Maria replies.

"What a nice surprise."

*Just wait for the real surprise!*

Maria and her mom are talkers, and we stand in the kitchen chatting for what feels like forever. This is just the pre-talk before we sit down to talk-talk. I'm bouncing awkwardly from one foot to the other, bursting with excitement and nerves, waiting for a sign from Maria that it's time to tell.

*What was she thinking not having a plan? You should always have a plan!*

"I'm almost done knitting the blanket for your sister's baby," her mom says. Maria's sister is due in a few weeks. Maria gives me a sideways glance.

*That's her signal. She wants me to tell her mom now.*

"You better make two blankets," I say, a smile spreading uncontrollably across my face.

"Huh?"

"One for Annie's baby and one for ours." I'm beaming, but they're both looking at me like I am completely socially inept.

Her mom's eyebrows curl as she processes the unexpected news. "Wait, what?"

"I'm pregnant, Mom. I have no idea why Mark would tell you like that." Maria looks at me, turns her palms up and squints, which I read as "what were you thinking?"

*I guess I misread the signal?*

❖

"I have some news to share," I say from the passenger seat of David's truck. Laura's sister is in the backseat, and we're on the way to their house for dinner.

Telling Maria's mom about the baby was easy, even if I did botch the timing a little. But this is different. I've been so nervous about telling Laura's family. They don't even know Maria exists, which is ridiculous because everyone except for them knows about Maria, and everyone knows I haven't told them about her too. Theresa sees Laura's family all the time, but I've asked her not to tell them. It's been almost three years since Laura died.

When I first met Maria, I was afraid to tell Laura's family about her because I worried it would hurt them. I was ashamed of having a new girlfriend and worried they might think that Laura didn't matter to me as much as she did. In the beginning, I also thought the relationship with Maria wouldn't last, so it didn't matter anyway. After Maria and I were together a while,

I had a different problem: I was afraid they'd be angry that I'd been hiding it from them for so long. I continued to live a double life, spending most of my days with Maria and pretending she didn't exist whenever I was with Laura's family.

Maria's pregnancy has forced the issue. I suspect Laura's family might notice if I suddenly have a baby, and I *want* them to know Maria and our baby. I want *my* family to be a part of *their* family. I know it's absurd that I'm hiding this huge part of my life from them.

"I'm going to be a dad," I tell them, bracing for a barrage of questions, including but not limited to "who's the mom?"

When I look over at David, and then back at Laura's sister, neither of them looks surprised. "We already know, Mark. We know about the baby, and we know about Maria," David says. He gives me the same wisened look he'd given Laura when he was lecturing her about credit card debt or finishing school. He's not mad. He's just *disappointed*.

One of Laura's friends, one of my friends, who'd lived with Laura when we were dating told Laura's other sister when she bumped into her a few weeks ago. She knew I'd been keeping it a secret, but I think she was tired of the charade. Who could blame her? I'd been asking everyone who knew Laura's family to participate in the lie.

"I wish you had told us about Maria a long time ago. When did you meet her?"

I can't tell him it was literally two months after Laura died. I'm still so ashamed of it. It was too soon. I should have mourned longer. How could I even look at another girl so soon after Laura died?

"It wasn't that long after Laura died, and I was afraid it would hurt you. Then I didn't tell you for so long that I didn't know how to bring it up. I didn't know *when* to bring it up"

"You're going to be a great dad," Laura's sister, who is sixteen, announces from the back seat.

"She's right, Mark. And we're happy for you. You're a good man, and you're going to be a good dad too. When do we get to meet Maria?"

We head to their house for dinner. Laura's mom is icy at first, but she shakes it off and is as lovely and gracious as always. Nobody says it, but I'm sure they're all thinking the same thing I am— that without the crash, this is when we'd be celebrating that Laura was pregnant. I still get to be a dad, but they aren't becoming grandparents, and Laura will never get to be a mother. It's not the first time I've thought about it. I'm ecstatic that Maria and I are having a baby. But I also know it's another thing I've taken away from Laura and her family. It's another thing I planned to do with Laura, but instead, I'm doing it with Maria.

# CHAPTER 32

*"Do you remember when we went to that Red Sox game, and I got the ball?" I ask her.*

*"I remember the goofy grin on your face when you got it, like a little boy who got away with stealing a piece of chocolate while nobody was looking." Laura smirks at my immature exuberance over grasping my first major league baseball the summer before she died.*

*Her analogy to a stolen piece of cake is apt. I didn't catch the ball in the traditional way.*

*I'd never attended a professional sports event until I was fifteen years old. Military bases were remote, so for most of my childhood there hadn't been any teams close by. Plus, my family didn't have the kind of money to make a trip out of it. So the first time I saw a live professional sport was after we moved to Maryland when I was in 7th grade and attended a Red Sox game against the Orioles in Baltimore. Since I'd never had any local teams to attach to, I'd adopted all my dad's teams and loved the Red Sox since I was a child. Seeing them in person for the first time had been one of the most magical experiences of my life.*

*Ever since that day, I'd maintained a practice of showing up an hour early to every game I attended and watching batting practice from the first row of seats behind the center field wall in hopes of catching a fly ball hit by one of my Red Sox idols. I figured I had a better shot when the stadium was relatively empty than I did once the game was underway. When Laura and I started dat-*

*ing, she'd become a Red Sox fan too—she was loyal like that—and accompanied me on my missions to attempt to catch a ball before the games we attended.*

*"That guy was being such a punk," I reminisce with her now.*

*"He was just messing with you. It was funny," she laughs. 3*

*One of the Red Sox players had strolled along the outfield wall, casually tossing a ball in the air, just out of my reach and the reach of every other schmuck hoping to get their hands on a real life major league baseball. I'd managed to barely reach the ball a couple times, but it had rolled off when I tried to close the fingers of my baseball glove around it. After a few near misses, I lunged over the wall, nearly falling onto the field, and captured the ball with great satisfaction. The outfielder looked up at me and shrugged, recognizing he'd been beaten. And I held the ball up triumphantly for Laura to see.*

*"You were so happy. It was cute."*

*"I used to think you were like that ball."*

*"How so?"*

*"I wanted you so badly, but for years you seemed like something I'd never have. I had you on such a pedestal. You were magical to me. And then you were mine."*

*"You're sweet. I was just a girl."*

*"You were so much more than that. I loved you before we ever started dating."*

*"That's what my dad said."*

*"He's a smart guy."*

*We're sitting in the grass of the field at Oriole Park now. She's resting her head back on my chest, and she turns to look at me.*

*"You said you used to think I was like the ball. You don't anymore?"*

*"Now I think you're like the ones that kept slipping off the end of the glove. I could just barely reach you, possess you for a moment, but you were always going to fall away," I tell her.*

*"The ball you caught won't last forever either, my love. Nothing does. But that doesn't mean it isn't real."*

❖

My first impression of Rich, the new therapist I'm meeting for the first time, is that he's both older than my previous therapist, Kara, and more serious too. She was what I needed after Laura died, a compassionate ear to guide me through the new emotions I was feeling. He may be what I need now, someone to coach me through the last stages of my transformation from the boy I was before the accident to the man I'm trying to become and the father I need to be. Rich has a Mr. Rogers thing going on with short graying hair, a tie, and a sweater vest. But he isn't quite as soft as Mr. Rogers.

"Why don't you just start by telling me what brings you here to see me?" he asks like we didn't talk on the phone the other day. But I'm not annoyed. I'm not the broken person I was last time I started therapy either. I'm actually doing pretty well.

"Do you want the short version or the long?"

"I'll take the long version."

I give Rich the highlights and the lowlights from the last three years: Laura, the car accident, David, Maria, going to jail,

CRASHING I LOVE YOU. FORGIVE ME.

coming home, finding work I love, all the issues with probation and addiction treatment, the problem with my community service, and my absent probation agent. Since before I started my job at Jericho, more than years ago, she'd never shown up for any of our appointments. And she'd never answered any of my phone calls or attempted to communicate with me.

"'She isn't here today.' For eighty-some weeks in a row, that's all they said," I explain to Rich. "After a while, I stopped sticking around long enough to ask if she was there. I knew she wasn't. I didn't mind. I just didn't waste my time pretending she might show up. I signed in, took the drug test, and left."

The probation office still hadn't resolved the issue with the community service. I'd gotten Rocko licensed as a therapy dog, and we volunteered together at the library helping kids practice reading. I'd also arranged some speaking engagements at schools and summer camps to talk to young people about the crash and its consequences, hoping that the story would keep some of them from making the same bad decisions I made. But none of it counted toward my sentence, and nobody at the probation office would talk to me about how to complete the community service requirement.

"Then, two weeks ago, my phone rang, and when I looked down at the caller ID, it said 'Probation.' I picked up, expecting to finally talk to my probation agent," I now explain. "But when the woman on the other end spoke, I knew it wasn't her."

"This is Agent McKay," she said. "From the Maryland Department of Public Safety and Correctional Services. I'm your new probation agent."

She sounded professional, nice, like she enjoyed her job and took it seriously. I thought that while the system she worked for was dysfunctional, many people work for probation and parole to help others get back on their feet.

"Wait. So, it wasn't her?" Rich asks. "It wasn't . . ."

"No," I start to reply.

"Your probation agent. The one who never showed up to all those appointments."

"Exactly. It wasn't her. And she seemed nice."

I said hello to Agent McKay, the new agent, and she politely asked why I hadn't shown up for any probation appointments in over a year or completed the court-ordered community service.

"I told her that wasn't true. I'd shown up every Friday morning, the first or second person in line before the office even opened. And I told her I never missed any appointments. I'd taken a drug test and signed in to meet with my previous probation agent every time I was supposed to. And I told her the receptionist kept telling me the agent wasn't available to meet."

She asked who my probation agent was, and I started freaking out a little, mentally cataloging the proof, all the ways to show I'd been calling regularly and showing up to appointments: phone records, receipts, sign-in sheets . . .

"I'm thinking, 'I don't have the sign-in sheets! How could I not think to take photos of the sign-in sheets?' because I know enough about the system to understand that even though I've shown up for every appointment, I could still wind up back in jail for their oversight."

Rich nods along and writes on his yellow notepad.

"So, I tell Agent McKay my old probation agent's name, and you'll never guess what she says."

Now Rich looks up.

"She hasn't worked there for *two years*. The entire time I've been showing up to all those appointments, there hasn't been anyone even working there to meet with me. Agent McKay sounded like she was mortified that her office was so incompetent, but I was still nervous."

She asked about the community service, and I told her about helping kids practice reading at the library with Rocco—I had documentation of that—and the public speaking I'd been doing—I could probably get documentation of that.

"But, I haven't been getting any credit for the community service because of the debacle with the court's community service program," I explained to her.

"I told her that none of it has counted toward my sentence because I'm not allowed in the court-supervised community service program," I continue telling Rich. "And she asked what my other probation agents did about it, so I told her the truth: 'Nothing. It's been three years, and they haven't done anything as far as I can tell.'"

"This sounds like a mess. Why don't you come down to the office tomorrow, and we'll figure it out?" she'd said to me kindly.

"That works for me. I'll see you then." I'd said back.

"It felt promising," I tell Rich. "She didn't sound angry with me." And even though the probation office was incredibly dysfunctional, I also knew these systems sometimes give people second, third, and fourth chances before sending them back to jail. But I was still worried her call was a ruse to get me to the probation office so they could arrest me for not attending my probation appointments, quitting addiction treatment, or failing to complete my community service.

"But Agent McKay wasn't as miserable looking as everyone else who worked at the probation office. You could see from her eyes that she smiled a lot. She was super nice when she greeted me, and then I wasn't too worried. She would have had to be a real psycho to smile like that and then arrest me."

She told me she'd read my file, and she was sorry for everything I'd been through. She asked about my family, and I told her about Maria, how we met after the crash, and that we were expecting a child. I explained that I had to choose between treatment and starting a job at Jericho, and nobody from probation would answer my calls or meet with me to find a solution, how much I loved my job at LAC, and how awful and unhelpful treatment had been.

"To be honest, sitting in a group of strangers and reliving the worst night of my life over and over made me feel so much worse," I told her. "Those places are dumps, and I can't imagine they help anybody."

Before sharing my story with students and campers, I'd get anxious, and afterward, I'd feel emotionally drained. Even though it was rewarding, it usually left me feeling depressed for days. Being put on the spot in treatment groups carried all the anxiety and emotional exhaustion of talking to young people, but without the reward of knowing I might be making a difference and with the added elements of shame, exploitation, and humiliation.

"So then she says, 'Your sentence says you have to complete treatment, so what would work for you?' And my jaw just dropped," I explain to Rich. "Out of a dozen or so probation agents and drug counselors, she was the first one to ever ask me what I thought would help."

I told her I wanted to see a psychologist to work on grief and trauma, and she said that if I found a therapist who would also address substance use, that would satisfy the probation requirement.

Kara didn't do counseling for drugs and alcohol, and I was a little embarrassed to go back to her, like I was failing as a graduate of therapy, so I decided to look for someone else who specialized in grief, trauma, and addiction. If I found the right person, I could meet the requirements of probation while addressing the mental health issues that were really affecting me—anxiety, frustration, grief, internal conflict over my happiness, and fear that fate would once again sweep away everything good in my life.

"So that's when I found you on the insurance website and saw that your practice treats people for substance use."

"Really? I'm not sure why," Rich says. "I have some patients who've struggled with addiction, but it's not something I specialize in."

"That's fine with me. I don't need drug treatment. I drink every now and then, but it's never been my problem."

"We can talk about drugs if that's what probation requires, but it sounds like we should probably spend more time talking about this family you're starting. What did your new probation agent say about the community service?"

"She told me to find a therapist, and she'll figure out the community service. I'm cautiously optimistic. She seems good."

"That was a long story you shared with me, but we do have some time left. Maybe you could tell me a little more about where you are now. Mentally and emotionally."

"I thought the crash destroyed me," I say, looking over to the photos of Rich's family sitting on the dark wood bookshelf by the door to his office. "But in some ways, I think I'm a better person for having gone through it." I've struggled with crushing grief, trauma, and existential turmoil, but I've also gained a new appreciation for life, invested more in relationships than accomplishments, and found a career that is more meaningful than the tax law career I'd been planning.

"It's not all great though. I still miss Laura. I think about her every day, and if I'm honest, the work I'm doing feels meaningful because I'm trying to make up for what I did to her," I tell him. "I stopped wanting to die a couple years ago, but until recently, I wasn't afraid to die. I was kind of indifferent about it. But with the baby on the way, I'm scared. I think something bad is going to happen to me, and I won't be here to take care of my family. I'm even more terrified something will happen to Maria or our baby. Maybe it will be my fault again. Every time Maria gets home later than expected, even a few minutes, I just assume she's dead."

Maria can talk for hours, and after photographing a wedding, she often sticks around chatting with the bride or guests. She keeps her phone in her camera bag while she works, so she doesn't hear it when I call. I sit at home assuming she's dead, and so is our baby, certain she's been in a car crash on the way home. I start planning for how I'm going to cope with their deaths.

"I'm glad you've been able to rebuild your life in so many ways. Trauma is so painful and debilitating that people don't often hear about the positive sides of experiences like yours," Rich says. "It's not uncommon for people who have been through a tragedy to report profound and positive changes in their life afterward."

"But it also sounds like you're still suffering a great deal," he says. "It's natural to worry about Maria and your baby after what you've been through. Your brain has been re-wired to expect the worst."

We talk about how rare it is for people to die suddenly, and he reminds me that just because something bad happened in my past doesn't mean something bad will happen in my future. Life is random, and anything can happen by chance, but the vast majority of people live longer, healthier lives than ever before.

"There are no guarantees, Mark. But you can't live in fear. You don't want your child to grow up with a father who is constantly scared and full of anxiety. Is that the life you want to give your family?"

"I'm not sure it's something I can turn off."

# CHAPTER 33

"Why are you driving in the right lane?" Maria yells.

"Please don't mess up my car!" Tom yells back.

The Fourth of July fireworks were last night, so even though we were three weeks away from our due date, and even though it was ninety degrees outside, we spent the day at Maria's annual family gathering on the shore of Middle River in Baltimore County.

Maria was uncomfortably pregnant, and we set up a place for her to sit in the shade of one of the big maples out back. Maria's six-month-old niece, born on New Year's Eve, played in a bouncer beneath the tree as Maria and her sister chitchatted about the sensations of pregnancy and birth. Maria said her belly felt tight, and her sister, a mom of three, told her it was her muscles strengthening for when she delivered the baby in a few weeks.

As day turned to twilight, Middle River filled with boats, their passengers clamoring for space to watch the fireworks. The show was spectacular, and afterward we headed to a nearby bar where Maria's brother-in-law was performing with his Nineties cover band. We sang and danced until Maria was exhausted enough to agree to leave. She hates to miss a party.

A few hours after getting home from the bar and going to sleep, Maria woke me up excitedly, her hand holding her belly.

"It's time," she said.

"Are you sure?" I asked, squinting to keep from meeting

the full strength of the sun streaming through the gaps in the blinds in the bedroom.

"I've been tracking the contractions for a while. I'm sure." She showed me the notes app on her phone and all the contractions she'd tracked over the previous hour. The baby was coming early, but not so early that it was a concern.

We spent the next few hours trying to distract Maria from the pain of her contractions. We took a shower. I rubbed her back. Rocko joined us for a walk in the park by our house. People looked at us like we were insane when a contraction sent Maria to her hands and knees, and I stood there rubbing her back while video recording the whole thing, the camera on a selfie stick in my other hand. "Who cares how we look?" I thought. "We're having a baby!"

I'd recently gone to renew my driver's license and found out it was revoked after I was convicted of killing Laura. The notice had been sent to the house Laura and I shared in Magothy Manor even though I'd updated my address with the motor vehicle administration months before. I was in jail at the time they'd sent the notice, and I never received it, so I'd been driving on a revoked license for a several years without knowing it. Thank God I'd never been stopped, or I could've gone back to jail on a probation violation.

Since my driver's license was revoked, Maria and I had a list of friends and family who'd offered to drive us to the hospital when Maria went into labor. After we tried a couple friends from the neighborhood, Jessica and Tom, two of Maria's best friends from high school whose wedding we'd attended the year before, said they'd pick us up. When they arrived, Jessica went upstairs to check on Maria, who'd been curled up on the bed, moaning in pain. She took one look at her and said, "It's time to go. Now. Like, right now."

I helped Maria into the backseat of the car so Tom could drive us the twenty minutes from downtown Baltimore to the hospital in the suburbs. He took Charles Street, notorious for massive bumps in its right lane wherever there was a drain in the road. Over thirty miles per hour, you could get airborne if you went over them right. Nobody drove in the right lane if they didn't have to. And nobody drove right over the dips without slowing down, either. Nobody except Tom, that is. Tom apparently didn't care about the bumps. He's been driving in the right lane, and he's been driving fast, tossing Maria around in the backseat as she moans.

Maria's been yelling at Tom about his driving since we left the house. Tom's been begging Maria not to have a baby in his car. He brought a metal bowl and put it in the back seat next to Maria in case her water broke. Like us, he has no idea what he's doing. I've just been rubbing Maria's arm in the backseat, thrilled that soon I'll get to meet my son or daughter.

We arrive at the hospital, and I run inside to grab a wheelchair. I push Maria to the labor and delivery unit and ring the bell by the locked door over and over, but nobody comes. I bang on the door like I'm going to knock it down. Finally, a nurse comes over and opens it.

"Can I help you?"

I gesture to Maria. "My wife. I think she's ready to go!" It feels strange to call her my wife, *but it is technically true.*

I have great health insurance through my employer, but even though the insurance would cover our baby once he or she was born, Maria and I learned several months ago that the pregnancy and childbirth would be considered healthcare for Maria, not our baby, and therefore would have to be covered by Maria's health insurance. Her insurance didn't include maternity coverage because she hadn't planned on getting pregnant. Between prenatal appointments and labor and delivery, having our baby was going to cost about $25,000, money we definitely didn't have.

Even though it was going to be expensive, neither of us wanted to get married just because we were having a baby. We were starting a family unexpectedly, but we still wanted to do it on our terms. We looked at the itemized cost breakdown from the hospital and realized we could save a few thousand dollars Maria delivered the baby without any pain medication. *No pain meds.* That's how desperate the medical costs made us feel.

We took a natural childbirth class to prepare for the no-drugs delivery. The instructors taught Maria breathing techniques, muscle relaxation, and other strategies for managing labor pain. They taught me to help her relax and take her focus off the pain. The classes were empowering for her, and I was grateful that I'd have a role in the delivery. Becoming a childbirth team bonded us even more closely. Maria got me a green and blue "Labor and Delivery Coach" shirt to wear to the hospital and a red "Papa Bear" shirt to wear after our baby was born.

We made a childbirth plan in our class. We didn't need to

get to the hospital early for an epidural, and we didn't want Maria to be stuck in a hospital bed for hours for no reason. That's why we stayed home so long after her labor started. The goal was to get to the hospital when she was nearly ready to push. But because it was our first time, we had *no idea* if we waited long enough.

We're not sure if Maria's labor has progressed enough for us to get admitted into the hospital, and even if she's far enough into labor to get admitted— if this is, *in fact,* labor— I hope we're closer to the end than we are to the beginning and stare at the nurse in anticipation.

She looks at Maria, then turns back to me and, with a look not quite of alarm but certainly of urgency, says "follow me." I exchange a satisfied look with Maria, both of us relieved to know she's far enough along to get admitted to the hospital.

I push the wheelchair hastily down the hallway—one third walking, one third jogging, one third skipping. Serious excitement and giddy anticipation build as the institutional tiles glide by underfoot.

But back to that whole "wife" thing. I moved into the house Maria was renting in South Baltimore in April. I hadn't been ready to live together before she got pregnant, but knowing the kind of parent and partner I wanted to be made living together a necessity. I wasn't ready for our lives to be so intertwined, but the baby made that a moot point: our lives *were* so intertwined. I wasn't going to miss a second of our baby's life. Part of my reluctance to live together had been knowing that losing Maria could be as crushing as losing Laura if we were building a life together. Once she was becoming the mother of my child, that concern seemed moot too. Losing her would turn my life upside down regardless. Her roommate moved out of their house and in with her boyfriend so I could move in, and my roommate moved out of our place and in with his girlfriend so we could give up our lease. Our baby was making everyone's relationships more serious.

Even without the extra childbirth frills, like pain medication, having our baby was going to cost about $20,000, and we thought about all the other uses to which we could put that money: a future wedding, a down payment on a house, or a college savings account for our baby. Then a month ago we decided to get married in a courthouse and enroll Maria in my health insurance plan. By saying "I do," the cost of childbirth went from $20,000 to a $100 co-pay.

We invited our moms as witnesses, and we agreed that the courthouse wedding was only a financial transaction that in no way precluded a real proposal, a real engagement, and a real wedding, when and if we decided to get real married. It was just paperwork like all the other paperwork we had to fill out to complete her insurance enrollment. When Maria said "I do," it really just meant "I do *need better health insuranc*e."

Approaching the courthouse in Baltimore, I was aware that last time I walked into one of these places, it was to plead guilty to killing Laura and receive my sentence. Harry invited me to court when I was working with him, but I could never bring myself to go inside. The memories of a courtroom were too painful. But on my technically-a-wedding day, I felt optimistic, like it was a good omen of some kind to be in the court-house for something positive. And despite the marriage being nothing but a financial transaction, it also felt momentous, like a step forward in my journey "back to normal." As we stood in the courtroom and exchanged vows, I looked at the glow of pregnancy on Maria's face and scanned down her dress to the round belly holding our child. "We're a real family," I thought.

Even though our courthouse wedding eliminated our concerns about the cost of childbirth, we were so invested in preparing for natural childbirth that we decided to go ahead with the no-drugs plan anyways. Now that we're at the hospi-tal, it's my job to get Maria everything she needs and set up the environment she wants in the delivery room.

"Can we have the birthing ball and the lights turned down?" I ask, and the nurse looks at me like I'm crazy.

"She's too far along for the ball, but we can turn the lights down."

The nurse leaves the room, and I open our baby-day bag to change into my "Labor and Delivery Coach" shirt, set up the electric tea lights around the room, and put on our James Taylor playlist to set a calming mood.

Maria's contractions are getting more intense. I rub her back as she moans and curls herself around the pain. I pull out my video camera and take some footage of her laboring. The nurse comes in and tells me I can't film, but I pull the camera back out and continue recording as soon as she leaves the room. Maria doesn't notice that I'm filming again, but she's a photog-rapher, and I know she'd understand.

Maria's doctor arrives just as Maria's water breaks. The pain builds and makes her cry out. I wipe the sweat off her forehead and hold her hand, surprised by the strength of her grip as she crushes my fingers. The doctor announces that Maria is eight centimeters dilated. Two more centimeters, and it will be time to push. The contractions are getting longer and more frequent. There is barely any time for her to catch her breath between each one. I see her clenching her jaw and try to remind her to relax like they taught me to do in our classes.

"You're doing great. I love you. You're doing great."

"Ten centimeters, time to push," the doctor declares. I put one hand behind Maria's head, and the other under her right knee. A nurse does the same on the other side, and we squeeze her legs to her abdomen as she pushes through a contraction. She yells not only from the pain but also from the effort, like a weight lifter pushing the limits of her strength. The intensity of her determination narrows her eyes as she seems to look first at me and then through me.

"I can see a head!" I shout to her excitedly. "You got this! You're doing it!"

Maria pushes again, harder, and the doctor pulls our son into the world. A rush of joy quickens my heart and warms my whole body. I love him so much; I would do anything for him.

"It's a boy," one of the nurses says.

We didn't find out if our baby would be a boy or a girl. I wanted to, but Maria didn't. I'd been reading all the dad-to-be books, and one of them said that the moment a dad finds out the sex of his baby when it's born might be the only time in his life when he knows more about the baby than the mom does. I closed my eyes and relished the vision of our baby's birth and the moment I'd tell Maria, "It's a boy!" or "It's a girl!"

"Hey, I'm supposed to tell her!" I shout.

Before I get the words out of my mouth, the nurses sweep our son away to the other side of the delivery room.

"What are you doing?" I ask frantically, following them across the room.

"What is it, Mark?" Maria asks urgently.

"Don't worry," the nurse says as she pushes me back. "You need to give us space."

They're pushing a tube down his throat and sucking fluid out of his lungs. He's turning blue, and it looks like he's gasping for air.

*God, please. I can't lose him.*

I've been trying to control my irrational fears that something will happen to Maria or the baby, but in the moment, it doesn't feel like my fears are irrational. Something is definitely wrong. Maria is being tended to, and I'm pacing back and forth, checking on her, then on him, then on her.

"He's perfect," I tell her, though inside I'm struggling to hold it together and terrified they won't be able to get him breathing.

After a minute, the nurse puts her hand on my back. "He's fine. You can relax. He got a little meconium in his lungs, but we got it out. It's okay."

*Thank you, God. Thank you. What's meconium?*

I get my video camera back out, and nobody seems to

mind my recording now.

We've narrowed our list down to two boy names: Finnegan, from a book of Irish names I downloaded, or Linz, Maria's maiden name she wanted to pass on in honor of her father. I prefer Finnegan. Maria prefers Linz.

"Does he look like a Finnegan or a Linz?" she asks.

I fight the urge to just pick my preferred name and look closely at his squinty eyes already trying to open, his little rosebud mouth, and the tight curls adorning his head, and I know.

"Finnegan." It's a no-brainer. He's a total Finnegan.

"Finnegan," she whispers back.

The nurses clean him up and put him on Maria's chest. It's the most captivating thing I've ever seen, and I know I could stare at them forever. After the nurses leave, I change out of my "Labor and Delivery Coach" shirt and into my "Papa Bear" shirt.

Later that night, as we snuggle with Finnegan, I look at them both with the most overwhelming, awe-inspiring, indescribable love and joy I've ever felt.

Finnegan is asleep on Maria's shoulder, and I pull them both closer. "I've wondered for so long what my purpose for still being on this earth is." I thought it might be to do some good in the world to make up for the terrible thing I did. "Now I know. I'm supposed to be a daddy." I need to make the world a better place not out of guilt but because if I do, he'll grow up in a world that's better than the one we brought him into.

Maria smiles up at me, a tear welling in her eye. She squeezes it shut, and the tear rolls down her cheek as she sighs and drifts off to sleep.

# CHAPTER 34

I'm not at all nervous standing in front of the chicken coop waiting for Maria to walk down the aisle. Finnegan—or Finn or Bug, as we call him—is one. It's been four and a half years since the crash, three and a half years since I got out of jail.

Becoming a father turned my life upside down. There's nothing in the world I care about more than Finn. I never realized how important I was to myself until I stopped being important. I thought I would never be head-over-heels, can't-think-about-anything-else in love again. Not with Maria. Not with anyone. I figured after Laura, I just didn't have that in me. I was grateful to love Maria. I was in love with her. We just skipped the infatuation phase and jumped to attachment, bonded in our raw grief. But seeing her with our child, I became firmly infatuated. I'd do anything for her. I'd do anything for Finn. They became everything.

When Finn was a month old, Maria returned to work for a wedding on Maryland's Eastern Shore. Hurricane Irene was on its way, but the bride and groom didn't want to postpone the wedding. They decided to have the wedding and then have their guests hunker down for the weekend. I thought it was crazy, but Maria couldn't back out; there was a contract, and her business depended on being reliable. I was alone with Finnegan and a bunch of frozen breast milk as the hurricane battered the east coast. I worried about Maria's safety, but I was thankful for the alone time with Finn and the opportunity to meet all his needs. When Maria returned the next day, we explored the damage in our neighborhood. Rocko ran around the park sniffing all the fallen trees. Finn nuzzled into Maria's chest and fell asleep.

Maria's second wedding after Finn was born was in Philadelphia. Finn and I tagged along with Maria to Pennsylvania and spent the day visiting the historic sites in the city. The day after the wedding, we went to a vineyard and ran into another couple whose wedding Maria had previously photographed—Maria, of course, becomes friends with most of the families she photographs—and joined their family for wine and lunch.

It was going to be a big day, but Maria didn't know it yet. I had the engagement ring in my pocket, and I told her friends at the vineyard that I planned to propose later in the afternoon. Maria couldn't understand why everyone kept toasting us as we all happily passed around the babies—these particular friends had a newborn too, born the same month as Finn—and bottles of wine.

Maria didn't drink the wine because she was breastfeeding, and after the vineyard, she drove us to Longwood Gardens, breathtaking European-style gardens set on an old du Pont family estate in southeastern Pennsylvania. There were flowers in bloom in every direction, beautiful fountains, ponds, stone walkways and perfectly sculpted shrubbery. In one corner, a large conservatory housed tropical plants with flowers that bloomed all year round.

A fireworks show was lighting up the grounds as we

crossed the gardens and entered the conservatory. Maria was wearing Finnegan in a wrap on her chest. He was cozied into her and asleep when I asked her to give me her camera so I could get a passing couple to take our picture. I whispered conspiratorially to the couple about my plan to propose and asked them to wait to take the picture until I was down on my knee.

We were in the Tropical Terrace section of the conservatory, surrounded by lush foliage, long vines, and large blooms. I walked over to Maria and slid my arm around her back as if to pose for a photo standing by her side, then reached with my other hand to grasp her fingers and turn her toward me. I held her two hands in mine for a moment, lowered myself to my knee, and pulled out the ring.

"I love you, and I love this family with all my heart. Will you marry me?" I asked, smiling up at her.

"Oh, yes. I will," she replied, already extending her fingers for the ring and bouncing with excitement (or maybe to soothe Finn and keep him from waking up).

We'd shopped for rings together, so I knew she would love the one I bought. I was also pretty confident she'd say "yes," especially since I was already married to her. But hearing her say it still made my heart feel too big for my chest, like it was pushing to come up through my throat, and I couldn't swallow to make it go back down.

I placed the ring on her finger as a tear slid down her cheek. Finnegan looked up curiously, and Maria swung her hips back and forth in a wide arc to calm him back to sleep. I kissed her and then kissed Finn on his head, so grateful for the sublime happiness of the moment and the promise of happiness to come.

Planning for the wedding was mostly complete by the time we finished our steak dinner that night. After photographing so many special days for others, Maria knew the venue for her wedding—our wedding—and had a vision for every bit of the flowers and decorations. I was just glad to know I wouldn't clash with the decor.

The farm we chose—Maria chose—was rustic and picturesque, a short distance from Deep Creek Lake in western Maryland. Her mom rented a big cabin on the lake, and we stayed there with her family all week.

There's a long tree-lined driveway from the road to the farm with a turquoise antique truck we leaned on for some of the pre-wedding photos we took an hour ago. It's sunny out, and the smell of earth and grass rides on the early fall breeze. There are wildflowers in every direction and a patio with a gazebo in front of a pond. That's where most couples get married, but we decided—Maria decided—we would get married in front of the chicken coop instead. That's where I'm waiting for her now.

Chris is a groomsman, and he's standing behind me. Theresa is sitting in the first row holding the paper with the reading she'll do during the ceremony. To my surprise and relief, she and Maria have bonded. Nobody ever judged our relationship as harshly as I did, and Theresa never held it against Maria that she came after Laura.

As Maria and I worked on our guest list for the wedding,

I wondered whether to invite Laura's family. They never said they were angry about Maria, but our relationship felt tense after they found out about her. I wasn't sure if it was because I got to start a family while Laura didn't or because I hid my relationship with Maria for so long. Maybe it was both. Or maybe I imagined it because I would be mad and because I wanted them to be mad. I asked Theresa what she thought. She was Laura's best friend, after all, and she was close with Laura's family. She didn't say they were mad at me, but she thought coming to the wedding might be too painful for them. I didn't invite them, but I'm still not sure if that was the right decision.

One of our friends is playing the fiddle as the bridesmaids process in. Finnegan and Rocko walk down the aisle next as Best Dog and Best Guy. Both are wearing bow ties, looking at once cute and suave. Then the music stops, and everyone instinctively quiets.

I look around the pond to see Maria and her mom walking toward us. The fiddle begins to play again, and a lump forms in my throat as Maria walks toward me. I look up to the sky to keep the tears at bay.

Maria is stunning in her strapless white dress, lacy veil, and dangly earrings, her cowboy boots adding a touch of fun. I catch my breath as I take her arm, and we turn to face each other in front of our friend who is officiating.

After the I do's, Finnegan goes home with a babysitter, and we take some more pictures in the wildflowers while our guests enjoy cocktail hour. Pro tip: if you marry a wedding photographer, expect to take *a lot* of photos on your wedding day. *A lot.*

Our brother-in-law's Nineties band is playing at the reception, and he announces our wedding party as they enter the reception and form a semi-circle around the dance floor. Our brother-in-law, lead singer and wedding MC, leans into the microphone.

"Ladies and gentlemen. It is now my distinct pleasure to introduce to you, for the very first time, Mr. And Mrs. Mark and Maria O'Brien!"

Maria and I walk into the spacious barn to the standing applause of our friends and family. I twirl her around as the first notes of *All for One*, the nineties power ballad from *Three Musketeers,* play— it's the only recorded music at our wedding; the rest is performed by our friend on the fiddle and our brother-in-law's band— and Rod Stewart begins to sing. I pull her close, and she grins sweetly up at me as I kiss her forehead.

"You look beautiful, *Mrs.* O'Brien."

"You clean up okay too, Mr. Maria," she replies with a mischievous raise of her eyebrow. We both laugh.

After the first dance, we sit amidst the smell of wine and roast duck, beaming at each other and our guests. The sound of a spoon on glass signals another kiss, and we happily oblige. The round tables of eight are on either side of the dance floor, and our bride-and-groom table-for-two sits in the middle. We listen as Maria's sisters and my best man give their toasts through toasts. Then we eat dinner and visit each table to greet our guests before heading to the dance floor for the rest of the night.

When the reception ends, we pack up the leftover wine and catch a ride back to the cabin, spend some time alone, and hop in the hot tub to relax after all the dancing.

"It's so crazy all the build up to today, and now it's over," Maria says.

"I know. But I'm really excited about Belize."

Maria and I didn't think we'd be able to take a honeymoon outside of the country because of my probation, so we originally decided to go camping in Montana or Wyoming. But then my probation agent—Agent McKay, the new, good probation agent—set up a court date with Judge Hackner to straighten out the situation with my community service. He was angry at first; he'd given me a very short jail sentence, and it appeared to him initially that I'd failed to do one of the few things he required.

"Do you have anything to say for yourself?" he asked me.

I explained the conundrum with the community service—the program he required me to complete was off limits because of my offense— and that I'd been doing the volunteer work he ordered; I just hadn't gotten any credit for it because it wasn't court sanctioned.

"I am really grateful for the second chance you gave me," I told the judge. "If it's okay, I'd love to tell you more about what I've been doing with it." I pointed to Maria and Finn in the courtroom and talked about our new family.

"And I've been working on criminal justice and addiction policy in Washington, DC to try to make a positive difference with my career."

His demeanor softened, and he told me he was proud of what I'd done. He had a room full of probation violation hearings, and many of the people in the room were about to get in trouble for violating his orders.

"This is what I expect you to do when I give you a second chance," he intoned, looking out over the courtroom.

I wondered if any of them ever really had a second chance like me. I'd seen what probation and parole were like and knew most of the people behind me had been set up to fail, but I wasn't there to argue with the judge.

"How many hours of community service would you have left if you were getting credit for the volunteer work you've done?"

"Probably fifteen," I replied.

"Do another fifteen this month, and after I receive the documentation, your probation is over," he said. "Dismissed."

I threw my arms around Agent McKay and thanked her for everything.

"Good luck, Mark," she said. "I'm proud of you."

Maria and I changed our camping plan and booked a honeymoon in Belize. Finn will be staying home with family so we can enjoy some time alone.

"Are you happy?" Maria asks me, leaning into my shoulder and gazing out to the stars shining off the lake.

"Yeah. I haven't been out of the country in twenty years. It's going to be a great trip."

"No. I mean, *are you happy?*"

"Yeah. I know. I was just playing with you. Of course, I

am. I'm in love."

"I love you too, Mr. Maria," she teases again.

I pull her closer and reach my arm around her waist, and our breathing synchronizes in a deep and slow rhythm as we both close our eyes.

"Just promise me nothing will ever happen to you."

# EPILOGUE

It's been eleven years since the crash. Finn is seven years old, and our family has grown.

Our second child, a girl named Charlie, is five now. The day she was born, I was on my way to work at Legal Action Center when I got the call from Maria. "It's time," she said. "You need to come home." I'd gotten my driver's license back, and I turned around to head home and take Maria to the hospital.

A few things were the same as our last childbirth experience. We were in the same hospital. I was wearing my "Labor and Delivery Coach" shirt. Maria wasn't taking any pain medications. I dimmed the fluorescent lights in the delivery room and put out our tea lights. We put on our James Taylor playlist, and I pulled out the video camera.

A few other things were different. Labor was longer than last time, and there was a lot more pushing with Charlie. Maria was exhausted before we could even see her head. I was running out of steam from holding Maria's leg and sandwiching her with each push. "That was really hard for me," I said afterward, teasing her.

Later that evening, Finn came to the hospital to meet his baby sister. The love I felt for them both was like nothing else, and I was so grateful for them, so eager to see them develop and encourage them as they discovered the world. My joy and the overwhelming love I felt for Finn and Charlie helped me to better understand how precious Laura had been to her parents, the magnitude of what I'd taken from them, and how unbelievably incredible their forgiveness was.

I stopped talking to Laura's family for a while after my wedding because I felt like I'd done too much damage to our relationship. My continued presence in their life could only be a source of pain for everyone, I'd thought at the time, but I reconnected with them before Charlie was born.

The night before Theresa's wedding in the Outer Banks, she and her husband threw a bonfire party on the beach. Laura would have loved the beach party, the smell of smoke and salt air, and the blazing fire casting dancing shadows all around. She would have been the maid of honor. I was a groomsman, and I felt like I was there representing her too. When I saw Laura's family across the beach, I walked over awkwardly to say hello. They were as kind and welcoming as ever. David wrapped me in a bear hug.

"When are we going to see Maria and Finn again?" he asked.

After Finn left the hospital the day Charlie was born, I called David to tell him the news.

"What's her name?" he asked.

"Charlotte Marie," I told him. Marie was Laura's middle name, and Charlotte was Laura's beloved aunt.

"I like that. I like that a lot, Mark. I'm really happy for you and Maria."

A few weeks later, I picked up the phone to call David again. I'd been thinking a lot about him since Charlie was born. I had a daughter now too, a sweet girl baby to nurture and protect so she could grow up to be the daddy's girl Laura had been for David. David was a good father, and he'd shown me what it meant to live with grace. His forgiveness remained the most astonishing and treasured gift I'd ever received.

I told him we were planning her baptism and wanted to make sure the date worked for him. Then I got around to the real reason we wanted to schedule the sacrament around his availability.

"Maria and I would be honored if you'd be her godfather," I said. There was nobody else in the world Maria and I would rather have as an example to her of what it means to live a good life.

"Of course, I will, Mark. I love you guys," he said.

Maria and I had our third child, a daughter named Penny, just 18 months after Charlie, proving that two-thirds of the time when Maria and I have a kid, it's a surprise. The day we brought Penny home from the hospital, Finn and Charlie were waiting for us with Maria's mom and sister, our brother-in-law, two of our nieces and our nephew. The little ones all ran outside to greet us.

As everyone walked inside, I thought about how much of life Laura missed out on. She would have been a great mom. She would have loved having children. We would have had a happy marriage. So much of what made my life fulfilling were the things I took from her.

As I've settled into the patterns of family life, I occasionally run into old friends I haven't seen in years. They've aged, grown, and changed. Like me, they're in new phases of life, different from the last time I saw them. They're no longer the people I knew when we were younger, but Laura never changes. She's timeless now. The woman she'll be forever has become too young for the man I've become. I'm a dad with graying hair now. If she saw me on the street, she wouldn't take a second look. Or maybe our souls would still know we were for each other.

I wonder what her life would be like if I'd been the one who died. Would she have a happy life like I do? Would she have a husband and children? I hope that she would sit in the living room of her home surrounded by her family as they cooed over her baby. Maybe she would think of me as I think of her, and she'd smile like I smile at her memory, the grief of loss tempered by time and mingled with the happiness of our memories, the gratitude for having known me at all.

With our brood of three, our family outgrew our home, a charming end-unit townhouse with beautiful natural light and enchanting little gardens I'd spent years learning to care for. We bought a larger single-family home in Baltimore County, near where Maria grew up and where her mom and sisters still lived.

Finn, Charlie, and Penny know that Laura was my girlfriend. There are photos of Laura and me displayed around our house, and we talk about her often. They know we were in a car crash, and they know Maria and I met after Laura died. They know David is Laura's dad and an important part of our lives. What they don't know is that I caused the crash and went to jail for it.

A couple years ago, Finn asked me about my job. I told

him I helped people who were coming home from prison start their lives again. "But isn't prison for bad guys?" he asked. He was in a superhero phase, and he had a sense that the world was divided into good guys and bad guys. I told him most people aren't all good or all bad, and my job was to help people who got on the bad guy side to get back on the good guy side. I knew prison wasn't full of bad guys, but it seemed like the best way to explain my job to a four-year-old. Everyone could turn their lives around, I explained, and a world where people had second chances was a better world for him to grow up in.

A few days later, I saw him playing with his superheroes, and Batman put the Joker in jail. After a few minutes, Batman let Joker out and invited him to join the good guys.

But even though he understood that people could change, I've dreaded telling him the whole story of the crash, my role in it, and what happened afterward. When he was younger, I knew he wouldn't understand. As he grew, I didn't want him to think differently of me. I loved the boyish way he looked at me as the dad who could do no wrong. I didn't want to deprive him of his image of me. And I didn't want to deprive myself of the way he looked at me either.

Losing Laura taught me to be vulnerable and open with the people I love. I want to show him what openness means, and I want him to know that I trust him enough to share my most painful experiences with him. I decide it's time to be honest with him, and I walk to his room to tuck him in for bed. Some of the most meaningful conversations I have with my kids are when I'm tucking them in at night.

"Hey, Bug. I need to tell you something," I say, sitting down beside him and shaking with anxiety. I take a deep breath, and he can tell from my body language and the tone of my voice that the conversation we're about to have is important. He's quiet and attentive, his eyes wide and curious.

"You know how Laura died in a car accident, and I was in it too?"

He nods, a blonde curl falling over his forehead.

"I was actually driving drunk. It was my fault. I broke the law, and I went to jail for it."

At first, he's shocked. Then he's confused. He knows drinking and driving isn't safe, and he knows it's against the law. But he doesn't understand how drinking and driving means you're responsible for someone's death in a car crash.

"But it was an accident," he implores; he doesn't want her death to be my fault.

"That's true. But sometimes when we make a bad choice and it has a bad outcome, we have to take responsibility for the consequences."

"On TV, they say the food in jail is bad. Is that true?"

"Yeah. It's not very good."

"I'm sorry that happened to you, Daddy," he says, curling up with his head in my lap.

I run my fingers through his soft hair.

"I know you miss Laura," he continues. "You get sad when we talk about her."

"I do miss her. I miss her a lot."

He asks if I wish she were still alive, and I tell him that

I do.

"But you wouldn't have us or know Mommy if she was still alive." He wants me to choose between the life I have with him and the life I would have had with Laura. "I wouldn't even be alive if she was alive."

"That's not how life works, bud. If there were some magical world where I could bring Laura back, I'd have you in that world too. But in the real world, we don't get to change the past. I made a bad choice, and it still hurts. A lot. I wish I could change it, but I can't. And it's also true that I would never trade the life I have with you, Mommy, and your sisters for anything in the world."

I used to think about Laura every second, then every minute, then every hour, then every day. Recently, I realized I no longer thought of Laura every day. At first, it saddened me. I wondered if she'd become less important to me. But I knew that couldn't be true. She didn't matter less; I just didn't need to think constantly about what losing her meant anymore. Loving and losing Laura was a part of me the same way being right-handed was a part of me. I wasn't in the process of understanding the loss anymore. I was living out the change it created in me. Laura was a part of who I was every second of every day, whether I was thinking about her or not.

As Finnegan closes his eyes, I'm glad that in his innocence he doesn't know that nothing in this life is permanent, not the things we love nor the suffering we all must endure. The crash taught me so much that I want my kids to know. I think about what I would tell them if they were old enough to understand.

I'd tell them I'll always be there for them, but they'll also experience pain I can't make go away. When they do, I'll silently hold their hands and cry with them. I won't rush them through their feelings or tell them how to feel. They'll learn to deal with pain in their own ways and in their own time.

I'd tell them that as long as they are breathing, there is hope that things will get better. Never, ever, give up hope. And never, ever, let the circumstances you find yourself in make you into something you don't want to be. You can always control how you respond to adversity, and that's also true of good fortune. Regrets are a part of life, but dwelling on them means living in a past you can't get back, slowly starving for a present and future you'll never have. You have to let go of regrets and live the best you can, starting wherever you find yourself.

I'd want them to know that a meaningful life isn't one spent grasping for riches but one spent finding passion and purpose. Meaning comes from being a part of something bigger and more important than yourself. They'll know they did it right if, at the end, the world is a better place than they found it.

I'd tell them there is no strength in hiding your true self. It takes courage to be who you are and share your heart. Be open with the people in your life. Give them a chance to love all of you and show them that you love all of them. Speak the truth as you understand it, but be open to being wrong and learning new ways of thinking. As you open yourself to others, be open to them and their ideas.

Perhaps the biggest lesson would be about forgiveness.

Nobody is beyond redemption. That includes you when you make the mistakes you surely will. And that also includes everyone else, even when you hate what they've done.

While forgiveness is good for the person in need of it, it's sometimes as important for the person who chooses to forgive. This was David's greatest lesson. David was heartbroken after the crash, but he never let his grief turn to bitterness. After the crash, I'd expected him to hate me for the terrible thing I'd done to his family, but David never let his pain turn to cynicism or his anger change his fundamentally buoyant and loving character. Mercy wasn't just a gift he gave to me; it was also a part of David's healing. He was honoring Laura by treating me with the love she would have treated me with and letting go of the anger that would have changed the father she loved if he'd let it consume him. If David had let hatred grow in his heart after Laura's death, he would have lost not only his daughter but also himself.

I had to learn that lesson for myself because I was both the perpetrator of the horrible crime that took Laura away and one of its victims. By the time Finn was born, I understood that my responsibility for the crash didn't make me a bad person. I'd forgiven God for taking Laura, and I'd forgiven Laura for leaving me behind. But I was still furious with myself for what I'd done. David's example helped me understand that I didn't continue suffering because I was unforgiven. I was suffering because I was angry. I needed to forgive myself not because I deserved to be forgiven but so that I could put down the heavy burden of anger I'd been carrying since Laura's death.

I still worry that something terrible is going to happen to my family. Every time Maria is late coming home, I immediately assume she's dying and brace for all the pain that is coming. Going to the doctor with a sick kid terrifies me. I'm not sure that will ever stop. Lying in Finn's bed, watching him sleep, I have a different but related worry: that something will happen to me before I can pass on the lessons I learned from the crash.

Determined not to let that happen, I step quietly out of his bed and turn off the light in his bedroom. I look into their rooms at Penny and Charlie, already breathing deep sighs of sleep. Then I walk down the stairs to my living room, open my computer, and begin to type: "It's so cramped in the car, all crushed around me…"

# ACKNOWLEDGMENTS

This book would not exist without the encouragement, guidance, and effort of so many. I'd like to especially thank a few people whose contributions stand out. Maria O'Brien, my wife, supported this effort with compassion and patience, shared her recollections of many of the events in this book, and had an uncanny ability to show up with coffee refills at the exact moment they were needed. Morgan Gliedman, my friend and editor, provided countless rounds of comments and revisions; this story would not have come alive without her. John Michael Daga's advice on storytelling and structure was indispensable. Andrea Seydel from Live Life Happy Publishing took the words in my manuscript and turned them into the book you're reading. Thank you, also, to the many others who shared their memories of events in this story and inspired me to continue writing on the days when it hurt to keep going.

# ABOUT THE AUTHOR

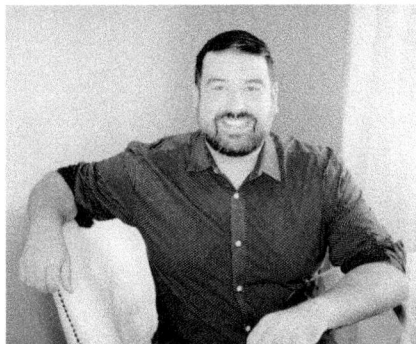

Mark L. O'Brien is a leading advocate and change-maker in trauma, substance use, mental health, and criminal justice. He is the founder and executive director of Trauma Informed, Inc, where he designs and leads programs to support trauma survivors and improve the way organizations respond to trauma; founding partner of Springlake Solutions LLC, where he provides strategic consulting to mission-driven organizations working in behavioral health and public safety; adjunct professor of political science at Towson University; assistant instructor at the University of Pennsylvania Positive Psychology Center; and a master's level positive psychology practitioner and posttraumatic growth coach. Mark L. O'Brien lives in Lutherville, Maryland with his wife, Maria, their three exuberant children, and a goofy pup named Otis.

Learn more about Mark's work and connect with him at www.marklobrien.com.

LiveLifeHappy
Publishing

www.livelifehappypublishing.com

www.ingramcontent.com/pod-product-compliance
Lightning Source LLC
Chambersburg PA
CBHW051412090426
42737CB00014B/2630